P. J. Kenny. 1841.

Metropolis

Metropolis

FROM the DIVISION of LABOR to URBAN FORM

Allen J. Scott

University of California Press

Berkeley • Los Angeles • London

University of California Press
Berkeley and Los Angeles, California

University of California Press, Ltd.
Oxford, England

Copyright © 1988 by The Regents of the University of California

First Paperback Printing 1990

Library of Congress Cataloging-in-Publication Data

Scott, Allen John
    Metropolis : from the division of labor to urban form / Allen J.
Scott.
        p.   cm.
    Bibliography: p.
    Includes index.
    ISBN 0-520-07198-0 (alk. paper)
    1. Metropolitan areas—United States—Case studies.
    2. Urbanization—United States—Case studies.   3. Division of labor—
Case studies.   4. Industrialization—United States—Case studies.
    5. Labor suppy—United States—Case studies.   I. Title.
HT334.U5S36 1988
307.7'64'0973—dc19   87-30168
                                                                        CIP

Printed in the United States of America

1   2   3   4   5   6   7   8   9

The paper used in this publication meets the minimum requirements of
American National Standard for Information Sciences—Permanence of
Paper for Printed Library Materials, ANSI Z39.48–1984. ∞

Contents

Preface

This book represents an attempt to construct and substantiate a problematic of industrialization and urbanization focused above all on the dynamics of the division of labor. It advances the claim that the phenomena of production, work, and community can be usefully analyzed as basic and mutually reinforcing elements of the urban process in capitalism. I attempt to develop this claim within a broad structure of theoretical argument illustrated with a series of dense empirical case studies.

Some half-dozen years ago, I made a first foray into an extended essay on urbanization with a book entitled *The Urban Land Nexus and the State* (Scott, 1980). In this earlier book I tried to conceptualize the urban dislocations and planning problems of the 1960s and 1970s in terms of a general theory of intraurban location and land use. I was already eager to take my distance from much prior urban analysis. I had made up my mind as to the importance of industrialization for urban development, and I argued that a coherent and politically relevant urban theory needed to insist on the primary significance of the production system in any account of the locational structure of intraurban space. In spite of this commitment, I did not succeed in fully working out its many and complicated ramifications. The account that I gave of the formation and dynamics of the production space of the city was rudimentary, and, as a corollary, my efforts to identify a geographical logic of urbanization were notably deficient. The present offering is an attempt to redress some of these deficiencies and to pursue more fully the agenda of inquiry first alluded to in the crucial chapter 6 ("Urban Patterns I: Production Space") of *The Urban Land Nexus and the State*.

Upon completion of the latter work, I set off on an extended research program designed to fill in some of the more important gaps that I had encountered in my own thinking and in the literature as I set about writing that crucial chapter 6. Eventually, this research program took me into the whole problem of the organization of production systems in capitalism, and, on that basis, into a major reinvestigation of the theory of industrial location and the logic of the modern space-economy. The present book is intended as a modest summing up of what has been accomplished thus far in this research program, but because the research is still far from complete, this book is very much a beginning rather than an ending. I am, in particular, very conscious of the fact that one of the things that is missing from the book is a really coherent account of consciousness, culture, and politics in urban communities and their role in shaping the socioeconomic life of cities. An urgent next step, no doubt, is to incorporate these issues into the analysis and to show how production, social existence, and political action all condense around one another in the urban sphere and thereby generate much of the observable complexity of the modern metropolis.

A large part of my more recent research has involved not just theoretical but also detailed empirical investigations into problems of industrialization and urbanization. Much of the empirical work has focused on the case of the Los Angeles urban region, and this accounts for the dominating (though by no means exclusive) role of this case in the empirical studies that constitute the core of chapters 6, 8, and 9. I make no apologies for this empirical bias. On the contrary, it seems to me to add a certain spice to the proceedings, for it so happens that Los Angeles (and more broadly the whole of the great megalopolis of Southern California) is now certainly one of the premier growth regions of the United States, if not, indeed, the world. It is probably not too exaggerated a claim to describe Los Angeles and its surrounding region as one of the paradigmatic cases of late capitalist industrialization and urbanization, just as Chicago was widely taken to be the paradigmatic expression of the industrial metropolis of the 1920s. It is thus a dramatic exemplar of the new patterns of industrialization and urbanization that are now making their appearance in the United States as the new regime of accumulation and its associated mode of social regulation ushered in by the crisis conditions of the 1970s begins to run its course.

The basic research and reflection on which the greater part of the book is based were accomplished in the framework of two projects funded by the National Science Foundation under grant numbers SES 8204376 and SES 8414398. I owe a special debt of gratitude to the Foundation, for without its generous support, I could never have carried out the detailed and costly empirical work that has proved to be so essential to the development of the ideas presented here. I also want to record my thanks to the John Simon Guggenheim Memorial Foundation for its generosity in awarding me a fellowship that was the catalyst allowing me to bring this book to fruition. I thank, in addition, the Institute of Industrial Relations and the College Institute of the College of Letters and Science, both at the University of California, Los Angeles, for their provision of supplemental funding that enabled me to take a full year off from my various teaching and administrative obligations and to devote myself wholly to the writing of this book. Several of the empirical studies that constitute the core of the book have been previously published in the form of journal articles, though all of this material has been significantly revised and rewritten for publication here. Chapter 6 is based on two papers published in *Economic Geography* (1983, 59:343–367, and 1984, 60:3–27); chapter 8 consists of excerpts from *Environment and Planning D: Society and Space* (1984, 2:277–307); and chapter 9 is a modified version of an article that appeared in *Urban Geography* (1986, 7:3–45). I am grateful to the editors and publishers of these journals for their permission to incorporate this material into the present book. Finally, I wish to pay tribute to those friends and colleagues at both the University of California, Los Angeles, and the University of Southern California without whose unstinting intellectual and social companionship this book might never have been written.

ACKNOWLEDGMENTS

The author and publisher are grateful to the following individuals and institutions for permission to reproduce copyrighted graphical materials:

A. Pred and *Economic Geography* for figure 2.1

M. J. Wise and the Institute of British Geographers for figures 5.1 and 5.2

P. G. Hall for figures 5.3, 5.4, 5.5, and 5.6

J. B. Kenyon and McGraw-Hill Inc. for figure 5.10

A. Takeuchi and St. Martin's Press Inc. for figures 5.11 and 5.12

P. Sheard and Monash University Publications in Geography for figures 5.13 and 5.14

J. B. Goddard and Pergamon Books Ltd. for figure 5.15

G. Gad and John Wiley and Sons Ltd. for figure 5.16

Urban Theory and Realities

How do cities develop and grow within the production system of modern capitalism? What forces govern the internal and external organization of their economies? How is the intraurban geography of production arranged, and how does it change through time? How is the labor of the citizenry mobilized over the urban system and deployed in productive work? What impacts does the economy have on the structure of urban life? Conversely, what influence does urban life have on the structure of local economic activity? These questions are not arbitrary. They represent preliminary windows onto a theoretical problematic of industrialization and urbanization whose outlines and substance will be discussed at length in this book, and they have important consequences for the ways in which we set about the tasks of understanding the modern metropolis.

My main objective here is to show how an urban process emerges—via complex patterns and dynamics of the division of labor—from the basic production apparatus of capitalist society. The attainment of this objective involves three major stages of analysis. First of all, I treat the broad problem of industrial production and the division of labor in capitalism, and I show how a theory of external economies can be rigorously identified on this basis. Second, I focus with special intensity on the ways in which the external economies engendered by the division of labor in capitalism give rise to significant agglomerations of capital and labor and hence constitute one of the fundamental conditions of large-scale urbanization as we know it. Third, I probe in great detail into the internal geography of production, work, and community in the modern large metropolis; I deal in turn with the genesis and characteristics of the urban economy, with the logic of local labor markets, and (more briefly) with the organization of intraurban

1

residential space; and I demonstrate how these phenomena constitute interpenetrating and mutually dependent facets of the modern metropolis with—again—the division of labor as an important and pervasive structuring relation.

Thus, in this book I argue for a perspective on the development of the metropolitan system that ascribes a strong analytical privilege to the functioning of the production apparatus and its expressive effects in the division of labor. I make this point right at the outset, knowing full well that it brushes against the theoretical temptations of a now-discredited base-and-superstructure account of capitalist society and of its different internal parts. Rest assured, however, that it is not my intention to try to cram the present analysis into this rigid conceptual machinery. I shall certainly attempt to show how the logic of capitalist industrialization processes is decisive in bringing large agglomerations of economic and social activity into existence. But the analysis is open from the very start to the intricate manner in which social life also shapes the urban process and restructures in various ways the dynamics of metropolitan development. In particular, the phenomena of residential activity and communal being have no simple one-to-one relationship to the production system, and they themselves have important repercussions on the ways in which the system functions. What is crucial about the production system, however, is that it creates the powerful forces that, first, give rise to metropolitan agglomeration as a purely locational phenomenon, and, second, influence in many intimate ways the workaday existence of the entire citizenry.

As the argument of the book unfolds, I hope to be able to demonstrate that this manner of approaching the metropolis (i.e., by maneuvering analytically from industrialization to urbanization by way of the division of labor) can contribute significantly to a revitalization of urban theory in general. My method in seeking to attain this goal involves a mix of abstract theoretical discussion complemented by a series of dense empirical case studies illustrating important and problematical conceptual details. My ambition is to show not only that industrialization, as I conceive it, is indeed frequently a major factor in the rise of large urban agglomerations but also that this view of things can help us resolve a number of significant subsidiary research questions. Among the latter are such issues as the formation of specialized industrial districts in intraurban space, the geographical decentralization of production, the logic of local labor markets, the impacts of occupational structure on patterns of urban social segregation, and so on. It is *not* my intention to assert that every form of urban agglomeration (in capitalism or otherwise) can be uniquely ascribed to the inexorable workings of the industrial system. On the contrary, we can point to many kinds of agglomeration—e.g., trade centers (central places), seats of government and administration, resort towns, retirement communities, and the like—which are patently not related to processes of industrialization. Nor do I propose to explain every possible facet of urban reality by proceeding in this way. There is much indeed (from housing markets to urban planning) that resists to a significant degree the kinds of explanatory devices that I seek to develop here. I do, nonetheless, make the definite claim that some of the most pressing theoretical and practical problems of metropolitan development in the advanced capitalist societies today can best be comprehended in light of the theory of the division of labor and urban form that I shall lay out in the chapters that follow; and I shall attempt to demonstrate that this theory provides a viable alternative to prevailing dominant viewpoints on contemporary urbanization processes.

Certainly, in the recent past, unmistakable signs of the intellectual enervation of many of these viewpoints seem to have become increasingly evident. Over the period stretching approximately from the mid-1950s to the late 1970s, urban studies had flourished remarkably well in almost all the social sciences, and something of a broad consensus about the main objectives of investigation was discernible. For much of this period almost all urban theorists seemed to be in at least tacit agreement that the central agenda of urban analysis should be concerned with what I shall call the social space of the city. In this way, they were all variously prolonging a tradition that had been initiated in the 1920s by the Chicago School of urban sociology. I make this comment even though I acknowledge forthwith that many of these theorists were at pains to keep their distance from the specific analytical commitments of the Chicago School. No matter how far they distanced themselves, however, they tended to remain part of a tradition that has consistently privileged the social space of the city as an object of theoretical inquiry, while neglecting or downplaying the role of production space. They were concerned especially with problems of housing, neighborhood formation, and collective consumption in the urban environment. Of course, there were also disagreements about just how to carry out analyses of these issues. On the one hand, neoclassical urban economists put their faith in behavioristic microeconomic processes of adjustment and liberalistic policy prescriptions (e.g., Alonso, 1965; Richardson, 1977). On the other hand, Marxist theorists rooted their version of urban analysis in notions of class struggle within the capitalist mode of production (e.g., Castells, 1973; Harvey, 1973). In spite of these important differences between the neoclassical theorists and the Marxists (as well as between each of these groups and the Chicago School itself), both sides seemed more than ready to acknowledge that the city as such could most effectively be understood as a locus of consumption activities and social reproduction. We might say that the urban theorists of the recent past were exercised by (and in several ways rose to the challenge of) the problems of everyday urban existence in welfare-statist capitalism. The theories that they developed over the 1960s and 1970s and the debates that ensued were for the most part quite explicitly geared to the tasks of comprehending the predicaments of urban life in a regime of welfare-statist capitalism and of identifying appropriate policy responses to those same predicaments. Concomitantly, they provided us with many important and durable insights into such matters as housing provision and finance, land-use conflicts, commuter transport services, urban planning processes, and all the rest.

After the late 1970s, however, urban realities began dramatically to change. The new neoconservative governments that came to power in the late 1970s and early 1980s, first in Britain and the United States, and then elsewhere, initiated programs designed to sweep away many of the old familiar arrangements of social administration and redistribution that had been built up after the Second World War. Large metropolitan regions were much affected by this process. Cutbacks in housing and welfare programs were promptly brought into effect; the redistributive functions of the state were steadily muted; reprivatization of economic and social affairs was both officially and unofficially encouraged; and, as the dissolution of popular social movements proceeded apace, large urban centers fell into an unwonted quiescence compared with the turbulent years of the 1960s. These developments did much to evacuate the relevance and urgency from the old urban theory and pushed it disconcertingly out of focus. This is not to say that the old theory was necessarily false or incoherent (indeed, as I have suggested, much of it was extraordinarily penetrating); I mean, rather, that if social theory is to be viable and relevant, it must not only adhere to purely formal criteria of truth, however conceived, but it must also—as Foucault (1980) and Habermas (1971) have taught us—shift its focus as the pertinent questions and human predicaments of the lived world change their shape and form.

As it happens, just at the time when the events described above were helping to remove the bloom from the old urban theory, an entirely new set of social problems and policy issues began to surface in the urban arena. By the second half of the 1970s, virtually all of the advanced capitalist economies were reeling from the effects of persistently high levels of job loss, unemployment, and chronic inflation. This was a time of dramatic economic dislocation and restructuring. As Bluestone and Harrison (1982) have shown, the 1970s witnessed an enormous amount of rationalization of industrial capacity in the Uni:d States via plant closures, mergers, and relocation. Similar events were having a devastating effect on most of the older industrial regions of Britain (Massey, 1984; Massey and Meegan, 1979). At the same time, in both North America and Western Europe basic industries were being thrown into crisis as a consequence of the intensified competition from imported goods manufactured in Japan and the newly industrializing countries. So marked were the economic depradations associated with these events that several observers of the advanced capitalist economies proclaimed that a literal deindustrialization was in progress (Blackaby, 1978; Bluestone and Harrison, 1982).

The major cities of North America and Western Europe were all deeply affected by these trends. In the United States, formerly prosperous industrial centers such as Buffalo, Detroit, and Pittsburgh were now faced with stagnation and decline as manufacturing plants closed down and as new capital investments were redeployed to cheap labor sites at peripheral and offshore locations. The endemic decentralization of productive capital from metropolitan regions became a rout, and as a consequence of this, large cities were increasingly burdened with difficult social and fiscal problems. In the mid-1970s, New York City itself came to the verge of bankruptcy as its economic position deteriorated and its tax base was eroded. Inner-city manufacturing districts and their attendant labor forces were especially affected by these developments, but even suburban areas (formerly zones of strong employment growth) were now also frequently showing signs of stress. Even in the mid-1980s, these processes are still apparent in numerous North American and Western European cities, though important indications of new growth are also widely detectable.

In fact, many forms of manufacturing activity continued to maintain a stubborn foothold in major cities over the period of turmoil and crisis in the 1970s. In many cases, this activity is now starting to flourish once more. Large numbers of new industrial growth centers in the Sunbelt and elsewhere were also expanding at a rapid pace during this period—especially those whose economies were founded on new high-technology industrial sectors—and in the 1980s, several of these centers have begun unmistakably to emerge as major urban regions. While all of this has been going on, the central office and service functions of cities have also grown with notable rapidity, and in numerous metropolitan areas of the United States today these functions dominate the entire pattern of employment.

In light of these developments, it is small wonder that the old urban theory (with its insistent fixation on the social space of the city) has taken on a superannuated look. Quite certainly, the major practical questions about urbanization have shifted their terrain. They are now to an ever-increasing degree concerned with the dynamics of the production system and its role in the growth, reproduction, and (and in some cases) stagnation and decay of metropolitan centers. By contrast, the old urban theory tended to relegate these dynamics to the status of mere background. Worse still, the production system was often simply assimilated, as Lowry (1964) had advocated in an influential statement, into the domain of the exogenously given—i.e., the nonproblematical. It no longer seems possible to continue with this self-defeating assumption about the limited role of production space within the modern metropolis. Rather, as I have already suggested, and as the chapters that follow argue in considerable detail, much that is most urgently in need of reconceptualization about the urban process today can best be seized via an inquiry into the operation of the production system (more especially of the *industrial* system) and concomitant structures of economic organization and work.

This claim about a fundamental interconnection between industrialization and urbanization is by no means new. In chronological order, Weber (1899), Haig (1927), Allen (1929), Perrin (1937), Florence (1948), Wise (1949), Lampard (1955), Hoover and Vernon (1959), Hall (1962a), Tsuru (1963), Sjoberg (1965), Thiry (1973), and Webber (1984), among many others, have all in one way or another alluded to the same idea. This conceptual lineage represents a sort of submerged tradition of urban studies, never as actively or coherently to the fore as Chicago School theory and its later transmutations, but always copresent through time. Nevertheless, this putative tradition has never succeeded in advancing any really sustained theoretical elaboration of this alternative view of urbanization, and it is my ambition in this book to redress somewhat this imbalance. I shall attempt to show how the modern metropolis emerges, at least in part, out of the fundamental logic of industrial production in capitalism, and how its geographical form is composed of interpenetrating production spaces and social spaces locationally dominated by the former. In this sense, the modern metropolis is both the creation of the social and property relations of capitalism and a specific condensation of them.

Before this analytical agenda can be set in motion, however, one further brief exercise in deconstruction and reorientation needs to be accomplished. Much has been made of late of the supposed actual or imminent transition to "postindustrial" society and, by extension, to the postindustrial city (Bell, 1973; Sternlieb and Hughes, 1975). Obviously, the basic theme of my book is an open challenge to the proponents of the postindustrial hypothesis, for my entire line of reasoning here is dependent on the notion of the continued basic importance of industrial production in capitalist society. I suggest, moreover, that this notion is pertinent not only to an examination of urbanization in the classical nineteenth-century period of capitalist development but also to any meaningful attack on the problem of urbanization in the twentieth century, and in late capitalism itself.

The postindustrial hypothesis strikes me as being seriously misleading in several of its major implications, and utterly wrong insofar as it points to the latent transcendence of capitalism by a sort of new information-processing mode of economic organization. Of course, we must acknowledge that contemporary capitalism is in part distinguishable from earlier forms by its greatly expanded dependence on white-collar workers, its burgeoning business and personal service functions, the massive increases in banking and financial operations that have taken place since the Second World War, and the greatly extended flows of information that have attended these outcomes. These phenomena are different in several important respects from previous forms of production and economic interchange, as the postindustrial hypothesis itself suggests. They are also typically growing with great rapidity in modern cities (Noyelle and Stanback, 1984) and hence we must treat them seriously in all that follows. To mistake them, however, for signs of a fundamental shift away from the structure and logic of industrial capitalism is to fail to understand their role and purpose in modern society. Three main points must be made in this regard.

First, many of these phenomena themselves represent simple forms of capitalist commodity production in the direct sense that their outputs are made by combining capital and labor, subject to the rule of profits. The fact that some of these outputs are intangible (like information or business services) does not detract from their common structural identity with sectors such as steel, cars, or electronics.

Second, among the most rapidly expanding sectors in American cities today are those that provide personal services (such as household finance, education, and health care). Some of these sectors are organized according to the logic of the commodity form; others are organized around the provision of public and semipublic goods. All of them, however, constitute essential underpinnings of the process of social reproduction in an increasingly human capital-intensive economy, and as such they are important components of and/or adjuncts to the basic structures of production and work in modern capitalism.

Third, and most important, a predominant subset of these phenomena (such as corporate administration, banking, insurance, accounting services, advertising, etc.) is posited on the immediate tasks of managing, commercializing, and financing the worldwide system of industrial commodity production. This system remains, as it always has been, the inner motor of the entire capitalist economy and the foundation of its central corporate institutions.

On all counts, then, these phenomena are directly or indirectly normal elements of the process of capitalist industrialization in its latest phase of development. They signify that a number of important changes have been taking place in industrial capitalism over recent decades, though they most certainly do not signify the passing away of capitalism as an organized system of commodity production. That said, and in deference to the substantive importance of these qualitative changes, I shall use the term *late capitalist industrialization* to designate collectively all forms of productive activity (ranging from manufacturing to the provision of financial services) in modern American society and to distinguish them from the specific forms of production that dominated in previous eras of capitalist development.

TWO

Structure and Change in the American Metropolitan System

Before the main theoretical arguments of this book are broached, I propose in this chapter to lay out in systematic fashion selected data on structure and change in the American metropolitan system. The purpose of this discussion is to set the scene for the subsequent analysis by identifying some broad empirical trends and highlighting a few preliminary questions. In line with the theoretical ideas alluded to in the previous chapter, I pay special attention in what follows to the structure of production and the changing employment base of large metropolitan areas.

GEOGRAPHICAL OUTLINES OF THE AMERICAN METROPOLITAN SYSTEM

In 1980 there were some 318 officially designated SMSAs (standard metropolitan statistical areas) in the United States. These SMSAs are widely scattered over the whole national territory, though an especially dense concentration occurs in the northeastern part of the country. This area largely corresponds to the old Manufacturing Belt, which, for the greater part of the present century, has constituted the industrial heartland of the United States and the principal seat of metropolitan development (see fig. 2.1).

The rise of large urban agglomerations in the Manufacturing Belt dates from the middle to the end of the nineteenth century. For some six or seven decades, down to the late 1960s, the region flourished on the basis of heavy manufacturing and large assembly industries. Productive activity in the region was devoted to such outputs as iron and steel, chemicals,

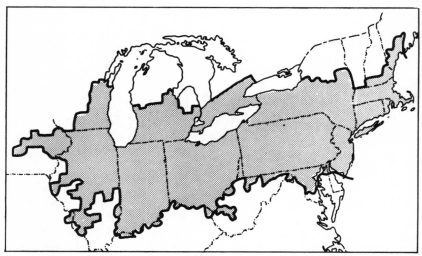

Figure 2.1. The Manufacturing Belt of the United States.
SOURCE: Pred (1965).

machinery, cars, electromechanical devices, domestic appliances, and so
on. The factories in which these outputs were produced congregated in
cities such as Baltimore, Boston, Buffalo, Chicago, Cincinnati, Cleveland,
Columbus, Indianapolis, Detroit, Milwaukee, Pittsburgh, St. Louis, and
so on. Within these cities, large pools of skilled and semiskilled blue-collar
workers were to be found along with growing numbers of white-collar
managerial and administrative cadres. In addition, many of the larger cities
were—then as now—important centers of small-scale and very labor-intensive forms of manufacturing activity serving final consumer markets in
clothing, footwear, furniture, hardware, and so on. The whole space-economy of the region was held together by a densely developed network of
water, rail, and road transport connections. Elsewhere in the United States,
outside of the Manufacturing Belt, industrial development was relatively
limited and widely dispersed, and urbanization was largely restricted to
localized resource sites, nodal points, regional trade centers, and small mill
communities and service towns.

By the late 1960s, this dominating configuration of the American economic and urban landscape was beginning to break up, and in its stead
the outlines of a new pattern became progressively more evident. This
shift was posited on fundamental changes going on in the American economy. The 1960s represents a period when the long postwar boom was
about to fade and when American industries were beginning to suffer in

a major way from the competitive incursions of cheap foreign imports. At the same time, the stagflationary crisis that set in toward the end of the 1960s and deepened over much of the 1970s resulted in a long-term profit squeeze for many sectors of production. These events created major difficulties for the older mass-production and consumer-oriented industries that had previously formed the basis of the prosperity of the Manufacturing Belt. The car industry in Detroit suffered greatly at this time, but so did many others, ranging from steel through electrical equipment to footwear and clothing. Furthermore, a steady stream of new investment capital was being to an ever-accelerating degree directed away from the Manufacturing Belt and toward peripheral areas in the United States and overseas.

This was a period during which the growth of the Sunbelt started to take off. By the mid-1970s, manufacturing employment was expanding much more rapidly in the Sunbelt than it was in the old Manufacturing Belt (or Frostbelt, as it was now being called). The latter region languished

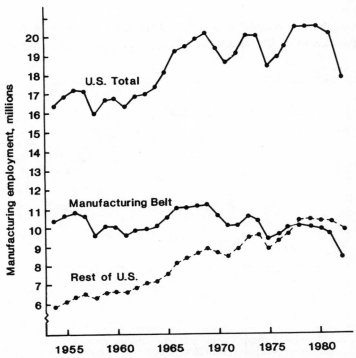

Figure 2.2. Manufacturing employment in the Manufacturing Belt and the rest of the United States, 1954–1981. Updated from Norton and Rees (1979, figure 1).

in stagnation and decline, and by the late 1970s its total manufacturing employment was actually starting to lag behind that of the former periphery (see fig. 2.2). Much of the new growth of manufacturing employment in the Sunbelt consisted of branch plants controlled from the old industrial heartland. To an ever-increasing degree, however, an autonomous internally generated process of industrialization was also going on in the Sunbelt, as expressed above all in the emergence of new growth centers founded for the most part on high-technology forms of manufacturing activity. By the 1960s, a series of major new centers of industrial production had appeared in Dallas-Fort Worth, Houston, Orange County, Phoenix, San Diego, Santa Clara County, and so on. Over the 1970s and 1980s, these centers continued to develop to the point where they now constitute some of the most dynamic and rapidly expanding foci of the whole American space-economy. These contrasts between developmental patterns in the Frostbelt and the Sunbelt are highlighted in figure 2.3, which demonstrates that between 1970 and 1980 the former was a region of significant urban decline while the latter was a region of rapid urban growth.

Over the last couple of decades, then, there has been a remarkable reorganization of the industrial-urban geography of the United States.

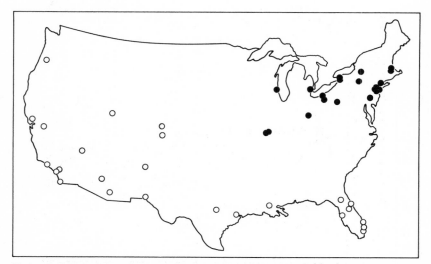

Figure 2.3. Population changes in metropolitan statistical areas, 1970–1980. Open dots indicate population growth greater than 30%; black dots indicate absolute population decline.

SOURCE OF DATA: U.S. Department of Commerce, Bureau of the Census, *Statistical Abstract of the United States,* 1984.

TABLE 2.1

METROPOLITAN AREAS WITH POPULATION EXCEEDING ONE MILLION IN 1980[a]

Rank	Short designation	Population 1970 '000	Population 1980 '000	Percent change 1970–1980
1	New York CMSA	18,193	17,539	−3.6
2	Los Angeles CMSA	9,981	11,498	15.2
3	Chicago CMSA	7,779	7,937	2.0
4	Philadelphia CMSA	5,749	5,681	−1.2
5	San Francisco CMSA	4,754	5,368	12.9
6	Detroit CMSA	4,788	4,753	−0.7
7	Boston CMSA	3,939	3,972	0.8
8	Washington, D.C. MSA	3,040	3,251	6.9
9	Houston CMSA	2,169	3,101	43.0
10	Dallas-Fort Worth CMSA	2,352	2,931	24.6
11	Cleveland CMSA	3,000	2,834	−5.5
12	Miami CMSA	1,888	2,644	40.0
13	Pittsburgh	2,556	2,423	−5.2
14	St. Louis CMSA	2,429	2,377	−2.2
15	Baltimore MSA	2,089	2,200	5.3
16	Atlanta MSA	1,684	2,138	27.0
17	Minneapolis-St. Paul MSA	1,982	2,137	·7.8
18	Seattle CMSA	1,837	2,093	13.9
19	San Diego MSA	1,358	1,862	37.1
20	Cincinnati CMSA	1,613	1,660	2.9
21	Denver CMSA	1,238	1,618	30.7
22	Tampa-St. Petersburg MSA	1,106	1,614	46.0
23	Milwaukee CMSA	1,575	1,570	−0.3
24	Phoenix MSA	971	1,509	55.4
25	Kansas City CMSA	1,373	1,433	4.4
26	Portland CMSA	1,047	1,298	23.9
27	New Orleans MSA	1,100	1,256	14.2
28	Columbus MSA	1,149	1,244	8.2
29	Buffalo CMSA	1,349	1,243	−7.9
30	Indianapolis MSA	1,111	1,167	5.0
31	Norfolk MSA	1,059	1,160	9.6
32	Sacramento MSA	848	1,100	29.8
33	Providence CMSA	1,065	1,083	1.7
34	San Antonio MSA	888	1,072	20.7
35	Hartford CMSA	1,000	1,014	1.4

SOURCE: U.S. Department of Commerce, Bureau of the Census, *Statistical Abstract of the United States 1984.*
[a] CMSA = consolidated metropolitan statistical area; MSA = metropolitan statistical area.

The center of gravity of that geography has been shifting steadily away from the North and East toward the South and West. As part of this change, there have been important changes in internal processes and patterns of urbanization as well as marked shifts in the geographical distribution of political and cultural power within American society at large.

TABLE 2.2

NUMBER AND POPULATION OF CMSAs AND MSAs BY POPULATION SIZECLASS
1970 AND 1980

Size class of metropolitan area	Number of areas in 1980	Population 1970 '000,000	Population 1980 '000,000	Percent change 1970–1980
5,000,000 +	5	46.5	48.0	3.4
1,000,000 – 5,000,000	30	53.6	59.8	11.4
500,000 – 1,000,000	33	20.4	23.3	14.2
250,000 – 500,000	57	17.1	19.8	15.5
100,000 – 250,000	122	15.7	18.5	17.9
< 100,000	28	2.1	2.4	13.4
Total	275	155.4	171.8	10.5

SOURCE: U.S. Department of Commerce, Bureau of the Census, *Statistical Abstract of the United States*, 1984.

INTRAMETROPOLITAN DEVELOPMENTS

Metropolitan size and growth. In table 2.1 are listed all metropolitan areas in the United States with populations in excess of one million at the time of the 1980 *Census of Population and Housing*. The table also shows population changes in these areas between 1970 and 1980. The contrast between decline in the Frostbelt and growth in the Sunbelt is again observable in these data. Absolute declines of metropolitan population between 1970 and 1980 are confined to the Frostbelt, whereas all significant growth (say, of the order of 20% or more) is in the Sunbelt.

At the same time, and cutting right across the Frostbelt-Sunbelt split, there has been a tendency in recent years for an inverse relationship to develop between the growth rate and the total population of U.S. metropolitan areas (table 2.2). From 1970 to 1980, metropolitan areas with populations of five million or more grew at an average rate of only 3.4 percent, whereas metropolitan areas ranging in size from 100,000 to 250,000 grew at a rate of 17.9 percent on average. Even the smallest metropolitan areas with populations below 100,000 grew at an average rate of 13.4 percent, and several commentators (e.g., Morrison, 1975; Vining and Strauss, 1977) have pointed to an actual recent rapid growth of nonmetropolitan areas as well. Of course, metropolitan areas in the Sunbelt have tended overall to grow more rapidly than those in the Frostbelt. However, in the Sunbelt itself, some of the largest metropolitan areas (such as Los Angeles, New Orleans, and San Francisco) have grown at rates that are far below broad local standards. It would seem that strong diseconomies of agglomeration are now starting to hamper expansion of the largest metropolitan areas, irrespective of location. Many kinds of manufacturing activity, in particular, are now declining rapidly in metropolitan areas all over the U.S. This state of affairs is echoed in recent developments in large British and European cities, which are also currently shedding manufacturing jobs on a major scale (Fothergill and Gudgin, 1979; Hall and Hay, 1980).

Manufacturing activities in metropolitan areas. Table 2.3 shows employment of manufacturing production workers in most of the large U.S. metropolitan areas in 1967 and 1982. As the table suggests, a long-run process of manufacturing job loss has been occurring in many metropolitan areas over the last few decades. The table shows employment change categorized by central-city area, suburban ring, and total SMSA. Observe that central-city areas have tended to lose production-worker jobs. Even the central-city areas of such dynamic Sunbelt SMSAs as Atlanta, Denver, and Los Angeles experienced absolute losses of these jobs between 1967 and 1982. In some metropolitan areas, such losses are more than compensated for by corresponding gains in manufacturing employment in suburban rings, which, on the whole, have grown with notable rapidity in the postwar decades (table 2.4). Nonetheless, many suburban-ring areas are themselves beginning to lose manufacturing employment as much industrial activity continues to spread out into peripheral areas. Again, it is preeminently the metropolitan areas of the Frostbelt that have suffered the most in this respect.

These remarks may be further illustrated by reference to table 2.5, which shows detailed manufacturing employment changes in the Philadephia SMSA from 1958 to 1984. These changes are representative of the experience of almost all large cities in the Manufacturing Belt over the last couple of decades. Table 2.5 shows that manufacturing employment in the Philadelphia SMSA as a whole expanded consistently if irregularly over the 1960s, but then fell steadily over the 1970s. Most of this fall is accounted for by severe contractions of manufacturing employment in the central city; but over the 1970s, even employment in Philadelphia's suburban ring also dwindled quite markedly.

These remarks all indicate that in recent years manufacturing employment has tended to decline precipitously in old, large industrial cities of the Frostbelt, and especially in the core areas of those cities. Sunbelt cities, by contrast, have fared relatively better, though even here manufacturing growth in central-city areas has been severely curtailed.

The white-collar metropolis. The phenomena discussed above are inscribed

TABLE 2.3

EMPLOYMENT OF MANUFACTURING PRODUCTION WORKERS, THOUSANDS, CENTRAL CITY AND SUBURBAN AREAS IN MAJOR SMAS 1967–1977[a]

	Central City			Suburban Ring			Total SMSA		
	1967	1977	Percent change 1967–77	1967	1977	Percent change 1967–77	1967	1977	Percent change 1967–77
New York	593.0	386.9	−34.8	156.6	102.1	−34.8	749.6	489.0	−34.8
Los Angeles-Long Beach	211.2	209.8	− 0.7	368.1	340.5	− 7.5	579.3	550.3	− 5.0
Chicago	382.2	241.2	−36.9	301.4	326.6	8.3	683.6	567.8	−16.9
Detroit	149.6	107.5	−26.8	247.4	262.1	5.9	394.3	369.6	− 6.3
Boston	53.9	32.2	−40.3	155.8	127.2	−18.4	209.7	159.4	−24.0
Houston	63.1	85.9	36.1	25.3	40.6	60.5	88.4	126.5	43.1
Dallas-Ft. Worth	74.8	67.1	−10.3	24.2	104.6	332.2	99.0	171.7	73.4
Cleveland	114.8	78.9	−31.3	95.1	97.0	2.0	209.9	175.9	−16.2
Miami	14.5	15.1	4.1	29.8	50.7	70.1	44.3	65.8	48.5
Pittsburgh	40.3	22.9	−43.2	156.8	131.0	−16.5	197.1	153.9	−21.9
St. Louis	92.8	63.5	−31.6	110.4	99.3	−10.1	203.2	162.8	−19.9
Baltimore	77.7	52.2	−32.8	68.9	57.3	−16.8	146.6	109.5	−25.3
Atlanta	37.0	26.8	−27.6	41.8	59.3	41.9	78.8	86.1	9.3
Minneapolis-St. Paul	42.6	30.6	−28.2	82.1	96.8	17.9	124.7	127.4	2.2
Seattle	37.0	34.5	− 6.8	29.6	42.3	43.9	66.6	78.6	18.0
San Diego	25.6	33.3	30.1	16.6	17.9	7.8	42.2	51.2	21.3
Cincinnati	50.9	33.1	−35.0	46.6	64.1	37.6	97.5	97.2	− 0.3
Denver	27.4	27.0	− 1.5	34.2	37.7	10.2	61.6	64.7	5.0

Tampa-St. Petersburg	13.5	14.9	10.4	19.8	25.7	29.8	33.3	40.6	21.9
Milwaukee	82.6	60.5	-26.8	67.0	78.2	16.7	149.6	138.7	-7.2
Phoenix	25.6	35.1	37.1	11.4	16.0	40.4	37.0	51.1	38.1
Kansas City	15.7	15.0	-4.5	74.7	62.6	-16.2	90.4	77.6	-14.2
Portland(Ore)	28.7	27.5	-4.2	29.7	40.4	36.0	58.4	67.9	16.3
Columbus	43.1	34.3	-20.4	13.3	28.8	116.5	56.4	63.1	11.9
Buffalo	48.9	33.4	-31.7	80.1	68.7	-14.2	129.0	102.1	-20.9
Indianapolis	59.2	59.4	0.3	37.3	23.7	-36.5	96.5	83.1	-13.9
Sacramento	6.9	7.1	2.9	9.2	11.1	20.7	16.1	18.2	13.0
Providence	31.7	26.6	-16.1	77.1	80.7	4.7	108.8	107.3	-1.4
San Antonio	17.8	22.6	27.0	2.0	6.1	205.0	19.8	28.7	44.9
Hartford	16.8	6.8	-59.5	53.8	42.9	-20.3	70.6	49.7	-29.6

SOURCE: U.S. Department of Commerce, Bureau of the Census, *Census of Manufactures*, 1967, 1977.
[a]SMSAs shown all had populations of 1,000,000 or more in 1980; Philadelphia, San Francisco, Washington D.C., New Orleans, and Norfolk are omitted because of incomplete data.

TABLE 2.4

MANUFACTURING EMPLOYMENT IN 245 SMAs IN THE UNITED STATES, 1947–1967

	Employment '000 1947	1967	Absolute change	Percent change
Central cities	7,356.7	7,063.4	−293.3	− 3.9
Suburban rings	4,141.7	8,044.0	3,902.3	+94.2
SMSAs	11,498.4	15,107.5	3,609.0	+31.4

SOURCE: Berry and Kasarda (1977), table 12.1.

within a number of deeply rooted changes in the structure of the American labor force. Over the last couple of decades, the number of white-collar workers in the labor force as a whole has grown with considerable rapidity, whereas the number of blue-collar workers has grown at a very sluggish pace, and from 1980 to 1982 actually declined (table 2.6). These changes in the division of labor are further captured in figure 2.4, which reveals

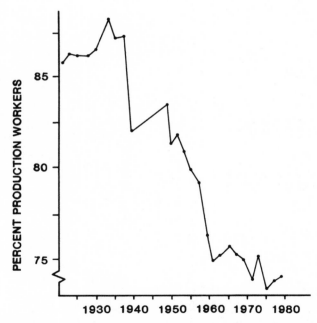

Figure 2.4. Production workers as a percentage of all workers in U.S. manufacturing, 1921–1979.

SOURCE OF DATA: U.S. Department of Commerce, Bureau of the Census, *Annual Survey of Manufactures* and *Census of Manufactures*.

TABLE 2.5

Philadelphia Standard Metropolitan Statistical Area: Total Employment in Manufacturing, 1958–1984

Year	City of Philadelphia '000	% Change from previous year	Suburban fringe '000	% Change from previous year	Total SMSA '000	% Change from previous year
1958	—	—	—	—	533.4	—
1959	—	—	—	—	546.6	2.5
1960	—	—	—	—	555.4	1.6
1961	—	—	—	—	544.2	− 2.0
1962	—	—	—	—	546.3	0.4
1963	—	—	—	—	536.7	− 1.8
1964	—	—	—	—	533.3	− 0.6
1965	—	—	—	—	551.3	3.4
1966	—	—	—	—	579.1	5.0
1967	—	—	—	—	583.1	0.7
1968	—	—	—	—	582.8	− 0.1
1969	252.5	—	329.4	—	581.9	− 0.2
1970	237.5	− 5.9	311.5	−5.4	549.0	− 5.7
1971	215.5	− 9.2	293.6	−5.7	509.1	− 7.3
1972	207.4	− 3.8	298.2	1.6	505.6	− 0.7
1973	203.8	− 1.7	308.2	3.4	512.0	1.3
1974	189.0	− 7.3	312.8	1.5	501.8	− 2.0
1975	163.0	−13.8	287.2	−8.2	450.2	−10.3
1976	158.7	− 2.6	284.4	−1.0	446.1	− 0.9
1977	153.7	− 3.2	292.7	2.9	446.4	0.1
1978	150.3	− 2.2	300.7	2.7	451.0	1.0
1979	143.4	− 4.6	310.6	3.3	454.0	0.7
1980	134.9	− 5.9	305.2	−1.8	440.1	− 3.1
1981	129.2	− 4.2	302.0	−1.0	431.2	− 2.0
1982	115.3	−10.8	286.3	−5.2	401.6	− 6.9
1983	109.2	− 5.3	279.8	−2.3	389.0	− 3.1
1984	108.4	− 0.8	287.9	2.9	396.3	1.9

SOURCE: U.S. Department of Labor, Bureau of Labor Statistics, *Employment, Hours, and Earnings, States and Areas, 1939–82*, Bulletin 1370–17, and *Supplement to Employment, Hours and Earnings, States and Areas, Data for 1980–84*, Bulletin 1370–19.

TABLE 2.6

U.S. OCCUPATION OF EMPLOYED WORKERS ('000)

	1960	1970	1980	1982
Total employment	65,778	78,678	99,303	99,526
White-collar workers	28,522	38,024	51,882	53,470
Professional & technical	7,469	11,149	15,968	16,951
Managers & administrators	7,067	8,295	11,138	11,493
Sales workers	4,224	4,857	6,303	6,580
Clerical workers	9,762	13,723	18,473	18,446
Blue-collar workers	24,057	27,807	31,452	29,597
Craft & kindred workers	8,554	10,164	12,787	12,272
Operatives	11,950	13,916	14,096	12,806
Nonfarm laborers	3,553	3,728	4,567	4,518
Ratio of blue-collar to white-collar workers	0.84	0.73	0.61	0.55

SOURCE: U.S. Bureau of Labor Statistics, *Employment and Earnings*.

that within the manufacturing labor force alone the percentage of blue-collar (production) workers has declined fairly regularly over the last five or six decades. This decline has been associated with large extensions of bureaucratic activity in the manufacturing system and a concomitant increase in managerial and secretarial personnel. This change runs parallel to large increases in employment in business and professional service industries generally, whether integrated directly with the manufacturing sector or not.

All major metropolitan areas in the United States contain large and growing numbers of white-collar workers. Even the crisis-ridden urban regions of the old Manufacturing Belt, many of which are otherwise losing considerable quantities of manufacturing employment, are still experiencing gains in various kinds of office and service employment (fig. 2.5). Thus, as shown by table 2.7, employment in business services increased substantially in the three largest SMSAs in the United States (i.e., New York, Los Angeles, and Chicago) even in the economically turbulent period stretching from 1972 to 1977. This type of employment also continues to concentrate heavily in central-city areas, as shown again by table 2.7, which reveals that employment in business services in the cores of the New York and Los Angeles SMSAs grew by 6.4 percent and 13.9 percent between 1972 and 1977. Nevertheless, there is evidence that growth in office and service employment in central-city areas may now be slowing

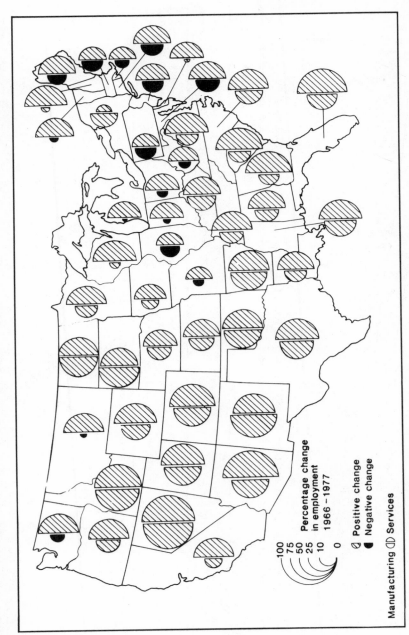

Figure 2.5. Changes in U.S. manufacturing and service employment by state, 1966–1977. Based on data in Norton and Rees (1979, p. 143).

TABLE 2.7

BUSINESS SERVICE EMPLOYMENT (SIC 73) IN NEW YORK, LOS ANGELES AND CHICAGO, 1972–1977

| | Central City | | | Suburban ring | | | Total SMSA | | |
	1972	1977	Percent change	1972	1977	Percent change	1972	1977	Percent change
New York	185,430	197,235	6.4	26,650	34,053	27.8	212,080	231,288	9.1
Los Angeles	69,962	79,682	13.9	47,964	61,167	27.5	117,926	140,846	19.4
Chicago	74,611	74,313	-0.4	36,158	52,420	45.0	110,769	126,733	14.4

SOURCE: U.S. Department of Commerce, Bureau of the Census, *Census of Service Industries*.

TABLE 2.8

FINANCE, INSURANCE, REAL ESTATE EMPLOYMENT IN NEW YORK

	New York City		Rest of SMSA		Total SMSA employment '000
	Employment '000	Percent of SMSA	Employment '000	Percent of SMSA	
1950	336.2	—	—	—	—
1955	357.4	—	—	—	—
1960	384.4	97.0	11.8	3.0	396.2
1965	389.8	96.6	13.7	3.4	403.5
1970	458.2	96.6	16.3	3.4	474.5
1975	420.1	95.7	18.8	4.3	438.9
1980	448.1	95.4	21.6	4.6	469.7
1982	487.1	95.5	23.2	4.5	510.3

SOURCE: U.S. Department of Labor, Bureau of Labor Statistics, *Employment, Hours, and Earnings, States and Areas 1939–82*, Bulletin 1370–17.

down somewhat, and it is perhaps symptomatic that central Chicago showed a small decline in business service employment from 1972 to 1977. The growth of white-collar employment in city centers seems to be reaching a plateau, though the expansion of such employment in suburban rings continues apace. Thus, whereas central-city areas remain the preponderant focus of white-collar employment, their relative weight in the whole metropolitan system is declining somewhat. Consider, for example, table 2.8, which provides details of employment in finance, insurance, and real-estate services in New York from 1950 down to 1982. The table indicates that both the city of New York and the rest of the SMSA have experienced an increase in this form of employment over the designated time period. The relative weight of the core area, however, has been shifting slowly but steadily downward over the same period.

Further evidence of these same trends can be gleaned from figure 2.6, which displays the headquarter locations of the 500 largest industrial corporations in the United States in 1984. It is apparent that these headquarters are in general firmly tied to major metropolitan centers. However, there is also a considerable spread of headquarter functions over the whole urban hierarchy and over many different types of regions. In fact, if we compare the geographical distribution of headquarter functions in 1984 with comparable data from a decade earlier (with, say, the data given in Dicken and Lloyd, 1981, or Pred, 1974), it is clear that a persistent process of spatial dispersal of these functions has been operating.

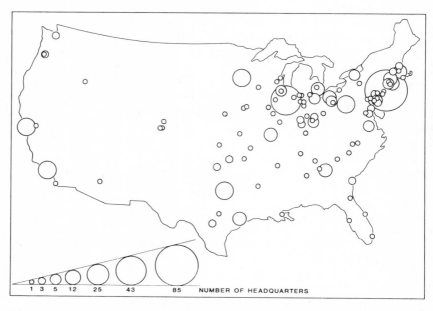

Figure 2.6. Headquarters locations of the 500 largest industrial companies in the United States, 1984.

SOURCE OF DATA: Fortune, *The 1984 Directory of U.S. Corporations.*

These findings suggest that large metropolitan regions (and especially their inner cores) in the United States are evolving in the direction of proportionately less manufacturing activity and more white-collar work. High-level office and service functions are particularly prone to seek out locations in the cores of large metropolitan regions. However, just as there has been an observable decentralization of manufacturing employment, so too can we observe—but lagged in time as it were—an analogous decentralization of some kinds of white-collar functions (Nelson, 1986). That said, the economies of the cores of large metropolitan regions are still dominated by white-collar employment, most especially high-level management and control activities together with attendant business and financial services. All the evidence suggests that there is likely to be some continued growth of these activities in core areas, though no doubt at a diminishing rate.

CONCLUSION

The findings presented in this chapter run parallel to the propositions of Hall and Hay (1980), who suggest that urban growth impulses in the advanced capitalist societies are passing:

(a) *outwards* from core areas to suburban rings;
(b) *downwards* through the urban hierarchy; and
(c) *across* from older industrialized regions to newer industrializing regions.

We should not deduce from these remarks, however, that American society is now entering into a phase of increasing deurbanization. The current conjuncture, rather, seems to be one of reorganization and restructuring within existing large agglomerations of capital and labor, combined with much new agglomeration at selected locations elsewhere. As we shall see in great detail below, there is no reason to suppose that processes of industrialization and urbanization have become permanently subdued in contemporary capitalist social formations. Even some of the old metropolitan regions of the Frostbelt are nowadays starting to give signs of an economic renaissance, though this has perhaps not always been an unmixed blessing in view of the important role that sweatshop industries and unskilled service activities have frequently played in this process. Above all, the balance of metropolitan growth in the United States appears to have shifted decisively to the Sunbelt, and it is here, more than anywhere, that jobs and population are regrouping on the economic landscape. In many ways, the recent rapid growth of the Sunbelt is reminiscent of the growth of the American Manufacturing Belt and the old industrial regions of Western Europe in the nineteenth century. That earlier growth ushered in radical shifts in the economic and urban geography of North America and Western Europe; and, similarly, these new developments prefigure dramatic geographic transformations. It is the purpose of the chapters that follow to provide some theoretical underpinnings for an understanding of these events and of their impacts on intraurban form.

THREE

The Logic of Industrial Production and Organization

I now seek to develop the basic theoretical framework on which much of the rest of this book hangs. My point of departure consists of a brief sketch of the fundamental macroeconomics of commodity production in capitalism. I then develop an overview of the problem of the division of labor and industrial organization. On this basis I trace out the lineaments of a theory of the firm as both a functional and a spatial phenomenon. From here I move forward into an elaborate account of locational activity and the structure of the modern space-economy.

COMMODITY PRODUCTION

The active core of capitalist society consists of a set of technical and social relations built up around the central institution of commodity production. Commodity production itself comprises a system of labor processes in which workers (in exchange for a wage) manipulate tools and equipment—i.e., capital—so as to bring forth sellable outputs. The broad reproducibility of the system hinges on two key conditions: (a) the continued acceptance on the part of the labor force of the legitimacy of the wages system, and (b) the ability of firms to sell their outputs at a price that fully covers all capital and labor costs and also yields up a normal rate of profit on all the capital that they advance. Recovered capital costs and profits are typically reinvested in new rounds of production, and in this manner the whole apparatus of production grows and develops over time. This definition of commodity production depends in no way on the physical form or character of outputs, but only on the specific (capitalistic) social relations that govern their production. By this definition, therefore, such intangibles as information, news, and advice are commodities, just as raw materials and manufactured outputs are.

At a basic technical level, commodity production can be conceived as an ensemble of simple input-output activities. In order to clarify this point, let us consider the case of an economy comprising n sectors of production, where each sector, of course, is made up by an aggregation of individual producers. Let the total *physical* input from any sector, i, to any other sector, j, be defined as x_{ij}. The total labor input to sector j is given as ℓ_{ij}, and the total output from the same sector is written, simply, as y_j. We can forthwith lay out the generalized structure of an intersectoral input-output system as follows

$$
\begin{array}{ccccccc}
x_{11}, & x_{21}, & \ldots, & x_{n1}, & \ell_1 & \to & y_1 \\
x_{12}, & x_{22}, & \ldots, & x_{n2}, & \ell_2 & \to & y_2 \\
\bullet & \bullet & & \bullet & \bullet & & \bullet \\
\bullet & \bullet & & \bullet & \bullet & & \bullet \\
\bullet & \bullet & & \bullet & \bullet & & \bullet \\
x_{1n}, & x_{2n}, & \ldots, & x_{nn} & \ell_n & \to & y_n.
\end{array}
\tag{3.1}
$$

This system identifies all the aggregate physical transactions and labor demands in the economy as an implicit function of the underlying physical/technical processes that regulate the transmutation of inputs into outputs.

As already indicated, commodity production also consists of a set of social relations superimposed on and intersecting with these physical input-output structures. Two such relations are of primary interest and significance here. The first is the price system, and the second has to do with the social arrangements that govern the distribution of the economic surplus into profits and wages. Let us define some terms: p_j is the production price of the jth commodity; w_j is the wage rate in sector j; and r is the normal rate of profit on all capital advanced. Note that r will tend to be constant over all sectors as a consequence of the dynamics of the equalization of the rate of profit in capitalism. We can combine these new variables with our basic input-output system so as to define an elementary macroeconomic model *à la* Sraffa (1960) as follows:

$$
\begin{array}{l}
(x_{11}p_1 + x_{21}p_2 + \ldots + x_{n1}p_n)(1 + r) + \ell_1 w_1 = y_1 p_1 \\
(x_{12}p_1 + x_{22}p_2 + \ldots + x_{n2}p_{n2})(1 + r) + \ell_2 w_2 = y_2 p_2 \\
\quad \bullet \qquad \bullet \qquad\qquad \bullet \qquad \bullet \qquad \bullet \qquad \bullet \\
\quad \bullet \qquad \bullet \qquad\qquad \bullet \qquad \bullet \qquad \bullet \qquad \bullet \\
\quad \bullet \qquad \bullet \qquad\qquad \bullet \qquad \bullet \qquad \bullet \qquad \bullet \\
(x_{1n}p_1 + x_{2n}p_2 + \ldots + x_{nn}p_n)(1 + r) + \ell_n w_n = y_n p_n.
\end{array}
\tag{3.2}
$$

The jth equation of this system signifies that (a) total capital advanced in sector j, i.e., $x_{1j}p_1 + x_{2j}p_2 + \ldots + x_{nj}p_n \ (= k_j)$, plus (b) normal profits, i.e., $k_j r$, plus (c) wages, i.e., $\ell_j w_j$, must all be equated at equilibrium to (d) total sector revenue, i.e., $y_j p_j$. In this simple version of the model, all capital inputs are assumed to be fully used up in one production period. We may append to this system of equations any arbitrary numeraire, say,

$$y_1 p_1 + y_2 p_2 + \ldots + y_n p_n = \Upsilon, \tag{3.3}$$

where Υ is gross income for the whole system.

We now take all wage rates, $w_1, w_2, \ldots, w_n$, as being defined exogenously by a series of historical and social circumstances—such as levels of worker organization, political conditions, and the like—that lie outside the strict economic logic of the equations themselves. Thus, given the $n + 1$ equations as represented by 3.2 and 3.3, we can compute the numerical values of the $n + 1$ unknowns consisting of the price vector $p_1, p_2, \ldots, p_n$ and the rate of profit r. It is evident that values of r are inversely correlated with wage rates so that any rise or fall in the latter will be followed by a decrease or increase, respectively, in the former. This correlation suggests that the takers of wages (workers) and the takers of profits (firms) must, on these grounds alone, be endemically susceptible to collisions with one another over their respective shares of the social surplus. Indeed, workers frequently organize in order to press their wage claims more effectively, just as firms periodically take strong measures to evade the high costs of labor and thus to increase rates of profit. The whole system of equations is like a skeletal representation of a capitalist social formation: it identifies a given configuration of the forces of production (i.e., input-output technologies) intertwined with and structured by a dominant set of social relations governing prices and income distribution. It is now possible to dress out this skeletal framework and to imbue it with innumerable additional details.

For present purposes, an especially urgent set of details concerns the institutional context of production. There is, running all the way through this abstracted model of a capitalist production system, a series of important relationships having to do with the firm, the division of labor, and the organization of production. These relationships, indeed, have major effects on the way the whole system functions; they are embedded in its logic, but they also in turn have a great impact on the way that logic operates. Thus, we cannot move unproblematically from the aggregate equations 3.2 and 3.3 to the individual unit of production and back again without first of all inquiring into the structure of these relations. What is more, it is precisely at the level of the firm, the division of labor, and the organization of production that the locational projection of this system out into the space-economy and the urban environment can be most effectively seized. Before we can deal with such geographical matters, however, we have much to do by way of preliminary investigation into the institutional structures of production. We begin with an account of the division of labor internal to the firm, and we then build up from this account to the problem of industrial organization at large.

THE DIVISION OF LABOR
WITHIN THE FIRM

There are innumerable divisions of labor in modern society. We may speak of divisions of labor according to skill, occupation, gender, industry, nation, and so on. For the moment, I propose to treat a rather special case of the division of labor involving the technical fragmentation of tasks *within* the individual firm. As the argument proceeds, I shall make increasing reference to a second case, namely, the social division of labor as represented by the (vertical) differentiation of tasks *between* independent firms. At a later stage I shall also deal with a third case, i.e., the spatial and/or international division of labor as described, for example, by Fröbel et al. (1980) and Massey (1984).

The individual firm can be viewed as a dynamic amalgam of interrelated labor processes separated from one another in a technical division of labor and coordinated by managerial authority. As both Leijonhufvud (1984) and Williamson (1985) have suggested, this way of viewing the firm provides us with a number of significant analytical possibilities that remain closed to us so long as we adhere to the neoclassical version of the firm as the embodiment of the standard production function, $y = f(k, \ell)$, which simply identifies output, y, as a mechanical function of capital inputs, k, and labor inputs, ℓ. The function yields a generalized definition of the quantitative relations between inputs and outputs, but it tells us nothing whatever about the detailed inner structural arrangements of the firm as a living social institution. Above all, it totally obscures for us the fundamental role of the technical division of labor in the functioning of the firm. It is of primary importance that we comprehend this role if our aim is to analyze the functional and spatial organization of production. We can initiate the analysis by means of a brief review of the account of the division of labor in pin manufacture with which Adam Smith (1776, 1970 ed.) opens his great book, *The Wealth of Nations.*

Let us imagine, to begin with, that pin manufacture is in a primitive stage of development such that the entire and undivided work of production is carried out by what Smith calls "country workmen" serving small localized markets. With increases in the extent of any market (and here Smith was thinking explicitly about *geographical* extent), the labor of pin making becomes divided into a series of specialized full-time tasks attended to by detail workers. This division is a reflection of the way in which the search for economies of scale drives forward the dynamics of the production system in capitalism. Thus, a reorganization of pin making activities now comes about, and labor processes are fragmented into such trades as drawing, straightening, cutting, pointing, grinding, head making, whitening, and so on. Smith observes that even the task of mounting the finished pins onto strips of paper for final sale is a trade in its own right. With increasing volumes of output, the division of labor tends to become increasingly more finely grained. As this happens, labor tasks become more routinized (which lowers skill requirements and hence wages), on-the-job learning is streamlined, and with the smoothing out of work rhythms, costly setup times and downtimes are minimized. Coincidentally, according to Marglin (1974), this same division of labor gives capitalists a greater measure of control over the labor process than they are able to exert where workers have discretionary command over a wider range of tasks.

A more analytical way of treating the technical division of labor can be developed by reference to figure 3.1. Assume that the situation depicted in figure 3.1 represents two possible techniques of production for a given firm. One technique involves the production of a quantity of output, y, by means of an undivided labor process whose average cost curve is defined by the function $f(y)$. The cost-minimizing level of production of this technique is given by the quantity $\bar{y}$; and the average cost associated with this level of production is α^*. The other technique is characterized by an internal technical division of labor in which y is made in two stages. In the first stage, a quantity, x, of an intermediate good is made (e.g., semifinished pins) and this then becomes an input to the second stage in which a quantity, y, of final output is produced (finished pins). We may take it that the average cost functions associated with x and y under conditions of divided labor are $g(x)$ and $h(y)$, respectively, and we shall assume for simplicity's sake that these functions are separable and additive. This technical division of labor makes it possible for the firm to operate in any one

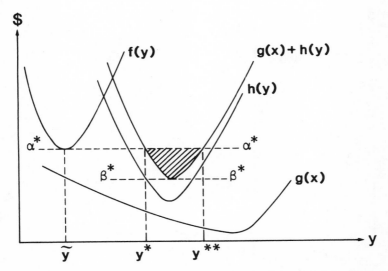

Figure 3.1. The simple dynamics of the technical division of labor; f(y) is the total average cost curve before division; g(x) + h(y) is a possible average cost curve after division.

of several different organizational configurations. I shall describe two polar cases of this phenomenon.

In the first place, let us assume that x and y are produced in perfect balance with one another in the relation x = y. The total average cost of production will be, simply, g(x) + h(y). Figure 3.1 has been constructed for illustrative purposes so that g(x) + h(y) ≤ α* over the interval y*, y**. Hence, if the market can absorb the increase in y, then, the firm will tend to switch to this configuration of the divided labor technique (as and when its blueprint is developed) rather than continuing to produce according to the undivided function f(y). The minimum value of g(x) + h(y) is given by β*.

In the second place, it may well be feasible for the firm to produce x and y in an unbalanced relation and to deal with excesses or deficits of x relative to internal needs by means of market transactions. In this event, x is likely to be produced at or close to its minimum average cost, which is shown in figure 3.2 as γ*. The firm's composite average cost of producing y will now be γ* + h(y). The condition γ* + h(y) ≤ α* holds over the interval y', y'', so that the firm will, again, prefer this alternative divided labor technique to the technique whose average cost function is f(y). At the same time, we also have the condition γ* + h(y) ≤ β* over the

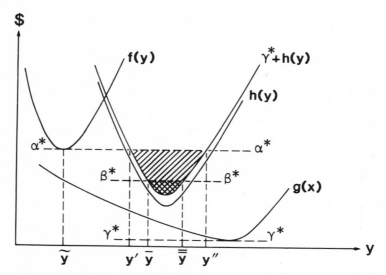

Figure 3.2. The simple dynamics of the technical division of labor continued; the line labeled β* is transferred from fig. 3.1.

interval $\tilde{y}$, $\bar{y}$. All else being equal, then the firm will opt for the divided labor technique in which x and y are produced in an unbalanced relation and where x is produced at its absolute minimum average cost. This option assumes that the firm can dispose of its surplus production of x with little or no damage to its overall profitability level; it assumes, for example, that surplus production can be marketed without a disproportionate increase in the firm's administrative costs.

It need scarcely be stressed that the relationships sketched out in figure 3.1 and 3.2 are illustrative only. These figures do not define any irrevocable theoretical necessities in the temporal sequencing of switches in production technique. Their main purpose is to provide us with a simple analytical vocabulary that can be put to use in carrying the argument forward. They do, nonetheless, capture some of the operative mechanisms that underlie the deepening and widening of the internal division of labor in any given firm; e.g., as the production system evolves from craft labor to deskilled detail work, or from batch manufacturing processes to assembly-line methods, or from grocery stores to supermarkets, and so on. That said, it is important to add the proviso that the internal organization of firms does not by any manner of means evolve invariably down the simple one-way street of endlessly fragmenting work tasks. Technical advances in production methods are sometimes associated with a narrowing of the internal division of labor. This is what Robinson (1931) has referred to as the *resynthesis* of labor processes in which a single unit of fixed capital substitutes for what was previously done in a series of discrete operations. Hence, we might envisage pin manufacture as evolving into a further stage in which the internal division of labor is entirely swept away and in which production is henceforth assured by a pin-making machine (run by a single operator) that does the entire work of fabrication from beginning to end. This example suggests that technical change in industry may well sometimes be associated with downsizing of production units in terms of employment levels, and even, occasionally, in terms of output levels.

INDUSTRIAL ORGANIZATION AND THE DIVISION OF LABOR BETWEEN FIRMS

Consider, once again, the division of labor in pin manufacture. We have dealt with this phenomenon so far as something that is contained within the walls of one large workshop. Various other possibilities are apparent, however. One is that the workshop breaks up into a series of specialized and geographically separate branch establishments under common ownership; this is the problem of the multiestablishment firm, which we will address at a later stage. Another is that the *technical* division of labor is transformed into a *social* division of labor in which the different trades involved in pin manufacture separate into independent and individually owned workshops. If this latter case should occur, the workshops will become linked in a system of input-output transactions and will thus constitute an elementary *industrial complex*. Where the social division of labor is accompanied by falling overall production costs, it will tend to deepen and widen, leading to the creation of expanding pools of external scale economies. In a now classic paper, Young (1928) has alluded to this phenomenon in terms of increasing returns via the intensifying "roundaboutness" of production. This raises at once the question of the structure of vertically organized systems, i.e., the *problem of the vertical integration and disintegration of production*. We start out with a description of production processes as a set of transactional activities and corresponding scope effects.

Transactional activities and scope effects. When we speak of the division of labor, we are by the same token making implicit reference to production activities as a series of labor processes that are linked by means of transactional interconnections. Indeed, in his pioneering inquiry into industrial organization, Coase (1937) suggested quite explicitly that we can think of production in one sense as a network or complex of transactions. On the one hand, the firm with its technical division of labor is constituted as a set of internalized transactions ruled over by a managerial hierarchy. Within the firm, transactional behavior is guided by administrative structures and decisions and ruled ultimately by fiat. On the other hand, each firm is situated within a social division of labor and thus also transacts business with other firms across external markets. In these markets, transactional behavior is guided above all by price signals. The great insight of Coase was to pose the problem of the structure of production in terms of the changing interface between the internal and the external domains of transactional activity. He expressed this insight in the following celebrated passage, which amounts, in essence, to an organizational theory of the firm.

> A firm will tend to expand until the costs of organizing an extra transaction within the firm become equal to the costs of carrying out the same transaction by means of an exchange on the open market. [Coase 1937, p. 395]

At any given time, then, the line that divides the internal hierarchy of the firm from the external market (and thus identifies the individual firm) is fixed at the point where the relative efficiencies of managements (hierarchies) and markets are equal.

This issue may be highlighted by means of two simple illustrations representing vertical integration and vertical disintegration, respectively. On the one hand, markets in molten steel are by the nature of the case extraordinarily difficult to organize efficiently. However, rolling mills can significantly reduce their production costs if they consume molten steel as an input rather than steel ingots (which by definition have lost their economically valuable high temperature). Market failure in molten-steel transactions means that rolling mills have a very strong incentive to integrate backward into steel smelting and thus to achieve thermal efficiency in production. On the other hand, law firms typically make frequent use of printing services, which they usually purchase from outside because the transactional costs of managing joint in-house legal and printing functions are likely to be high. Vertical disintegration of legal and printing functions is all the more predictable in view of the efficiency that seems to characterize open markets in printing services.

An alternative way of expressing the same ideas is to say that *internal economies of scope* are present in the case of the steel smelting and rolling example, but that *internal diseconomies of scope* are present in the case of the legal and printing services example (see Panzar and Willig, 1981; Silver, 1984; Teece, 1980). In the terms defined by Panzar and Willig (1981), economies of scope are detectable if $g(x) + h(y) \geq c(x, y)$, where (a) x and y are (as before) quantities of output, (b) $g(x)$ and $h(y)$ are separable and additive average cost functions, and (c) $c(x, y)$ is the joint average cost of producing x and y in an integrated firm. Where $g(x) + h(y) \leq c(x, y)$, diseconomies of scope prevail. Note that economies and diseconomies of scope identified in this way refer generally not only to vertical forms of industrial organization but to conglomerate forms as well. These scope effects are ultimately defined by transaction costs that in turn have both institutional and technical foundations.

Vertical integration and disintegration. Let us now examine in a little more detail some of the ways in which transaction costs and their attendant scope effects influence the vertical organization of production. Unfortunately, it is extremely difficult to enumerate systematically all the concrete circumstances that affect the form and direction of these relationships. Here, for the purposes of simple illustration, I shall simply describe a few examples of such circumstances, and then, in the next main section of this chapter, I shall attempt to construct a more synthetic overview of the problem. Vertical integration and disintegration are in a sense mirror images of one another, and if a given condition engenders the one, the absence or reversal of that same condition is likely to give rise to the other. For convenience of exposition, however, I treat vertical integration and disintegration as two distinctive categories of phenomena, and I deal with each under separate subheadings.

Vertical integration:

Vertical integration tends to come about when the internalization of the transaction costs associated with different labor processes results in significant cost savings. Williamson (1975, 1979, 1985) has proposed in a series of powerful and influential analyses that this occurs above all where market failures in external transactions are the rule. He claims that such failures are most prone to make their appearance in situations where (a) critical information is unequally distributed over transacting parties, and (b) costly future contingencies are likely to arise, in the context of (c) a complex and unpredictable future. Given the difficulties and expense of writing and policing satisfactory contingent-claims contracts under these conditions, one or another of the transactors will have an inducement to resolve the problem by means of vertical integration. For example, a firm that purchases R&D services from an independent consultancy may find that it is subsidizing research breakthroughs in related areas that the R&D firm can then profitably market for itself. If these potential breakthroughs cannot be adequately dealt with in a contingent-claims contract, the first firm may well begin to provide its own R&D services internally. Alternatively, a firm that has to deal with monopolized input or output markets may find its future profitability compromised by rising prices on the one hand or restricted sales outlets on the other (Kaserman, 1978). This is precisely the kind of problem alluded to above, where molten steel passes from a smelting works to a rolling mill. In the absence of market flexibility in molten steel, the two must enter into some sort of long-term mutual dependence that makes each (under conditions of separate ownership) vulnerable to the opportunism of the other. This problem, again, can often best be resolved by vertical integration, i.e., by enlarging the scope of managerial governance of the firm (Williamson, 1981).

One of the very strong findings in much of the recent literature on industrial organization is that vertical integration tends especially to come about in situations where transactions involve firm-specific know-how and technological complementarities (see Armour and Teece, 1980; Levy, 1985; Masten, 1984; Stuckey, 1983; Warren-Boulton, 1978). In the semiconductor business, for example, R&D work, wafer diffusion, and testing are characteristically vertically integrated because there are significant, idiosyncratic, and extremely complex information feedback and feedforward effects from one stage to the next (Henderson and Scott, 1987). Semiconductor assembly, by contrast, may or may not be vertically integrated with these other functions, depending on the amount and kind of technological information that needs to be exchanged between transacting parties; and this in turn depends largely on the quality of the devices to be assembled (Scott and Angel, 1987).

Vertical disintegration:

When internal transaction costs exceed external transaction costs, labor processes are highly susceptible to vertical disintegration. One way of reexpressing this idea is to say that an upper limit on the number of functions that a firm can profitably operate is set by its internal information-processing capacities and effective managerial range. When the firm becomes overextended in these respects, it can no longer properly coordinate the functioning of its different parts, and it will thus begin to shed some of these. If market transactions are efficient and low in cost, this will be a further inducement to the firm to externalize selected functions in order to achieve economic viability.

Three special substantive cases where the ratio of internal to external transactions costs is high merit close attention in this context. The first is where markets for final output are extremely uncertain. The uncertainty is liable to be transmitted backward through the vertical structure of the firm leading to serious misallocations of resources (Carlton, 1979; Scott 1983a). The firm, however, can externalize much of the uncertainty by engaging in subcontracting activity. Moreover, if markets in subcontract services are extensive and highly solvent, then by the law of large numbers the overall level of uncertainty (and hence costs) in the whole system will be reduced. The second case is where a particular kind of production process can achieve economies of scale only if it serves several downstream customers at a time (as in the law firm/printing firm example cited earlier). Because of the need to set up specific external sales arrangements for the output in question, it is often most efficient to produce it in streamlined disintegrated firms that can concentrate their managerial energies on the necessary tasks of specialized manufacture and marketing. Finally, the third exemplary case is where segmented (or segmentable) labor markets exist. In this circumstance, large unionized firms employing expensive primary labor can usually reduce their costs by putting out packets of work to small nonunionized firms ensconced in secondary labor markets (Berger and Piore, 1980; Friedman, 1977).

Several analysts have further suggested that routinization of labor processes and standardization of outputs also encourage vertical disintegration. These attributes are associated with diminished technical complementarities between different tasks, and this then renders market transactions relatively straightforward (Masten, 1984; Monteverde and Teece, 1982; Scott, 1983a). These remarks underpin the earlier comment to the effect that transactions that involve firm-specific know-how and technological complementarities help to bring about vertical integration by increasing the likelihood of market failure.

Other approaches to the problem of vertical structure:

This brief description of industrial organization processes highlights the fundamental role of internal and external transaction costs in determining levels of vertical integration and disintegration. The competing theory of Stigler (1951) sees vertical disintegration as purely a function of scale economies where individual functions with increasing returns to scale are spun off from firms as markets grow in size. This theory has been widely and correctly judged to be inadequate by reason of its failure to address the basic issue of the intrafirm and interfirm transaction costs that different functions incur under different institutional arrangements (Levy, 1984, 1985). Similarly, the theory of Alchian and Demsetz (1972), which sees the firm as an expression of technically nonseparate activities, goes only part of the way to an adequate analysis, for firms can frequently be observed to exist even where simple technical separabilities are strongly in evidence (Williamson, 1975, 1985).

Neither scale economies nor indivisibilities alone, then, appear able fully to account for the observable phenomena of industrial organization. Even the transactional approach alone cannot do justice to the range and complexity of the problem as a whole, for we must in the end set transactional activities in the context of the various costs that are incurred as production proceeds. In light of this observation, I now attempt to provide an abstract synthesis of all the different elements that finally enter into the problem, and I also introduce an important new ingredient into the analysis, the multiestablishment firm.

THE ORGANIZATION OF PRODUCTION AND THE THEORY OF THE FIRM: A SYNTHESIS

Let us return to the example of two labor processes producing x and y, where x is an input to y. Again, $g(x)$ and $h(y)$ are separable and additive average cost functions, and $c(x, y)$ is the average cost of jointly producing x and y under conditions of vertical integration. We may take it that $c(x, y)$ exhibits the effects of economies and/or diseconomies of scope. In the present account, I identify these scope effects explicitly by means of a simple algebraic shortcut, i.e., $s(x, y) = c(x, y) - g(x) - h(y)$, where $s(x, y)$ is total economies or diseconomies of scope per unit of y. Thus, $s(x, y)$ is simply the residual element of $c(x, y)$ once we extract the effects of the separate cost functions $g(x)$ and $h(y)$. Note that where $s(x, y) < 0$, we have positive economies of scope, and where $s(x, y) > 0$, *dis*economies. With these definitions in mind, let us turn to figure 3.3.

The first panel (A) of figure 3.3 represents the case of full vertical and spatial integration of x and y. For ease of exposition, it is assumed here that x and y are produced in perfectly balanced proportions at every level

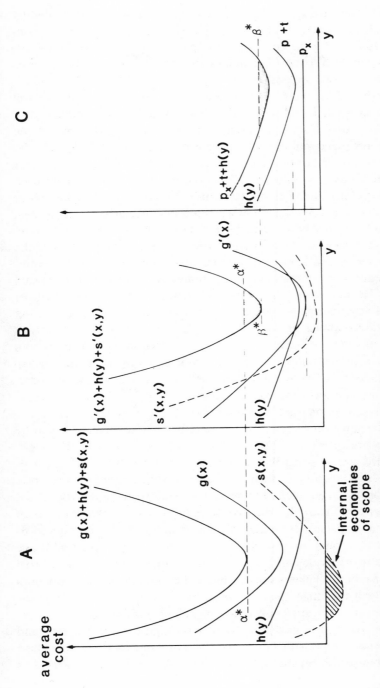

Figure 3.3. The intra and interfirm organization of production. (A) Vertical and spatial integration. (B) Vertical integration and spatial disintegration. (C) Vertical and spatial disintegration. The quantity $p_x + t$ is the market price of x; $s(x,y)$ represents intrafirm economies and diseconomies of scope; and t represents interestablishment transactions costs.

of output. Total average production costs in this case are represented by the curve labeled $g(x) + h(y) + s(x, y)$, whose minimum value is given by α^*. Observe that the curve $s(x, y)$ in panel A is drawn (for illustrative purposes) in such a way that it cuts through a region where internal economies of scope are positive.

In the central panel (B) of figure 3.3 it is assumed that x and y are still vertically integrated with each other but that x is now produced at a different location from y. In brief, panel B represents the case of the vertically integrated multiestablishment firm. The curves labeled $g'(x)$, $h(y)$ and $s'(x, y)$ are defined as in the previous case, but note two important qualifications to this statement. First, the function $g(x)$ has now been transformed into the function $g'(x)$. This is intended to reflect the change in location of the establishment in which x is manufactured. Such a change will often in practice be associated with a switch of production technique; and it will usually also be associated with changes in the price schedules of the materials and labor used as inputs to x. Second, the curve representing internal economies and diseconomies of scope has also changed in shape. The new curve $s'(x, y)$ has been drawn (for the sake of argument) in such a way that it now passes entirely through a region representing internal diseconomies of scope. In this new situation the curve $s'(x, y)$ includes an additional internal cost that is incurred in transferring x from its point of production to the location where y is manufactured. Thus, $s'(x, y)$ includes simple physical transport costs on x as well as any additional communication and coordination costs involved in spatially separating production of x and y from each other. Total average costs in the case of the situation represented by panel B are now therefore given by the curve labeled $g'(x) + h(y) + s'(x, y)$, whose minimum value is β^*. The shaded area in panel B defines a locus of points for which $g'(x) + h(y) + s'(x, y) \leq \alpha^*$. Here, then, vertical integration and spatial separation of functions will be preferred to full vertical and spatial integration.

In panel C of figure 3.3 the two labor processes are taken to be both vertically and spatially separated. Producers of y will now be obliged to buy input x through external market transactions. The input will hence be valued at its market price, p_x. Given the dissolution of the internal institutional bonds linking x and y, internal economies and diseconomies of scope will no longer play a role in fixing their joint average costs. However, external transaction costs (including transport costs) will assuredly be incurred in mediating input x through the open market, and these are simply represented by the constant unit quantity t. Total average costs of production in this fully disintegrated case can be expressed as

$p_x + t + \text{h}(y)$. The condition $p_x + t + \text{h}(y) \leq \beta^*$ prevails over the shaded area of panel C, and this signifies that full disintegration is the most economical form of production in this given example.

Observe at once that figure 3.3 (like figures 3.1 and 3.2) does indeed only represent an arbitrary example, and there is no intention here of tendentiously asserting that (a) integrated single establishment forms of production are always inferior (from the viewpoint of costs) to multiestablishment structures, or that (b) multiestablishment structures are always inferior to full functional and spatial disintegration. On the contrary, many other possible orderings of these organizational forms are conceivable in theory and observable in practice. What figure 3.3 seeks to accomplish is simply to portray the sort of interplay that comes into effect between the major variables that control the functional and spatial relations of vertically adjacent labor processes.

On the basis of the analysis carried out with the aid of figure 3.3, we are now in a position to affirm that the interpenetrating levels of the functional and spatial organization of production are determined by internal and external transactional relations (as expressed in economies and diseconomies of scope) in the context of variable scale effects and their expression in production costs and market prices. Any coherent theory of industrial organization and location must deal with all of these relationships in their full simultaneity.

TOWARD AN ANALYSIS OF LOCATIONAL AGGLOMERATION AND DISPERSAL

The discussion above reveals that there is a necessary positive relationship between vertical disintegration and the proliferation of externalized transactional activity in any given production system. The more the system breaks down into specialized industrial establishments, the denser the web of interlinkages between those establishments becomes. In this manner, the outlines of an interconnected complex of industries take shape, and if vertical disintegration is also accompanied by *horizontal disintegration* (i.e., increasing numbers of establishments per quantity of total output), then the labyrinth of interlinkages is likely to become particularly convoluted. Each unit of production performs a series of specialized tasks within the complex, and each in turn continually adjusts its internal operations as the whole complex evolves through time. No single unit can unilaterally create the conditions of its own existence, since each is dependent for its survival upon the successful reproduction of the entire social division of labor and concomitant external economies. Hence, we can only comprehend these sorts of disintegrated production complexes in their totality: they are not just simple aggregations of individual units of productive decision making and behavior, but also, and more significantly, they are integral totalities whose configuration is governed by structural laws of motion as whole.

One extremely important structural consequence of the disintegration of production is a propensity for those establishments that are caught up in tight transactional relationships with one another to gravitate location-ally toward their common center of gravity. We will deal with the intricacies of this idea in the next chapter. For now, we may simply aver that there is always considerable pressure *(ceteris paribus)* on producers in disinte-grated complexes to locate near one another in order to keep the costs of externalized transactional activity as low as possible. These remarks also imply the converse case: production systems that are undergoing integra-tion and resynthesis of their component processes are by the same token reinternalizing formerly externalized transactional relations; this alone will help to dissolve the bonds linking different units of production, and any preexisting complex will accordingly be susceptible to reconstitution within a few integrated establishments at widely scattered sites. Sometimes, depending on the structure of technologies and markets, we may find these contrasting principles of disintegration/clustering and integration/dispersal operating simultaneously in different segments of the same sector of pro-duction (Scott and Angel, 1987).

These remarks may be illustrated in a rudimentary and rather speculative way with some information taken from an early study by Chapman and Ashton (1914) of the British cotton textile industry at the end of the nineteenth century. Chapman and Ashton show that in Lancashire, the heartland of the British cotton industry at that time, some eighty-two percent of all textile mills were disintegrated into specialized spinning and weaving establishments. In the rest of the country, however (i.e., in what amounted to the geographical periphery vis-à-vis the cotton textile in-dustry), only forty-nine percent of mills were disintegrated.

This information prompts the interpretation that in Lancashire, with its dense assemblage of disintegrated producers, relatively smooth trans-actional relations between specialized spinning and weaving establishments were possible. These transactional relations were embodied in efficient markets in spun yarn of a wide variety of counts. However, outside of Lancashire, the relative sparsity of complementary producers made it nec-essary for cotton manufacturers to integrate vertically in order to produce efficiently. Chapman and Ashton further indicate that these vertically integrated manufacturers typically produced more standardized qualities of output than did manufacturers in the central Lancashire complex—a reflection, no doubt, of the pressure to economize on transactions in areas with relatively sparse endowments of both upstream and downstream externalities.

In a word, *increasing roundaboutness of production and expanding external economies of scale are at the very heart of concentrated regional and urban growth*. Conversely, diminishing roundaboutness—i.e., a narrowing of the social division of labor—is often a precondition for locational dispersal to occur. Where this latter tendency begins to undercut production in centralized disintegrated complexes, it can often help to initiate painful rounds of economic crisis and decline. Underlying these counterposed trends in the functional and geographical organization of production is the stubborn core of capitalist commodity production as defined by equations 3.2 and 3.3 above.

Agglomeration Processes and Industrial Complex Formation

For much of the recent past, geographers and regional scientists have tended to deal with matters of industrial development on the basis of the classical theory of location as originally codified by Alfred Weber (1929) and as subsequently reexpressed by neoclassical theorists such as Hoover (1937), Isard (1956), and Moses (1958). In this theory, location is typically treated as a problem in individual decision making and behavior relative to a given spatial environment. Each decision maker is assumed to seek out a location such that the transport costs incurred in assembling inputs from their (given) sources and in dispatching outputs to their (given) final markets are at a minimum. In more elaborate versions of the theory, decision makers are assumed to minimize the global costs of transport *and* production, so that important tradeoffs occur between transport inputs and other kinds of inputs in the final locational decision. Almost all versions of the theory also make reference to the role of agglomeration economies in locational decision making, though because of its limited sense of inter and intraindustrial dynamics, the conception of agglomeration that typically informs the Weberian theory of location leaves much to be desired.

Within its own frame of reference, this Weberian approach to locational analysis provides a number of useful insights, and I shall make reference to these from time to time. I want to stress at the same time, however, that the framework itself is seriously deficient in several important respects and above all by reason of its insistence on the primacy of the atomized locational decision maker. Weberian theory never really comes effectively to terms with the central question of the functional-spatial logic of the locational system *taken as a whole:* that is, it fails to deal with the system as an ensemble of events interlocked together within an evolving network of transactional relations. In the present chapter I shall explicitly address this latter issue, and attempt to develop what we may call a *post-Weberian* account of locational processes via a continued discussion of the logic of industrial organization. It is my hope in this way to be able to address a particular problem that the classical theory has never seemed able adequately to grasp, namely, intrametropolitan industrial location, and on this basis to work toward an attack on the wider question of industrialization and urbanization.

GROWTH CENTERS REVISITED

Even as early as the 1950s and the 1960s, a few analysts had attempted to go beyond simple Weberian location theory by means of investigations of the aggregate dynamics of growth poles and growth centers. These investigations were, like location theory itself, flawed in a number of ways, and they were above all silent on the crucial issue of industrial organization as described in the previous chapter. In spite of this failure, growth pole and growth center theory provides us with a useful preliminary sense of the development of major nodes of economic activity on the landscape, and I shall use it here as a point of departure for a more elaborate inquiry as to why the geography of capitalist society is so persistently characterized by uneven development in the form of privileged centers of concentrated economic activity separated from one another by large expanses of relatively less developed terrain.

To begin with, a growth *pole* is a sector of production with the special feature that it has many backward linkages (both direct and indirect) to other sectors of production. Thus, by definition, a growth pole occupies a central position in any input-output structure, and as such, expansion or contraction of the pole engenders much expansion or contraction (as the case may be) in the rest of the economy. The car and aerospace industries, for example, are powerful growth poles in the modern American economy, and as such they play a significant leading role in its cyclical upswings and downswings. Note immediately that this definition of a growth pole invokes the notion of location in economic space (i.e., the multidimensional input-output system), but is strictly noncommittal about location in geographical space. In other words, the definition tells us nothing about the actual geography of any given pole (Darwent, 1969).

In practice, a pole and its attendant constellation of upstream industries may occur in a diversity of geographical realizations ranging from the extremely dispersed to the extremely concentrated. Where the latter outcome prevails, say, because of the pressure of transport costs on interindustrial linkages, the lineaments of a *growth center* start to make their appearance.

Let us now suppose that a major polar industry locates at a given place on the economic landscape, perhaps in conformity with Weberian locational pressures, and that a local growth center takes shape around it. Accordingly, innumerable upstream industries begin to move into the local area in a process of regional import substitution. We would also expect some plants in downstream sectors to shift into the area in order to tap its readily accessible inputs. In these ways, the backward and forward linkages emanating from the pole become lines of gravitational force along which new units of production are drawn into its spatial orbit (Perroux, 1961).

A series of derivative but highly significant effects now typically come into play. First, many workers are attracted to the vicinity of the center, and if the production system is variegated enough, they will embody a corresponding diversity of skills and human attributes. This diversity in itself constitutes a locational attraction for new industries. Second, the wages earned by the labor force are spent locally on nonbasic goods and services, and the concomitant multiplier effects engender further rounds of economic growth. Third, the transport connections between the center and the rest of the world are likely to be intensified, which reinforces the dynamic of growth and encourages additional in-migration of new units of capital and labor. Fourth, and finally, beneficial agglomeration effects in the form of localization and urbanization economies as defined by Hoover (1937) become increasingly available; they include, in particular, infrastructural artifacts with high fixed costs such as shared loading bays, transport terminals, street networks, utilities, and the like. All of these effects help to consolidate the expansion of the center as a hub of intense economic and social life.

Some theorists, in particular Hirschmann (1958) and Myrdal (1957), have pushed these notions to a yet more general articulation of the whole problem of regional dynamics. They have suggested that the developmental trajectory of growth centers can best be described in terms of so-called "polarization" or "backwash" effects. These effects are substantively identified in terms of the supposedly parasitical relationship of growth centers to their hinterlands in which the resources, talents, and human energies of the latter are eventually drawn into the service of the former. Hinterlands are said to gain at best only residual benefits from this relationship via "trickle down" or "spread" effects. Thus, in this view, growth centers will tend to experience accelerated development at the expense of their dependent peripheral areas.

Not surprisingly, the crises of the core regions in advanced capitalist societies from the late 1960s to the early 1980s have to a large extent undermined the persuasiveness of these ideas about the structured growth patterns of major centers, and in recent years they have fallen into some neglect. They have also been in part superseded by a competing theoretical model that tries to account for the symptoms of these crises in terms of a so-called *product cycle*. In this model, the observable phenomena of deindustrialization in and decentralization from core areas are explained as an effect of the progressive maturation of manufacturing technologies and their concomitant tendency to disperse locationally to cheap production sites (Norton and Rees, 1979). I shall have more to say about the product cycle in chapter 10. We may simply note, for the present, that like the other theories described above, product cycle theory is highly suggestive of some important processes, but it fails to grasp them adequately by reason of its commitment to merely formal generalization of their outward empirical manifestations (see chap. 10).

Despite my reservations about these different accounts of the rise and fall of growth centers, they do give us a preliminary identification of several of the factors that contribute to the decidedly uneven spatial development of capitalist society. They also (unlike, say, central place theory) make some gestures in the direction of an urban theory that is sensitive to the fundamental significance of large-scale commodity production. However, considerable reconstruction of these accounts must be achieved if we are to go beyond what Storper (1985) calls their "essentialism." i.e., the erroneous assumption that the observed empirical tendencies of the recent past are universal and transhistorical in nature. As implied by the discussion in chapter 3, this must involve, at a minimum, a concerted attempt to build a systemic theory of the inner mechanisms of industrial organization, the social division of labor, and location. We now embark on the complicated task of deciphering the location-theoretic aspects of this agenda, and we begin with some modest and largely self-evident notions about linkage costs. Here, we are temporarily back in the world of the familiar Weberian locational decision maker.

INDUSTRIAL LINKAGES AND LINKAGE COSTS

Increasing disintegration of production processes is *ipso facto* associated with a widening network of interindustrial linkages, all of which incur various costs. These costs range from the strictly organizational (as in the case where disintegration leads to, say, increased errors in external transacting) to the purely spatial (as in the case of simple transport costs on physical movement). Reduction or elimination of the former costs encourages further disintegration, which in turn brings more of the latter costs into play. In this section, we concentrate above all on these spatial costs as a prelude to a more thoroughgoing synthesis of industrial organization and location processes.

Any interaction between economic agents in geographical space incurs a transaction or linkage cost in that (a) direct interpersonal contact and information exchanges are involved, and/or (b) a physical flow of some kind is incurred. The greater the distance over which the transaction occurs, the higher its cost. We know from Weberian theory that, all else being equal, producers will always seek out locations where total linkage costs are at a minimum. Such costs, however, are highly multidimensional, so that their effects on locational decisions are typically rather intricate. In addition, they are based on linkage attributes and structures determined within a social division of labor that is itself much affected by transport and communications costs (a relationship that is evident from the situation portrayed in fig. 3.3). What this means is that industrial organization and location are in certain important respects mutually interdependent phenomena.

Simple transport and communication costs. The first thing that needs to be said about simple transport and communication costs is that they are invariably a direct function of distance. However, the precise form of the function is very much dependent on the play of internal economies of scale in the transport process. Consider, for example, figure 4.1, in which the quantity of flow over a given distance is expressed as x, and its associated cost over the same distance is $t(x)$. The latter function displays a typical tapering effect as x increases in value. In the case where there are fixed costs (labeled c) attached to the flow, the total delivered cost of x will be $t(x) + c$. Unit delivery costs will then be $t(x)/x$ (if $c = 0$), or $[t(x) + c]/x$ (if $c > 0$). The latter costs will tend asymptotically to zero with increasing magnitudes of x. If we now hold x constant and allow distance to vary,

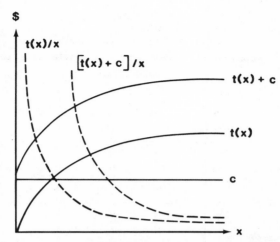

Figure 4.1. Transport costs as a function of quantity transported. x = quantity, $t(x)$ = variable transport tariff, c = fixed cost.

we will usually find that similar economies of scale are also present as a function of the distance over which x flows.

Tables 4.1 and 4.2 display data that exemplify these remarks. They show for the empirical case of trucking rates in southern Ontario that actual transport costs are strongly tapered per unit of flow as both quantity and distance increase. These discounting effects are the result of the marked lumpiness of transport services in general, and the high fixed costs that are frequently incurred even before the first unit of freight has been loaded and the first unit of distance has been covered.

Linkage attributes and cost structures. Just as linkage costs are highly susceptible to the effects of quantity and distance, so are they affected by

TABLE 4.1

TRUCK TARIFF ON STEEL PIPE TRANSPORTED BETWEEN TORONTO AND HAMILTON

Quantity of steel pipe	Unit cost of truck transport
Small amounts	$1.45
5,000 lbs	$0.69
24,000 lbs	$0.35
40,000 lbs	$0.23

SOURCE: Bater and Walker (1970).

TABLE 4.2

Truck Transport Rates from Toronto to Selected Cities in Ontario
(Class 70 Freight Rates, 1969)

Destination	Miles	500-lb. shipment		1,000-lb. shipment	
		Total cost ($)	Cost per lb. per mile	Total cost ($)	Cost per lb. per mile
Kitchener	70	14.35	0.041	21.10	0.030
Peterborough	80	14.60	0.037	21.11	0.026
London	111	15.35	0.028	22.00	0.020
North Bay	210	16.40	0.016	25.10	0.012
Sudbury	250	16.65	0.013	25.10	0.010
Timmins	430	18.75	0.009	36.80	0.009

Source: Hodge and Wong (1972).

various contingent attributes of any given flow. Four main points are necessary here.

First, linkage costs usually decline as the goods (or information) being transported are standardized with respect to shape, substance, quality, density, and so on. The greater the degree of standardization, the easier it is to order and reorder requisite quantities, to package them efficiently, and to predict the precise amount and form of needed transport services.

Second, if linkages are both recurrent and stable over space and time, various setup costs can be systematically lowered. This means that reordering is reducible to a simple routine. By contrast, if business contacts change frequently (as a result, say, of market uncertainties or product differentiation), then new contacts must be constantly rebuilt and significant search costs incurred. Further, spatio-temporal irregularity of linkages means that appropriate transport services cannot be precisely scheduled, with concomitant inflation of both fixed and variable costs.

Third, many transactions between business parties require careful and time-consuming intermediation that may be a source of extra costs. Sometimes, linkages cannot be set up by means of a simple order or command, and they may in fact be so difficult to manage that considerable time must be spent in negotiating various physical details and design specifications. This problem will be exacerbated where there are subtle questions of form, fit, color, texture, materials, and so on that must be resolved before a given transaction can be satisfactorily completed. Questions like these are especially prevalent in situations where subcontractors are involved and highly idiosyncratic instructions about work tasks need to be conveyed between linkage partners. On occasion, no doubt, these tasks of inter-mediation can be accomplished by mail or telephone or other electronic means; often, however, they can be effectively carried out only in the give and take of direct personal face-to-face contact. If this is the case, then the time and travel costs of those employees who participate in the contact must also be added to all the other costs of linkage.

Fourth, and by extension from the latter point, linkages sometimes do not entail any physical flow of goods whatever, but only the personalized exchange of intangibles. This is common in the case of transactions between office and service functions in the modern metropolitan economy. Such transactions may involve multiple meetings of several individuals at a time, and as Thorngren (1970) and Westaway (1974) have shown, the employees who are most likely to be involved are middle-level to high-level managers. The more complex and difficult the tasks of transacting are, the more experienced and highly paid the relevant transactors tend to be. Hence, face-to-face contacts over intricate and critical business decisions will be apt to have heavy time and space costs attached to them.

Linkage and location. These different aspects of linkage costs have mul-tiple implications for the unfolding of locational systems. Let us consider by way of illustration two contrasting scenarios.

On the one hand, where linkages are small in scale, unstandardized, unstable, and in need of personal intermediation, they will usually be associated with high distance-dependent costs per unit of flow. As a result, we may expect to find that small plants with variable production activities (hence with small-scale and problematical input-output relations) will tend to locate near their main linkage partners. The precise degree of convergent locational behavior will depend in part on the ratio of the value of output to the cost of linkage (a high value signifying relative insensitivity to proximity, a low value the converse), but this rough formulation of the problem will serve for the present.

On the other hand, where linkages are large in scale, standardized, stable, and easily manageable, they will tend to incur relatively low transactions costs per unit of flow. This implies that large plants with routinized and evenly regulated input-output relations will be correspondingly more free to detach themselves from their linkage partners and to locate at greater distances from them.

It should be added that transport and communication costs have fallen steadily over time in conjunction with the general development of the forces of production in capitalism. This has assuredly stimulated a general loosening of the bonds attaching different industries to one another across geographical space. Even so, there remain many sectors where, even today, producers have little option but to cluster tightly together in order to reduce the costs of their collective transactional activity. Furthermore, with the increasing importance of just-in-time delivery systems in modern manufacturing, this tendency to spatial agglomeration is being reaccentuated (Sheard, 1983a). Just-in-time systems involve contractual relations between firms such that inputs are delivered as they are needed in the production process rather than being stockpiled at the point of use. This arrangement depends to a great extent for its success on close geographical association between the different producers who participate in it. For the rest, office and service functions in the modern economy are also often tied together by costly (even though intangible) transactional relations, and this too induces much spatial clustering of these functions.

THE ELEMENTARY GEOGRAPHICAL DYNAMICS OF PRODUCTION COMPLEXES

From disintegration to agglomeration. As we learned in chapter 3, production processes sometimes have a strong proclivity, under identifiable circumstances, to break apart into vertically disintegrated units of activity. If internal economies of scale within these units are limited, then much horizontal disintegration will also come about. Such fragmentation leads directly to expansion of the external transactional structure of production and hence to increasing incidences of complicated spatially dependent costs, as discussed above. The higher these costs are per unit of output, the greater will be the inducement for producers to locate in close proximity to one another. Actually, even where these costs are not especially onerous, a proliferated structure of external transactions may still encourage clustering as a result of the opportunity costs that can often occur under conditions of dispersal. For example, where manufacturers are geographically isolated from complementary input suppliers, major disruptions to production processes may be incurred if particular parts or services (however small) are needed but cannot be readily obtained, or if equipment breakdowns occur which cannot be promptly repaired. The corresponding production delays may cost manufacturers considerable sums of money. Hence, locational association between interdependent producers can be a form of insurance against plant and equipment down time. It must also be pointed out that local labor markets play an important supplementary role in the process of agglomeration, but we will proceed for the present by holding this aspect of the problem in abeyance.

Vertical disintegration and the externalization of transactions are the dual faces of a single phenomenon definable as a switch in the overall technology of production away from hierarchies as a means of organizing labor processes and toward markets (Williamson, 1975, 1985). I use the term *technology* advisedly here; I intend it to denote not just the mechanical hardware of production but also the whole organizational disposition of the industrial apparatus. Vertical disintegration of that apparatus is especially probable where it is composed of easily disarticulatable labor processes in a multitask milieu and where internal economies of scope are weak. It will be even more probable if markets are in addition uncertain and highly competitive and where producers operate flexibly over a wide range of differentiated outputs. In these circumstances, producers characteristically seek to avoid investments in large units of fixed capital, and they are also likely to attempt to externalize those parts of the production process that are most vulnerable to rapid fluctuations in demand. As Piore and Sabel (1984) have suggested, the new flexible microelectronic production technologies now being installed in many sectors may eventually allow manufacturers to achieve high levels of product differentiation while reinternalizing elements of the production process. This remains very much an open question, however, and in any case, flexibility by definition is always greater at the level of the complex than at the level of the individual unit of production, which suggests that in a world of economic uncertainty and change some disintegration is always likely to prevail.

Producers who operate in disintegrated, multitask, and uncertain economic environments are very likely to be tied to one another in high-cost linkage networks in which transactions are numerous, small in scale, unstandardized, and unstable over space and time. They are therefore also likely to be found in mutually beneficial locational symbiosis with one another. Industries producing consumer outputs such as clothing, furniture, leather goods, or jewelry and serving competitive markets are very prone to this sort of organizational-locational outcome. So too are many basic industries whose outputs consist of variable small-batch items such as segments of the machinery, electronics, or instrument industries. Innumerable office and service functions have the same propensities. Even some large-scale mass-production industries are tightly organized within networks of small disintegrated plants providing all manner of specialized material inputs and services. For example, the car and aerospace industries are typically deeply involved with large numbers of localized suppliers and

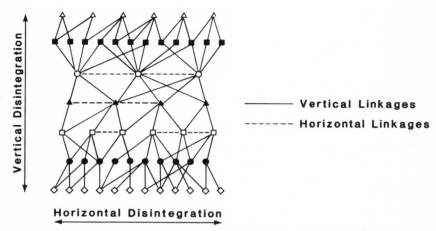

Figure 4.2. A network of external transactions within a fragmented production complex.

subcontractors even while they are at the same time engaged in massive transactional relations with much more distant linkage partners.

This reference to the car and aerospace industries provides an echo of growth center theory with its insistence on the privileged role of large propulsive sectors of production as the central axes of industrial complex development. However, it should by now be clear that the organization of industry and social division of labor represent a more fundamental set of variables governing spatial agglomeration and growth center development. As important as large propulsive industries may sometimes be in the emergence of major clusters of capital and labor, it is preeminently the externalization of transactional activities and the concomitant locational convergence of producers that are the proximate mechanisms of centralized growth. Functional polarity certainly reinforces agglomeration and economic expansion, but it is neither a necessary nor a sufficient condition for their occurrence.

Thus, where the structure of production is resolvable into dense networks of (vertically and horizontally) disintegrated production processes, there we will usually find the primary conditions of urban growth and development in modern capitalism. In this case, the production system takes on the form of a many-tiered constellation of producers divided from one another by complex internal diseconomies of scope and scale (see fig. 4.2). The net effect will be an intricate labyrinth of externalized transactions linking different producers, many of whom will coalesce in geographical space to form clusters and subclusters of agglomerated economic activity.

The special case of subcontracting. Subcontracting is a special and significant case of disintegration, and we can greatly extend the argument by means of an inquiry into some of its functional and locational characteristics. In particular, subcontracting plays a major (but hitherto largely unrecognized) role in the formation of localized industrial complexes.

Subcontracting involves the farming out of packets of work to independent producers who undertake to perform—according to given instructions—a specialized set of tasks. The work is then usually returned in semifinished form to its point of origin for further fabrication and finishing. The particular interest and importance of subcontracting reside in the fact that linkages between putting out and taking on establishments are often severely problematical in the sense that they can only be successfully consummated where there is considerable personal contact and exchange of information between the parties concerned. Subcontracting activities are also common where segmented labor markets prevail so that work can be put out from producers who operate in high-wage segments to producers in low-wage segments. Taylor and Thrift (1982a, 1982b) have suggested that subcontracting activity will be marked by rather unequal relations between producers because large, powerful primary firms can exert strong downward pressures on the subcontracting rates of smaller and less powerful secondary firms. Where this occurs, the rate reductions are then commonly passed on to the labor force in the subcontract sector in the form of reduced wages and inferior working conditions.

Two major species of subcontracting activity are recognizable. They are termed *specialty* and *capacity* subcontracting, (Holmes, 1986; Sallez 1972; Sallez and Schlegel, 1963). Specialty subcontracting involves the farming out of work that is complementary to the main functions of the putting out firm. Thus, specialty subcontracting is a form of vertical disintegration, as, for example, in the case of aerospace manufacturers who subcontract out their demands for aluminum castings. Capacity subcontracting consists of overflow work that can technically be done in-house but is nonetheless farmed out because of a temporary excess of orders over available capacity. Capacity subcontracting is therefore a form of horizontal disintegration, and by its nature it tends to be a cyclical phenomenon: it typically increases near the peak of the economic cycle and then diminishes again as the cycle begins its downward sweep.

Subcontracting of both main varieties can be seen in large degree as a further expression of the whole problem of uncertainty in production systems. It is, in fact, an effective method of safeguarding the overall profitability of production in situations where final output markets are

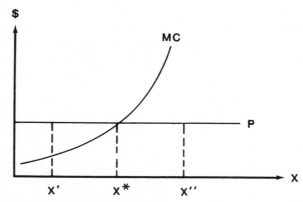

Figure 4.3. Marginal cost and market price with an inflexible production technology.

extremely unpredictable. By means of subcontracting, producers can evade overcommitments of capital and labor when markets are low, and under-commitments of capital and labor when markets are high. Consider, as an example, a vertically integrated clothing manufacturer with marginal cost schedule as shown in figure 4.3. Given the installed technology that generates this schedule, the firm's optimal profit-maximizing level of output is x^*, which coincides with the point where marginal cost (MC) and price (p) are equal. Suppose, however, that the firm's market is highly unpredictable and that over any given season its total sales may range anywhere and with equal probability from x' to x''. With its fixed technology, as represented by the situation portrayed in figure 4.3, the best that the firm can do in the face of this unpredictability is to continue to attempt to maximize profits by setting production equal to x^*. If the interval x', x'' is sufficiently large, however, the firm's realized profits may be severely restrained. Where, in any season, sales fall toward x', the firm will have to defray the heavy costs of unsold output. Where, by contrast, potential sales rise toward x'', the firm will incur large opportunity costs as a result of the shortfall between the amount actually produced (x^*) and total possible sales. If we are also dealing with a sector of production in which the possibilities of intertemporal readjustment by stockpiling and later sale are limited—e.g., by reason of frequent changes in marketable designs—then the whole problem of responding efficiently to market fluctuations will be all the more acute.

One way in which the firm may attempt to resolve these problems is by switching to an alternative, more flexible technology. Elements of such a technology can be attained through a strategy of extended subcontracting.

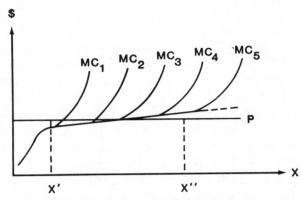

Figure 4.4. Marginal cost curves for a series of different subcontracting possibilities.

Imagine that a given firm has the option of using up to five subcontractors to perform a set of work tasks. The marginal costs of production associated with using from one to five subcontractors are shown in figure 4.4. The figure has been constructed in such a way that the marginal costs are close to the selling price of the putting out firm's product over the interval x', x'', an outcome that can be expected to occur in the long run as subcontractors compete among themselves over the going rates for subcontract work and as clothing firms adjust their final prices. The situation expressed by figure 4.4 signifies that the putting out firm can now rapidly expand or retrench its total level of production over a wide range while at the same time continuously maximizing its profits. Thus, as the market for the firm's output rises or falls, the firm can rapidly respond by switching forward and backward from one level of subcontracting to another. The net effect will be a significant improvement in the long-run profitability of capital.

Obviously, the entire feasibility of this organizational strategy rests on the possibility of the putting out firm being able to find appropriate subcontractors without incurring excessive additional transactions costs. Subcontractors, for their part, will want to be maximally accessible to the sources of their work. Hence, in the absence of countervailing forces tending to keep them apart, both putting out firms and subcontractors will usually find it much to their advantage to bunch together in geographical space. One such countervailing forces is the presence of abundant and cheap labor reserves in the Third World, and much subcontracting activity in modern industry now involves the putting out of work over long distances from core to peripheral areas. In spite of this, there continues to be considerable and intimate locational interdependence between many kinds of putting out and taking on firms in the large metropolitan regions of contemporary America. Moreover, subcontractors will also want to ensure for themselves as regular a flow of orders through time as possible, and all the more so where market uncertainty is prevalent. By the law of large numbers, temporal regularity can be enhanced if orders are pooled together and then shared among the set of subcontractors. An approximation of this pooling effect can be achieved by means of locational agglomeration. If subcontractors converge toward the center of gravity of putting out firms, they will be locationally indistinguishable from one another, which suggests that putting out firms will be to that degree indifferent as to which subcontractor they use; and this will in turn be translated into narrower fluctuations in the flow of work through subcontractors as compared with the case where individual subcontractors are spatially tied to particular putting out firms. By its nature, this locational strategy will reinforce clustering wherever it is put into effect. To express the matter in more general terms, where we have much uncertainty in a given productive system, disintegration and agglomeration can counteract its negative economic effects, for by the law of large numbers, the flow of work through the whole system is always less uncertain than the flow through any one vertically integrated channel.

PROTOURBAN FORMS

As all of these processes operate, functional and spatial complexes of productive labor come into existence on the landscape of capitalism. These complexes evolve through time as the size of the market increases and as the social division of labor expands. By the same token, the bonds that hold any given complex together grow tighter and the spatio-temporal structure of externalized transactional activity becomes more intricate. The net result is that production costs tend steadily to decrease everywhere on the terrain of the complex in sympathy with the widening rounds of specialization and diversification which are the inner symptoms of its growth. This process is the source, first, of deepening external economies of scale (which, as viewed through the analytics of Young (1928), is primarily a nonspatial phenomenon), and second, of powerful and explicitly spatial agglomeration effects. These phenomena are in turn the foundation of a distinctive *Verdoorn* process in which rising levels of output in a given region lead eventually to increments in industrial productivity

(Kaldor, 1970). As a result, organized industrial complexes are often the foci of self-reinforcing patterns of economic growth.

In the same way, the comparative advantages of industrial regions are not always based simply on given natural endowments. More significantly, they are also *socially produced* by the internal developmental logic of regional growth and change as described above. Certainly, we can point to many localized production complexes in the nineteenth and twentieth centuries that were founded on naturally occurring resources such as metallic minerals, energy deposits, or natural harbors, but the occurrence of such resources is by no means a necessary precondition of development. On the contrary, where processes of the social division of labor, industrial specialization, diversification, and so on come into play, development can frequently occur even where there is no underlying resource base whatsoever. Thus, regions that are lacking in natural wealth, or have little at the outset to differentiate them from scores of other similar regions, may sometimes take off into rapid industrial growth if an initial impulse, however fortuitous its origins, pushes them to the threshold of complex formation. This seems to have happened recently at a number of locations in the U.S. Sunbelt, as for example in the case of Silicon Valley, where high-technology industries have taken root and flourished on a major scale (Scott and Angel, 1987). Furthermore, as an emergent complex in any given area starts to expand, it becomes a potentially fertile locus of industrial innovation, and this adds fuel to its internal growth dynamic. The high potential for innovation resides in the innumerable market niches and new business opportunities created by the rich organizational networks that are intrinsic components of the complex as such. Many experienced entrepreneurs and workers participate in the daily activities of the complex, and they are therefore optimally positioned to take advantage of new technical and commercial opportunities as and when they become available. These innovative potentialities of expanding complexes are usually manifest in the hyperactive vertical and horizontal spinoffs that are typical attributes of their broad pattern of growth.

Once a localized production complex comes into being, it is then held together as a unit by the many additional agglomeration economies that come into being as part of its geographical logic. On occasion, several different complexes may develop side by side within a single metropolitan region (as, for example, in the cases of the aerospace, clothing, and film industries in Los Angeles), all of them functionally separated from one another but spatially interdependent as a result of the wider urbanization economies that they collectively engender. Any given complex in any given region will also invariably be linked to industries in other complexes at other locations via long-distance business transactions and commodity flows. The whole system of complexes, together with their satellite peripheries, then forms an interlocking network of economic activity with many local and nonlocal multiplier effects (Pred, 1977).

Growth centers thus expand over a complicated field of forces defined by the extent of the market, the social division of labor, the innovation process, industrial diversification, and locational activity. But they also sometimes contract over the same field of forces through accelerating rounds of restructuring, job loss, and unemployment leading to crisis and demise. I shall deal with these latter issues in chapter 10. For the moment, we are now in possession of the rudiments of a genetic theory of what we may call protourban forms—i.e., of spatially convergent production processes linked through webs of extended transactional relations. These webs are the very geographical core of the urban process in capitalism, though they are not yet fully and finally urban: to be so, they must be complemented by a work force together with all the emergent effects that are set in motion as workers seek out housing for themselves, participate in the routines of urban life, and bring forth the spatially segmented patterns of neighborhood development that are so characteristic a feature of the large metropolis in contemporary capitalism.

The Internal Production Space of the Metropolis: Some Illustrative Sketches.

INDUSTRIALIZATION AND URBANIZATION

In previous chapters, I have described how *protourban forms* emerge from the prespatial logic of commodity production, and how, through the intermediation of industrial organization processes, they take on definite geographical form. As I demonstrated, agglomerative tendencies will often appear with especial intensity in the vicinity of large propulsive industries. However, and more generally, I have also shown that the same impulse toward agglomeration can appear wherever any complex of interlocking units of production starts to develop and grow through the division of labor. Quite frequently, such units as these will consist only of small-scale, specialized, and highly disintegrated industrial establishments.

Much urbanization in capitalism is in fact posited upon various combinations of both large-scale basic industries and small-scale (often very labor-intensive) industries. The former industries were a notably important element of the landscape of the large metropolis over the period that saw the rise and consolidation of the American Manufacturing Belt and down through the era of Fordist industrialization stretching roughly from the 1920s to the early 1970s. Many of these industries—above all in the nineteenth century—depended on heavy and bulky input materials such as coal, ore, or agricultural resources. These materials were (then as now) difficult and expensive to convey over long distances, especially in view of the more primitive transport technologies that prevailed in the last century. Thus, industrial plants in these sectors regularly congregated around natural resource sites or at nodal points where basic inputs could be cheaply assembled. Many major cities in the nineteenth century grew up on the basis of this sort of large-scale materials-intensive manufacturing, as, for example, in the cases of Pittsburgh with its steel industries, Minneapolis with its flour milling operations, and New Orleans with its sugar refineries. But Chicago is the nineteenth-century city par excellence whose emergence and growth are founded on this kind of industrialization. Fales and Moses (1972) have painted an elaborate picture of Chicago in the 1870s as a major nodal center with a burgeoning industrial base comprising such materials-intensive industries as meat packing, blast furnaces, foundries, brick making, brewing, glass production, and so on. These industries located for the most part close to central transport terminals in the city so that they could easily gain access to the raw materials of the hinterland and just as easily dispatch final outputs to widely dispersed markets in the northern and eastern United States, and thence to the rest of the world.

Many elementary accounts of urban development have actually attempted to construct paradigmatic explanations of the origins of urbanization in the nineteenth century around processes of locational convergence of this (essentially Weberian) type. As significant as these processes have undoubtedly been in many individual cases, however, they certainly do not capture fully and in all its subtlety the central dynamic of industrialization and urbanization. Indeed, in many respects, they represent no more than a very special case. If urban growth were truly founded only on the locational attraction to cheap transport sites of simple basic industries, actual patterns of urbanization in the nineteenth and twentieth centuries would have taken on a radically different aspect from the one they actually have. They would almost certainly have consisted only of a few large conglomerations of manufacturing industry at major resource locations and nodal centers with a wide scattering of mill towns elsewhere. We would in all probability *not* have observed the large numbers of hyperenlarged urban areas with extremely variegated economic systems that are scattered across the face of the United States today. Even in the nineteenth century, cities such as Baltimore, Boston, Cincinnati, New York, and Philadelphia were patently very complicated geographical phenomena with highly differentiated industrial and trading activities and with considerable amounts of small-scale labor-intensive manufacturing in addition to basic large-scale materials-intensive forms. In the twentieth century, we can even point to some urban centers (the most dramatic case being, no doubt, Silicon Valley) that are effectively bereft of any pregiven locational advantage other than their own internal dynamic of growth and diversification. What is more, over the twentieth century, a very high proportion of the large-scale materials-intensive forms of manufacturing that formerly flourished near the core of the large metropolis has effectively been eliminated from the urban environment. Much of this industry has decisively decentralized to suburban and peripheral areas in response to rising land and labor costs in the core and to falling transport costs generally. Notwithstanding the systematic decentralization of this element of the urban economic base, and despite occasional crises of the urban system, cities in the major capitalist countries continue to grow as the division of labor moves forward and as new innovative sectors of production make their historical appearance. The tendency toward massive urbanization of the economy in capitalism will undoubtedly continue to manifest itself so long as the logic of fragmentation, interaction, and agglomeration proceeds within growing segments of the economy.

This same logic leads not just to generalized urban agglomeration but also to the emergence of multiple dense industrial districts *within* the metropolis. The internal production spaces of large cities are composed of mosaics of particular kinds of industrial land use focused on localized nodal clusters comprising activities that range from manufacturing to office and service functions. In what now follows I shall examine in detail a number of different cases of this phenomenon. I shall in fact consider five main empirical examples: (a) gun and jewelry manufacture in Birmingham, England; (b) the footwear industry of East London; (c) clothing production in New York City; (d) the motor-vehicle industry of Tokyo; and (e) office functions in the modern metropolis. I have chosen to examine these examples both because they illustrate different aspects of the theory of industrial organization and location as discussed earlier and because they represent especially clear cases of the internal specialization of parts of the production space of the large metropolis. At the same time, the secondary literature provides ready-made accounts of these cases that can be harnessed to the needs of the present investigation. The examples cut across a wide range of historical and geographical circumstances. As such, they illustrate both the generality of the problem of agglomeration and the wide diversity of concrete forms that it can assume under different conjunctural circumstances. In subsequent chapters I shall deal with some of the more detailed analytical issues raised by a perusal of these problems.

GUN AND JEWELRY MANUFACTURE IN BIRMINGHAM

From the end of the eighteenth century and over much of the nineteenth and twentieth centuries, Birmingham developed as a unique center of small-scale crafts and trades based above all on various forms of metal-working activity. At the height of Birmingham's prosperity in the mid-nineteenth century, its wealth was founded on four major staple industries, i.e., brass goods, buttons, guns, and jewelry, though a bewildering variety of other kinds of manufactures also flourished in the city: e.g., bedsteads, steel pens, locks and latches, pins, nails, and hardware of all varieties. Birmingham at this time was a living exemplification of Adam Smith's simple parable of the division of labor in manufacture. Virtually all of the specialized trades in the city were highly localized, and none more so than the gun and jewelry industries, in which the fragmentation of labor processes had proceeded very far indeed (Wise, 1949).

Gun manufacture. In the mid–nineteenth century, the Birmingham gun industry consisted of two major branches devoted to the production of sporting and military guns, respectively. At that time, vertical disintegration in the industry had advanced to a remarkable extent. Few if any guns were actually made from start to finish in one workshop. Instead, as Allen (1929) has indicated, a number of master gun makers organized the production process within two major strata of linkage relations. First, the master gun maker put out orders for various parts:

> He purchased materials from the barrel-makers, lock-makers, sight-stampers, trigger-makers, ramrod-forgers, gun-furniture makers, and, if he were engaged in the military branch, from bayonet-forgers. [Allen, 1929, p. 116]

Second, the parts thus acquired were then sent out to a wide variety of "setters-up," who performed the specialized functions leading to the assembly and the finishing of the gun:

> To name only a few, there were those who prepared the front sight and lump end of the barrels; the jiggers, who attended to the breech end; the stockers, who let in the barrel and lock and shaped the stock; the barrel-strippers, who prepared the gun for rifling and proof; the hardeners, polishers, borers and riflers, engravers, and finally the lock-freers, who adjusted the working parts. Some of these were individual outworkers employed by a particular master; others were shop owners working for several employers. [Allen, 1929, p. 117]

All of this fragmentation and interlinkage of gun making encouraged producers to converge locationally around their own center of gravity. In this manner, a specialized gun quarter came into existence close to the center of the city. Its endogenous transactional activities were visible in the very streetscape, for

> an army of boys was to be seen hurrying to and fro about the gun quarter performing the functions of porters. [Allen, 1929, p. 118]

Workshops accordingly huddled close together in order to expedite the whole process of disintegrated but interconnected production.

After the middle of the nineteenth century, there occurred a technological revolution in the process of gun manufacture. With the encouragement of the British government, capital-intensive, routinized, mass-production methods of gun making were imported from the United States, and these came rapidly to dominate the manufacture of guns for military purposes. Military gun production was now concentrated into a small number of large integrated plants located (significantly) in noncentral areas. The old centralized labor-intensive gun-making complex of Birmingham declined rapidly as a consequence. However, a rump of the old gun quarter has continued even down to the present day, though the workshops that now occupy the quarter produce only sporting guns for a rather restricted market. The geography of the Birmingham gun quarter as it was in 1948 is shown in figure 5.1—a shadow of its former self, but still giving evidence of considerable vertical disintegration and clustering of functions.

Jewelry manufacture. Like the gun industry, the jewelry trades are located in a specialized district near the core of the city. These trades have been an important sector of the economy of Birmingham ever since the early nineteenth century, and they have remained a strongly identified element of the city's landscape throughout the twentieth century. Over this long period of time, the jewelry industry has experienced many internal mutations as a result of the vagaries of demand and the intensity of competition.

One of the major characteristics of the industry is its proclivity to break up into an extraordinarily elaborate social division of labor. This leads directly to functional diversity and locational agglomeration. These phenomena have been described by Allen (1929, p. 56) in the following terms:

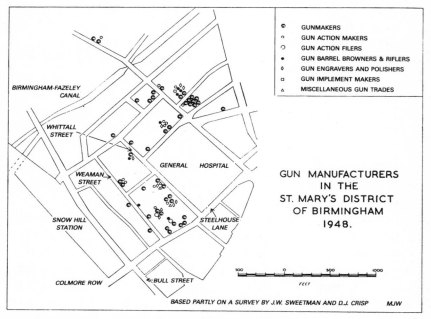

Figure 5.1. Gun manufacturers in the St. Mary's district of Birmingham, 1948.
SOURCE: Wise (1949).

As the [jewelry] trade grew, processes became more highly specialized and it became necessary for manufacturers who performed complementary operations on some article to be in close proximity to one another. Few makers of finished goods, moreover, were concerned with more than a narrow range of article, and it was an advantage for them to be grouped together since the factors through whom the jewelry was sold, and who required to purchase many different types, were then able to get in touch the more easily with their sources of supply.

Wise (1949) lists the following trades to be found in the central jewelry quarter in 1948: goldsmiths, silversmiths, electroplaters, medalists, gilt and imitation jewelry fabrication, gem sitting, stamping and piercing, engraving, polishing and enameling, die sinkers, jewelry repair, refiners, general outwork, factors and merchants, dealers in bullion and precious stones, jewelers' material suppliers, manufacturers of optical goods, watch-makers, and miscellaneous manufacturers. More than sixty percent of the firms in these trades had ten employees or fewer in 1948, and all were bound together in a dense structure of transactional interrelations. The net geographical result was a closely textured amalgam of workshops and

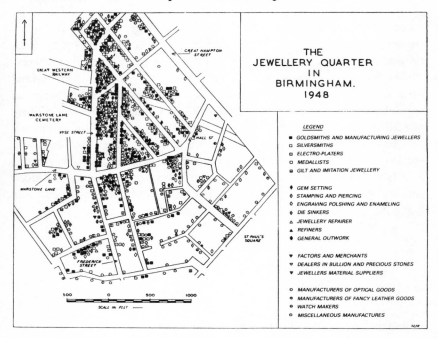

THE
JEWELLERY QUARTER
IN
BIRMINGHAM.
1948

LEGEND

■ GOLDSMITHS AND MANUFACTURING JEWELLERS
▫ SILVERSMITHS
⊟ ELECTRO-PLATERS
□ MEDALLISTS
⊟ GILT AND IMITATION JEWELLERY

◆ GEM SETTING
◇ STAMPING AND PIERCING
◊ ENGRAVING POLSHING AND ENAMELING
◐ DIE SINKERS
△ JEWELLERY REPAIRER
▲ REFINERS
◆ GENERAL OUTWORK

▼ FACTORS AND MERCHANTS
▽ DEALERS IN BULLION AND PRECIOUS STONES
▼ JEWELLERS MATERIAL SUPPLIERS

○ MANUFACTURERS OF OPTICAL GOODS
● MANUFACTURERS OF FANCY LEATHER GOODS
◉ WATCH MAKERS
○ MISCELLANEOUS MANUFACTURES

Figure 5.2. The jewelry quarter in Birmingham, 1948.
SOURCE: Wise (1949).

factories huddled together near the core of the city as shown in figure 5.2.

Local labor markets. Through much of their history, both the gun and jewelry quarters of Birmingham have developed in close association with their own specialized local labor markets. Both are defined in part by a series of surrounding residential neighborhoods in which an abundance of workers with locally useful skills and experience could be found. In the nineteenth century, residents of these neighborhoods also engaged massively in homework at reduced rates of pay, and this helped to lower the overall costs of production both by keeping expenditures on labor low and by eliminating the need for various manufacturers' overheads.

These processes seem in general to point in the direction of a spatially recursive determination of intraurban locational patterns. On the one hand, workers gravitate to residential neighborhoods surrounding their places of work. On the other hand, employers have an incentive to locate close to the center of their main sources of labor. In both cases, high levels of mutual accessibility are the result. At the same time, the more any given cluster of producers grows in size, the more it will tend to become locationally focused on the very center of the city in order to maintain accessibility to its total labor force. Conversely, smaller clusters with limited labor demands will be more prone to locate at less accessible locations where land prices are comparatively low. These tendencies will be variously played out in the context of intense competition for land by alternative uses, as described by classical Von Thünen land-use theory. In these ways, specialized and localized territorial complexes of production, work, and local labor market activity are (for a time at least) sustained and reproduced within the fabric of the metropolis. I shall return to these issue in chapters 7 and 8.

THE FOOTWEAR INDUSTRY OF EAST LONDON

Shoemaking is an industry that evolved over the eighteenth and nineteenth centuries from the fully integrated "country workman" stage of development to a highly disintegrated industry confined to a few major cities. In North America, the industry passed very rapidly through this evolutionary process some time in the early nineteenth century when it became largely concentrated in southern New England. According to Hoover (1937), this concentration was induced by the vast expansion of markets touched off by the rapid improvement of long-distance transport services at that time.

The changeover in the footwear industry from craftlike, integrated forms of production to finely grained fragmentation was signaled not so much by changes in technological hardware as it was by insistent division of labor and the development of specialized labor-intensive units of production. Mechanization of the industry was at first difficult to achieve because of the complicated geometric forms and variable sizes of shoes. Handwork predominated until the very end of the nineteenth century, and many different kinds of labor skills evolved within the industry. The net effect of these trends was that in both North America and Western Europe, the industry was locationally reconstituted in a few specialized centers of production. It was, in fact, drawn to major cities where it tended to occupy distinctive industrial quarters which were, in turn, the geographic foci of

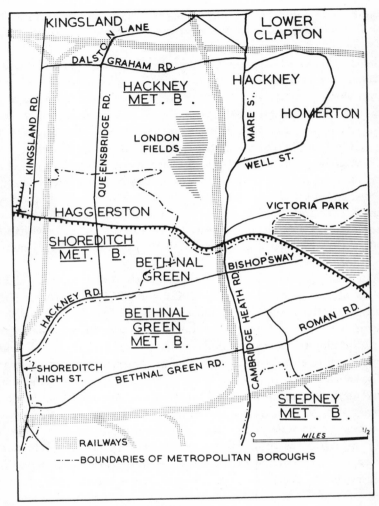

Figure 5.3. East London: General location map.
SOURCE: Hall (1962b).

dense residential neighborhoods from which the main labor force of the industry was drawn.

In London, as both Hall (1962b) and Munby (1951) have shown, the heyday period of shoe production was the 1880s and 1890s. During this period, the industry clustered in the East End of London (see fig. 5.3). Here, it lay in close proximity to a number of low-wage working-class and immigrant communities, the latter composed largely of eastern European Jews. In these same communities an abundant supply of outworkers was also to be found.

The division of labor in the East London footwear industry at end of the nineteenth century had proceeded very far indeed. Small workshops and outworkers specialized in one of five major branches of the trade. They were: first, *clicking*, which involved the cutting out of leather pieces to form the upper parts of the shoe; second, *closing*, which was an operation designed to join the pieces together to form a whole upper; third, *rough stuff cutting*, in which the soles were crudely cut out; fourth, *lasting*, which consisted of shaping the leather upper and attaching it to the sole; fifth, *finishing*, in which all the surplus leather still attached to the shoe was trimmed away and the shoe made ready for sale. These trades were organized into closely wrought networks of workshops and sweatshops through which the semifinished materials passed as they moved towards completion.

Figures 5.4, 5.5, and 5.6 show the geographical distribution of the shoe industry in East London in 1860, 1901, and 1951, respectively. These Figures trace the long-run locational evolution of the industry in East London. They reveal a pattern of considerable growth over the second half of the nineteenth century, followed by a long period of decline and stagnation throughout the course of the present century. Already by the 1880s, much of the handicraft labor in the industry was being made redundant by the introduction of power-driven machinery, and factory methods were now starting to drive out the old labor-intensive forms of production characterized by extreme vertical disintegration (Munby, 1951). Moreover, as large-scale factory production became increasingly prevalent, so the location of the industry shifted from London to the provinces, where cheap unskilled and semiskilled female labor could be readily obtained. The London industry dwindled considerably and was left to specialize more and more in those few lines of production where the small master system could still operate efficiently, namely, high-quality shoes calling for attentive labor-intensive methods of fabrication (Hall, 1962b).

Like the gun industry in Birmingham in the mid–nineteenth century, the footwear industry of East London was eventually all but destroyed by shifting industrial technology and the development of new, integrated, and capital-intensive methods of production. As we shall see in due course, this pattern of growth and creative destruction is a recurrent leitmotif of the history of cities in industrial capitalism.

Figure 5.4. The East London footwear industry in 1860.
SOURCE: Hall (1962b).

CLOTHING PRODUCTION IN NEW YORK CITY

The clothing industry is a metropolitan industry first and foremost, and New York City has been the primary center of the industry in the United States throughout the present century.

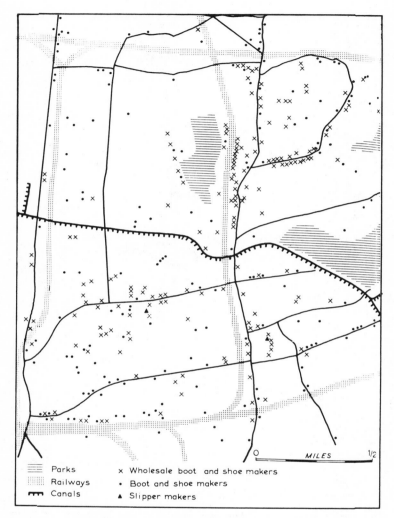

Figure 5.5. The East London footwear industry in 1901.
SOURCE: Hall (1962b).

The clothing industry is typically extremely volatile. Individual producers face uncertain markets, and they are constantly pushed into product
differentiation strategies as a means of warding off the market depredations
of their competitors. Consequently, the industry is characteristically organized around small labor-intensive plants producing restricted batches
of output in limited runs. This, at least, is overwhelmingly the case with

Figure 5.6. The East London footwear industry in 1951.
SOURCE: Hall (1962b).

the New York industry, which specializes in the more fashion-oriented and competitive end of the market. The New York industry is also much given to fragmentation and subdivision of production processes. Often, manufacturers are only to a minor extent involved directly in the physical production of their own output; rather, they concentrate their efforts on design and marketing and farm out the intermediate stages of manufacture to subcontractors. Such work as cutting, sewing, buttonholing, pleating, hem-stitching, and so on is widely subcontracted out. Indeed, vertical disintegration in the New York clothing industry has proceeded to such an advanced degree that scores of different types of ancillary services form an integral part of the overall complex. Helfgott (1959, p. 63) alludes to the following typical cases of this phenomenon:

> the design, display and selling of textiles, sponging (cloth shrinking); factoring (textile banking); trucking; agencies that provide . . . models; the supplying of thread and trimming; embroidery; the manufacture of belts; and the repairing of machinery,

and the list could undoubtedly be extended many times over.

All of these different productive activities interpenetrate with one another in a tangled network of linkages. By the same token, they cluster compactly in geographical space, and in this way they form a specialized garment district in the core of the city. This clustering is accentuated both by the small scale of most interactions within the industry and by the need for intense face-to-face contacts in order to negotiate the details of subcontract work and the precise specifications of needed inputs. It is even further accentuated by the elastic system that ties manufacturers and subcontractors together in mutual symbiosis. In this system, as Haig (1927, p. 81) has indicated, the manufacturer

> expands or reduces his group of contractors with the volume of the business attracted by his offering of garments. Because of the extreme uncertainty of this demand he delays his decisions regarding his models and the quantities until the latest possible moment. When he does arrive at his decision, action must be swift. He must engage sufficient contractors to supply the volume he has decided upon, and he must secure deliveries from them with a minimum loss of time.

This, of course, is precisely an informal verbal transposition of the abstract analysis of the logic of subcontracting under uncertainty as discussed in the previous chapter.

Figures 5.7 to 5.9 indicate the locations of men's and women's clothing manufacturers in Manhattan in the earlier part of the present century. Notice the extraordinarily dense spatial conflux of plants shown in these figures, and their collective tendency (especially among women's clothing producers) to move steadily uptown with the passage of time away from the financial center of Lower Manhattan and toward the major wholesale

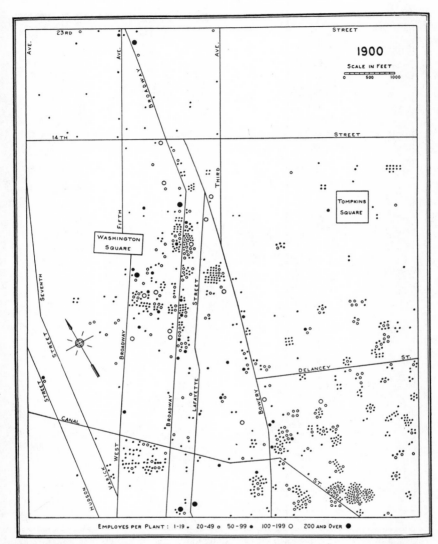

Figure 5.7. Location of plants in men's clothing industry in area of greatest concentration in Manhattan in 1900.

Source: Haig (1927).

and retail market areas that lie north of 34th Street (Hoover and Vernon, 1959). Today, the industry is heavily concentrated in the midtown area of Manhattan within the few blocks that run from 34th Street in the south to 40th Street in the north, and from Sixth Avenue in the east to Eighth

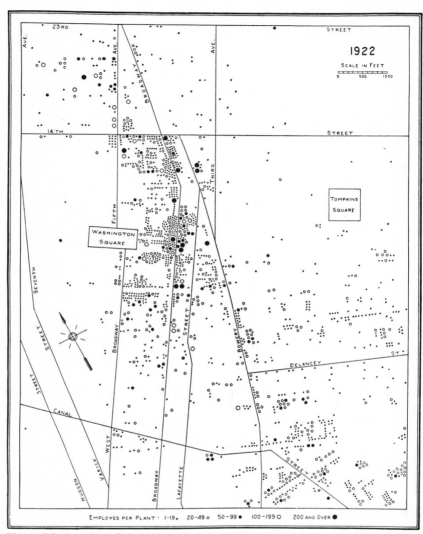

Figure 5.8. Location of plants in men's clothing industry in area of greatest concentration in Manhattan in 1922.

SOURCE: Haig (1927).

Avenue in the west (see fig. 5.10). This area is a veritable hive of vertically disintegrated production and small-scale transactional activity.

Notwithstanding this very definite spatial nucleation of the New York clothing industry, considerable decentralization of plants has also been

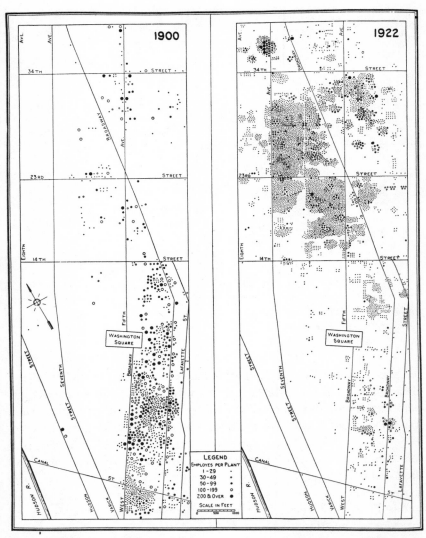

Figure 5.9. Location of plants in women's clothing industry in the area of greatest concentration in Manhattan in 1900 and 1922.

SOURCE: Haig (1927).

evident over the decades, and the industry is, indeed, organized at two different spatial levels. At its core in central Manhattan are those producers who are most directly involved in the high-fashion side of the market, where the style element is important, runs are short, and skilled labor

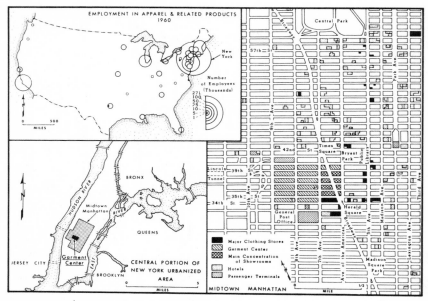

Figure 5.10. Midtown Manhattan garment center.
SOURCE: Kenyon (1964).

(especially for cutting and sewing) is much in demand. In the periphery, all around the fringes of the Greater New York Region are scattered large numbers of subcontract shops performing more standardized, large-batch low-skilled work (sewing above all) for plants located in the core, (Kenyon, 1964). These geographical relationships are illuminated by the data presented in table 5.1, which shows the spatial distribution of the women's dress industry in the New York metropolitan region in 1946 and 1956 cross-tabulated by a price index of quality. The table reveals two important trends. First, the women's dress industry decentralized systematically from the core to the fringe between 1946 and 1956. Second, however, this decentralization has been most pronounced among shops producing lower-quality and standardized outputs. Shops producing higher-quality, more fashion-oriented outputs scarcely decentralized at all over the specified time period.

In the 1950s, there was particularly active decentralization of large, rapid-turnaround subcontractors to the old textile districts of southern Massachusetts and the anthracite regions of eastern Pennsylvania, where much low-wage female labor could be readily found. These subcontractors

TABLE 5.1

GEOGRAPHICAL DISTRIBUTION OF THE WOMEN'S DRESS INDUSTRY IN THE
NEW YORK METROPOLITAN REGION

	1946		1956	
Quality of dress (wholesale price)	New York City	Rest of Metropolitan Region	New York City	Rest of Metropolitan Region
	(% of total payroll)		(% of total payroll)	
under $5.75	78.1	28.9	40.2	59.8
$5.75–$16.75	81.8	18.2	62.9	37.1
over $16.75	98.7	1.3	94.3	5.7

SOURCE: Helfgott (1959), p. 72.

were and are functionally connected to the industry of central New York,
but by reason of their large scale of operation and their relatively standardized linkages they have been able efficiently to exploit locations in the
periphery. Helfgott (1959, p. 105) has observed of this phenomenon:

> In the unit priced dress industry the cost of hauling fabrics to points in eastern
> Pennsylvania and the garments on hangers back to New York ranges from 4
> to 11.5 cents per dress, depending on the value of the dress. The slightest
> labor-cost differential between New York and out-of-town locations clearly
> compensates for the costs of trucking garments back and forth.

It should also be pointed out that these core/fringe relationships corre-
spond to technological differences between the plants located in the two
areas. Central-city shops tend to operate on a making-through basis,
(which means that a single operator does the work of making an entire
garment). But shops in the periphery are for the most part organized on
a section-work basis (which means that each garment is manufactured by
means of deskilled, technically divided labor processes). These differences
further accentuate the contrasts between the two areas, and in particular,
between the high-quality flexible forms of manufacturing in the core, and
the lower-quality routinized forms of manufacturing in the periphery.

In recent years, the New York clothing industry has suffered greatly
from continuing rounds of decentralization and from the increasing availability on the market of cheap imported clothing. The midtown section
of Manhattan, however, remains the privileged center of the high-fashion
garment industry in the United States. Here, conditions of flexible efficiency in the production system via vertical disintegration are still the
major underpinning of the continued existence of the industry. These

conditions have allowed the industry to survive and prosper even in the very heart of one of the world's largest cities.

THE MOTOR-VEHICLE INDUSTRY OF TOKYO

Car production in Japan grew with great rapidity in the postwar decades, and most of all in the period after the early 1960s. The core of the industry is located in the Tokyo region, which nowadays produces over thirty-two percent of all the country's vehicles.

The car industry in Tokyo forms part of a wider metals and machinery production complex covering the entire metropolitan area and its fringe communities. The spatial distribution of car and body makers and parts makers in the region is shown in figure 5.11. Supplementary cartographic information is provided by figure 5.12, which gives the distribution of subcontractors serving four major vehicle producers. The industry is spread out over the whole region, though there is a clear geographical focus in the Kawasaki-Yokohama area with its many assembly plants, parts manufacturers, and subcontractors. Several thousand producers participate in the industry in the Tokyo region, all of them linked together through a labyrinth of direct and indirect transactions. There is also considerable interlinkage between the car industry in the Tokyo region and the other manufacturing regions of Japan. As in the case of the New York clothing industry, there is evidently a rough correlation between size of plant in the Tokyo car industry and distance from the center of the whole system. In particular, many of the largest car manufacturers are scattered in a wide zone around the periphery of the region (see fig. 5.11).

The Tokyo region has ten main final assembly plants belonging to five corporations, i.e., Hino, Honda, Isuzu, Mitsubishi, and Nissan. In spite of the size of these plants, much of their production activity is actually externalized, and Takeuchi (1980a, 1980b) has indicated that more than sixty-five percent of any car (by cost) is made up of bought-in items. Each assembler lies at the center of a loose coalition of body manufacturers, parts makers, and subcontractors working in close cooperation with one another through the just-in-time (or *kanban*) system. The system is based on rapid delivery of parts as they are needed in the production process, and thus considerable locational interdependence between the different units that compose the system can be observed. The system has also evolved in the direction of an extreme form of multitier subcontracting (see fig.

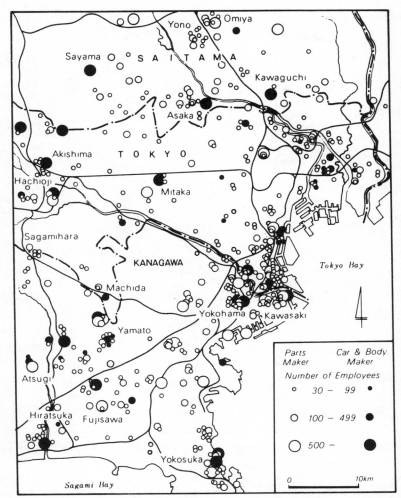

Figure 5.11. Distribution of motor-vehicle production in the Tokyo region, 1969.
SOURCE: Takeuchi (1980a).

5.13). Sheard (1983a, p. 59) gives an account of this in the following
terms:

A large stamping firm (first layer subcontractor) might undertake to supply a
side-door sub-assembly to a certain auto maker. The firm would use its large
transfer presses to make the large stampings but would farm out all smaller
stampings to a smaller firm (second layer subcontracting) which would use
smaller and less expensive presses. Even this firm would find it less costly to

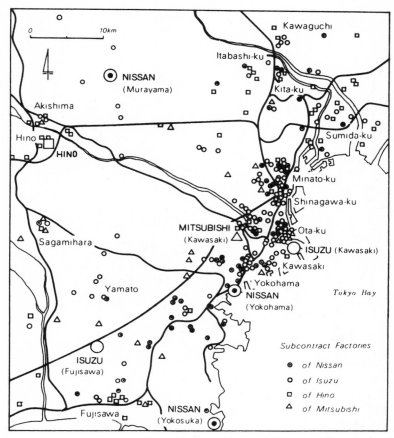

Figure 5.12. Distribution of motor vehicle subcontractors in the Tokyo region, 1972.
SOURCE: Takeuchi (1980a).

engage a local workshop (third layer subcontracting) to provide some of the component stampings.

Sheard has also estimated that any given major car maker in Japan will have on average 171 first-layer subcontractors, 4,700 second-layer subcontractors, and 31,600 third-layer subcontractors. This way of organizing the subcontracting process is extremely flexible overall, and it allows central assemblers to expand and retrench production with great rapidity as the market grows or shrinks.

At the same time, the hierarchy of subcontractors in the Japanese car industry corresponds to a highly stratified set of labor processes and employment conditions with many different wage levels. As we move down

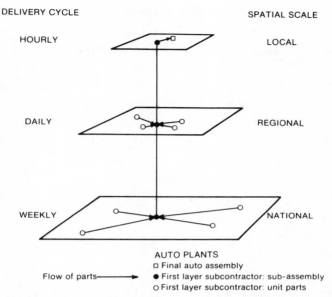

DELIVERY CYCLE   SPATIAL SCALE

Figure 5.13. Time-space organization in a Japanese motor vehicle production system.
SOURCE: Sheard (1983b).

through the hierarchy of subcontractors, we also move in the direction of smaller and more labor-intensive plants and very much lower wage scales (see fig. 5.14 and table 5.2). This suggests at once that the disintegrated organizational hierarchy of the Japanese car industry is not only an efficient production apparatus in the purely technical sense but that it also functions as a potent mechanism for controlling labor costs in different segments of the industry by systematically externalizing small-scale labor-intensive tasks to firms operating in secondary labor markets. Friedman (1977) has shown that an identical phenomenon exists in the British car industry. In Japan, enterprise-based unions and lifetime employment security at the topmost levels of the hierarchy of manufacturers certainly accentuate these contrasts.

In the Tokyo region, all of this finely grained organizational complexity is directly reflected in the geography of the industry. Producers are spatially arranged throughout the region in nuclei and subnuclei built up around localized webs of interlinkages. At the same time, the industry is so large and diverse in its constituent elements that it is not restricted (as in some of the other cases we have examined) to just one narrow quarter of the metropolis. It is widely represented throughout the Tokyo region (though

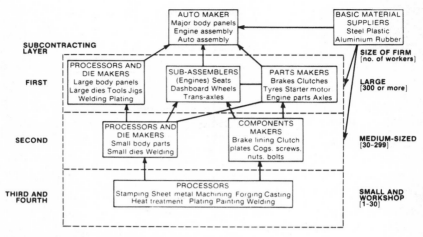

Figure 5.14. Subcontracting layers in the Japanese motor vehicle industry.
Source: Sheard (1983b).

in an uneven spatial pattern) and it is also connected by means of many long-distance transactional relations to a wider national and even international system of production. The industry will doubtless continue to ramify spatially in this manner so long as technologies, labor processes, and organizational structures sustain the complex in the form of myriad

TABLE 5.2

The Structure of Subcontracting in the Japanese Car Industry, 1976–1978

Employees per firm	Number of firms	Value added per employee ('000 yen)	Average wage per employee ('000 yen)	Percent of firms issuing subcontract orders	Average number of subcontractors used per firm
1–3	4182	1973	588	17	2
4–9	4832	2797	1424	46	3
10–19	1704	3546	1810	74	6
20–29	896	4024	1905	87	9
30–49	648	3937	2016	89	11
50–99	661	4290	2140	93	17
100–199	344	4892	2408	94	24
200–299	130	4810	2493	96	30
300–499	111	5135	2658	97	45
500–999	110	6020	2828	100	60
1000+	83	9263	3222	95	289

Source: Sheard (1983b), pp. 34 and 36.

interweaving units of production each performing a limited set of tasks within the entire chain of car-making operations.

OFFICE FUNCTIONS IN THE MODERN METROPOLIS

In chapter 2 we saw that office functions in the large American metropolis have continued to expand over recent decades, both in central-city areas and in suburban fringe areas. These functions comprise the central managerial, administrative, financial, and commercial tasks of capitalism. They typically exist in the city within dense networks of ancillary activities and supportive services.

Office functions are preeminently the preserve of a white-collar labor force. They emerge out of an advanced form of the division of labor, and in particular out of the separation of executive and clerical labor processes from direct physical production. They are frequently very labor-intensive, and they depend heavily on forms of activity that involve constant decision making and human interaction. That said, there is also much routinization of many types of office tasks, and this has been facilitated by massive incursions of new electronic technologies into the office environment over the last couple of decades. Despite the evidence of recent capital deepening, office functions tend generally to fragment into many specialized units that operate as cells of extensive communications and information networks. This fragmentation is a reflection of the innumerable, small, varied, and changeable transactions that are carried out by individual subelements of the system so that each can operate most efficiently as an independent economic agent rather than as part of a single, large, and unwieldy bureaucracy. Thus, the office sector is much given to vertical disintegration and to market intermediation of interoffice transactions. As a corollary, individual office units within any given complex invariably have access to scores if not hundreds of different inputs that are needed in widely varying mixes at different times. A cursory list of a few such inputs might include legal advice, management consulting, secretarial assistance, copy writing, banking services, accounting, factoring, public relations, marketing, software development, and the like.

Analysts such as Gad (1979), Goddard (1973), and Schwartz (1979) have commented on the dense development of the linkage structures that commonly tie offices together into functioning economic organizations. These linkages do not consist so much of material inputs and outputs as they do of flows of information via telephone contacts, personal encounters, and other means of communication. Face-to-face meetings are especially characteristic of interoffice contact systems, though they are usually costly, above all where several individuals at a time are involved. Thorngren (1970) has suggested that the expense of such meetings escalates rapidly upward with the complexity of the information to be transmitted, because the level of complexity is usually matched by the skill and experience (and hence the salary level) of the participants. Since office linkage costs can be very onerous (and would be even more so under conditions of wide dispersal), we observe much nodal clustering of interrelated offices in the central business districts of large cities. These central nodes form a distinctive part of the urban landscape, for they are usually housed in high-rise buildings whose intensive use of the land is a response to the inflated land prices that prevail at the core of the city.

In fact, this typical centralized locational pattern of metropolitan office complexes would seem to be doubly determined, as in the cases of the Birmingham gun and jewelry industries mentioned earlier. In the first place, offices congregate together because of their transactional interactions. In the second place, they also gravitate en bloc to the center of the whole urban mass in order to maximize their accessibility to the vast quantitites of labor that they consume overall. Thus, Schwartz (1979) has reported that there were 889,490 office workers in Manhattan in 1967, and Gad (1979) has indicated that in 1970 there were 192,000 workers in the four square kilometers that constitute the inner core of the central business district of Toronto. As I show in chapter 7, it is only by centralizing with respect to the total metropolitan labor market that large-scale office complexes can prevent their wage rates from spiraling indefinitely upward.

Within any given localized office complex it is usually possible to observe a subsidiary pattern of functional and spatial subnuclei composed of specialized clusters of functions. This internal disaggregation is based on the existence of strongly focused transactions around specific kinds of activities within any particular complex. Goddard (1973) has shown for the case of central London that contact patterns reach a peak of intensity within certain specified groups of offices. Consider, for example, the broad structure of interoffice telephone contacts in central London as shown in figure 5.15. Six distinctive groups of offices stand out in this figure, namely, publishing and business services, civil engineering, official agencies, commodity trading, fuel and oil, and banking and finance, all of them with strongly marked intragroup transactions. Gad (1979) has observed a sim-

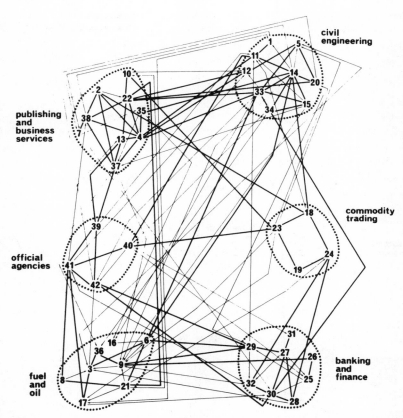

Figure 5.15. Telephone contacts in central London. Key: 1. Primary industry. 2. Food, drink, and tobacco. 3. Fuel and oil. 4. Chemicals. 5. Metals and metal goods. 6. Mechanical engineering and machinery. 7. Precision engineering. 8. Electrical engineering. 9. Transport equipment. 10. Textiles, leather, and clothing. 11. Bricks, pottery, glass, and cement. 12. Other manufacturing. 13. Paper, printing, and publishing. 14. General construction. 15. Specialist contracting. 16. Gas, electricity, and water. 17. Transport and communications. 18. Transport services. 19. Food wholesaling. 20. Other specialist wholesaling. 21. General wholesale merchants. 22. Retailing. 23. Export and import merchants. 24. Commodity brokers. 25. Insurance companies. 26. Other insurance. 27. Banking. 28. Stockbroking and jobbing. 29. Other finance. 30. Property. 31. Accounting. 32. Legal services. 33. Consulting engineers. 34. Architects. 35. Other specialist consultancy. 36. Nonprofit services. 37. Advertising and public relations.

SOURCE: Goddard (1973).

ilar sort of functional partitioning of offices in the central business district of Toronto. In this case, four main groups make their appearance, namely, financial activities, real estate developers and related functions, the media, and shipping and trading firms (see fig. 5.16). In Toronto, as in the central

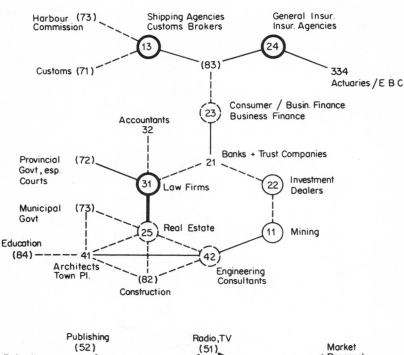

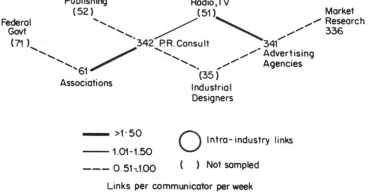

Figure 5.16. Office linkages in the central office complex of Toronto.
SOURCE: Gad (1979).

London example, intragroup transactions dominate over intergroup transactions, and this is testimony, in part, to the detailed patterns of disintegration that occur, even within specific sectors of the office complex.

As intimated earlier, these subsidiary groups of offices exist not only as

The Organization of Production and Intrametropolitan Location: Linkages and Subcontracting Patterns in Two Los Angeles Industries

INTRODUCTION

My objective now is to deepen the analysis of intraurban locational processes by looking in considerable detail at two extended case studies of industrial organization and location in the Greater Los Angeles Region (fig. 6.1). I examine specifically the women's dress industry and the printed circuit industry, both of which exemplify important aspects of the theoretical arguments laid out in chapters 3 and 4. Special attention is devoted here to the interwined problems of the social division of labor, interindustrial linkages, and subcontracting in these two sectors, and resulting patterns of intraurban location. The discussion is based on a detailed research project carried out in 1982, the results of which have been published at length elsewhere (Scott, 1983a, 1983b, 1984a). The reader is advised to consult these references for a full technical account of data sources, sampling procedures, statistical analyses, and so on. In the present context, I shall highlight only the broad outlines and conclusions of the research.

The women's dress and the printed circuit industries are characteristically made up of small single-establishment firms. There are a few exceptions to this generalization, but they are of negligible importance in the Greater Los Angeles Region. Frequency distributions of the sizes of establishments

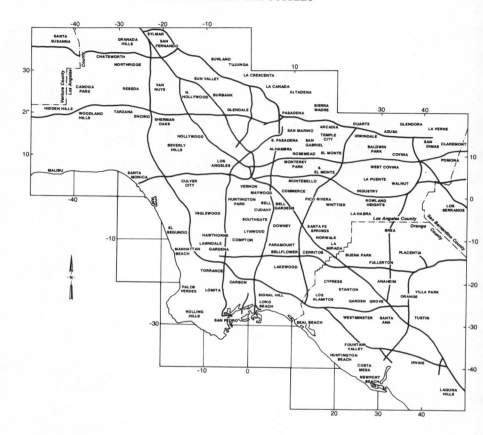

Figure 6.1. The Greater Los Angeles Region: General location map showing major municipalities and expressways.

for the two industries in the region are given in table 6.1. The variance of both distributions is high, and the statistical profiles that emerge are representative of skewed contagious distributions with long upper tails as discussed by Steindl (1965). What this implies, in practice, is that there is significant intraplant organizational variation in each sector (even such narrowly defined sectors as these) and hence significant contrasts in plant size. There are in total 135 women's dress plants in the region and 150 printed circuit plants. The two industries are extremely transaction-intensive, and they are characterized by detailed intrasectoral linkages as well as by strongly developed linkages to wider apparel and electronics production complexes, respectively. We now examine each industry and its peculiar intrametropolitan geography in turn.

TABLE 6.1

FREQUENCY DISTRIBUTIONS OF ESTABLISHMENT SIZES FOR THE WOMEN'S DRESS
AND PRINTED CIRCUIT INDUSTRIES IN THE GREATER LOS ANGELES REGION

Employment size category	Women's dress industry		Printed circuit industry	
	Number of plants	Relative frequency	Number of plants	Relative frequency
0–10	23	0.170	44	0.293
10–20	24	0.178	33	0.220
20–30	22	0.163	16	0.107
30–40	12	0.089	13	0.087
40–50	11	0.081	8	0.053
50–60	14	0.104	4	0.027
60–70	4	0.030	1	0.007
70–80	5	0.037	2	0.013
80–90	2	0.015	4	0.027
90–100	1	0.007	3	0.020
100+	17	0.126	22	0.147
	135		150	

THE WOMEN'S DRESS INDUSTRY IN THE GREATER LOS ANGELES REGION

Production processes and location. Like the apparel industry in general, women's dress manufacture is extremely labor-intensive and technologically static. Fabricating technologies are notoriously archaic and remain essentially at the rudimentary level of such simple mechanical devices as the cutting knife and the sewing machine.

The production process as a whole generally consists of seven basic steps, i.e., designing, pattern making, cloth cutting, sewing, finishing, packing, and sales. Many of these steps are in practice broken down into more minutely detailed operations, as for example in the case of sewing, which is often (though not always) organized as section work, in which operators specialize in the sewing of one specific part of a garment, such as sleeves, or hems, or pockets. High-quality producers are less inclined toward such divisions of labor, and, in these cases, sewing operations are recombined into a making-through process. In the women's dress industry, vertical disintegration of functions is common, and much work is subcontracted out. Cutting and sewing are especially susceptible to this. In everyday industry parlance, firms that subcontract out work are known as "manufacturers," even when little manufacturing is actually done on the premises and when in-house work is restricted to, say, purely white-collar activities such as designing and sales. A "contractor" is any firm that takes on work from a manufacturer.

Women's dress manufacturers face much economic competition and volatility in final products markets. These conditions are, at once, causes and symptoms of the rampant product differentiation that characterizes the industry and makes it difficult to stabilize outputs, and hence production routines. Moreover, the marked seasonality of the clothing trade means that output specifications must be periodically changed even where other tendencies toward product differentiation are eliminated. Firms ordinarily produce four seasonal "lines" (or collections of styles) a year. As a rule, only a limited number of styles in any line sell at all vigorously; and once manufacturers discover which of their styles in any season are most marketable, they then begin to produce these in quantity. Dresses are often, though by no means always, sold wholesale through showrooms located at the core of the city. In Los Angeles, the main focus of such wholesale activity is the California Mart, a large complex of offices, showrooms, business premises, and so on located at Ninth and Main Streets in the central-city area.

Labor employed in the women's dress industry is unskilled and semiskilled for the most part, though a few occupations in the industry are highly skilled, such as designing, pattern making, and cutting. Most dress-industry workers are female, and, in the Greater Los Angeles Region, the majority of these consist of Latinas and Asians. In 1982, the 135 women's dress plants in the region employed a total of 8,775 workers (giving an average plant size of 65.0). Most of the workers in the industry live in residential districts close to the center of the city, where they have immediate access to their places of employment.

The locational structure of the industry in the region is identified in figures 6.2 and 6.3. For ease of reference the system of coordinates shown on these figures is keyed in to the general location map of figure 6.1. A set of concentric circles has been superimposed over the spatial pattern of plants in figure 6.3. These circles are centered on the California Mart, and their radii increase at regular one-kilometer intervals from the center outward. The circles help to impose some sort of visual order on the copious amounts of locational data presented in figure 6.3.

Taken together, figures 6.2 and 6.3 reveal the dominant tendency for women's dress manufacturers in the region to gravitate overwhelmingly to the downtown area of Los Angeles. Indeed, some 72 women's dress plants (i.e., 53.3% of the total) are located within a range of one kilometer of the California Mart. Concomitantly, as distance from the California

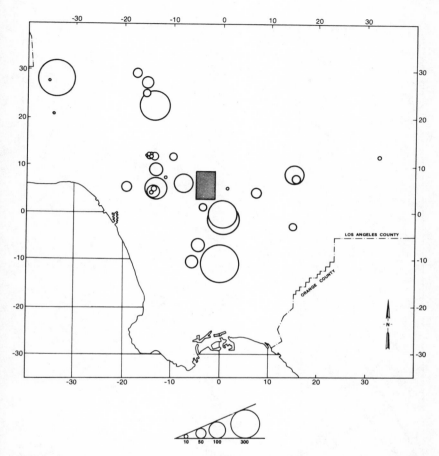

Figure 6.2. The location of the women's dress industry in the Greater Los Angeles Region. (See fig. 6.3 for inset.)

Mart increases, so plant locations become more and more dispersed, and, at least on the basis of visual inspection, plants also seem to become larger in size. More accurately, in the noncentral areas of the region, say, beyond five kilometers from the center, the composite geographical pattern of plants is made up of an irregular intercalation of small and large plants dominated by the latter. It would appear that these dispersed small plants occupy locational niches where locally favorable conditions (in such matters as transport services, labor supply, markets, and so on) are available. Large plants that are dispersed throughout the noncentral areas represent standardized capital-intensive producers whose locational pattern is a struc-

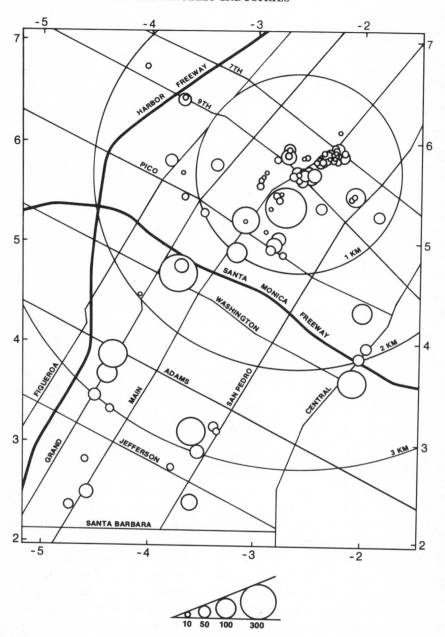

Figure 6.3. The location of the women's dress industry in the central area of Los Angeles.

tured outcome of their productive and organizational dynamics. These explanatory details will be dealt with more fully later.

Linkage patterns. The women's dress industry has a highly disintegrated organizational structure, and this is reflected in the very closely textured transactional relations that run from plant to plant. Virtually every plant in the industry has a bewildering variety of upstream materials and service inputs, downstream marketing contacts, and lateral subcontracting linkages. All of these transactions induce producers to converge toward a common center of gravity, thus forming a specialized garment district at the core of the city. Let us briefly consider the substantive nature of these transactions.

First, materials inputs in the dress industry are composed of an immense variety of items. Cloth is usually by far the main input in terms of value, but many smaller items are purchased at frequent intervals, and their cost represents a significant proportion of the total cost of production. Such items as trimmings, thread, linings, ribbons, needles and pins, buttons, buckles, fasteners, pattern-making equipment, sewing-machine parts, and so on are all part of the everyday paraphernalia of the dress industry. Unit transaction costs on all such inputs are typically high relative to their price, and they are kept down to manageable levels only by means of the mutual locational convergence of all participants in the industry. Thus, inputs are usually locally and cheaply available from the many wholesalers who crowd into the garment district. The same locational strategy makes it possible to service many plants' needs via networks of visiting sales representatives whose operating costs are dramatically reduced when the geographical distribution of customers allows them to make many visits in one day.

Second, sales of dresses are predominantly arranged through central showrooms located in the garment district. In Los Angeles, the key focus of this sales activity is the California Mart, which is a complex of hundreds of showrooms and wholesale clothing outlets. Here, manufacturers can rent space for short or long periods of time and make themselves collectively available to buyers who purchase items for subsequent retail distribution. The combined weight of this and similar complexes in the downtown area attracts buyers from all over the country and, indeed, the world.

Third, the kinds of work subcontracted out in the women's dress industry are many and various. Such activities as buttonhole making, pleating, quilting, shirring, trimming, screen printing, grading, and so on are all forms of work that are commonly put out to specialized subcontractors. Cutting and sewing, however, are by far the most significant forms of work regularly subcontracted out by dress manufacturers. Sampled plants in the Greater Los Angeles Region were found on average to subcontract out 47.8 percent of all their cutting and 88.6 percent of all their sewing. Both of these figures represent percentages of the total value of cutting and sewing done, respectively. They betoken a very powerful tendency toward vertical disintegration within the women's dress industry, which means, in turn, that there is a correspondingly intricate pattern of trans-actional activity linking manufacturers and subcontractors.

Cutting and sewing subcontracting activities. I now seek to probe more deeply into the functional and spatial logic of subcontracting activity in the women's dress industry in the Greater Los Angeles Region. I begin with a simple empirical description of the geographical location of cutting and sewing contract shops in the region.

The Spatial Distribution of Cutting and Sewing Contractors:

The locations of cutting and sewing contractors in Los Angeles are shown in figures 6.4 and 6.5, respectively. Cutting and sewing shops tend to specialize in serving particular segments of the clothing industry—some concentrating on shirts, some on sportswear, others on women's dresses, and so on—though they also shift with relative ease from one specialty to another. Unfortunately, it was not possible to obtain data on cutting shops by type of specialization, though it was possible to identify those sewing shops that specifically serve the dress industry. The map of cutting shops (fig. 6.5) simply shows all cutters in the Greater Los Angeles Region irrespective of any specialization they may have; and it is presumed that the designated spatial pattern is representative of the geography of those cutters who are explicitly linked to the dress industry. The data reveal a locational pattern that, in case of both cutting and sewing contractors, is strongly focused on the core of the region. In both cases, however, there is also an evident tendency toward outward dispersal, especially toward the ring of neighborhoods around the downtown area where cheap female Latino and Asiatic labor is readily available. Notice however, that decen-tralization of subcontractors in Los Angeles has not proceeded to anything like the same extent that it has in New York (see chap. 5). The reasons for this contrast remain unclear, but they are probably related to the much larger scale of the New York industry and the wider availability of cheap female labor in the fringe areas of the New York Metropolitan Region.

The spatial distribution of cutting and sewing contractors in Los Angeles was further scrutinized by means of some simple descriptive statistics.

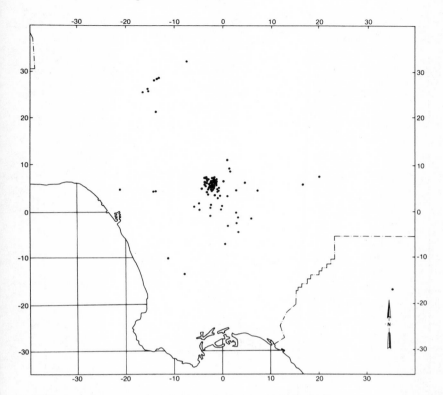

Figure 6.4. Cutting contractors in the Greater Los Angeles Region.

These statistics are arrayed in table 6.2, which is broken down by dress manufacturers, cutting contractors, and sewing contractors. For each type of activity, all distances to (a) the California Mart and (b) the center of gravity of the corresponding spatial distribution were computed. The means and variances of these distances were then calculated, and these are laid out in table 6.2. Note that all statistics shown in table 6.2 are unweighted by plant employment. These statistics bear witness, again, to the centralizing tendencies within the clothing industry in general. In all three cases the mean distance to the center is less than six kilometers. Nonetheless, the computed variances also imply that there is considerable subsidiary dispersal, for they are of the order of ten to fourteen times larger than the corresponding means. It would also seem that there is much similarity between the three spatial patterns as embodied in these statistics. Tests of differences of means as well as variance ratio tests indicate that there are almost no significant differences between manufacturers, cutting

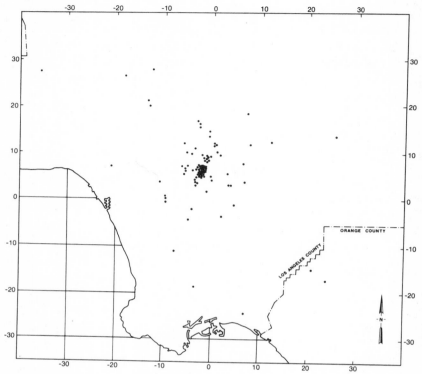

Figure 6.5. Sewing contractors serving the women's dress industry in the Greater Los Angeles Region.

TABLE 6.2

DESCRIPTIVE STATISTICS OF RADIAL DISTANCE RELATIONS FOR DRESS
MANUFACTURERS, CUTTING CONTRACTORS AND SEWING CONTRACTORS

	Relative to California Mart		Relative to center of gravity	
	Mean distance (kilometers)	Variance	Mean distance (kilometers)	Variance
Dress manufacturers (N = 135)	5.13	70.21	5.93	56.75
Cutting contractors (N = 90)	5.95	64.58	5.74	65.99
Sewing contractors (N = 140)	4.68	52.05	4.66	52.25

shops, and sewing shops in the matter of spatial distribution. Sewing activities, however, do appear to be slightly more centralized than the other two, and an F-ratio test of the variances of the distances of sewing shops and manufacturers from the California Mart reveals a just significant difference at the 95% confidence level. All other tests of differences were nonsignificant.

The Dynamics of Subcontracting in the Women's Dress Industry:

The degree to which any dress manufacturer subcontracts out cutting and sewing tasks was found to be inversely related to the quality of final outputs (Scott, 1984a). In this industry, quality is dependent above all on the amount of labor and skill invested in each dress, and it can most effectively be measured simply in terms of unit price. Define two variables, CC_i and CS_i, representing, respectively, the proportion of all cutting work subcontracted out and the proportion of all sewing work subcontracted out by the ith firm. Let p_i be the average wholesale price of dresses produced by the ith firm. For a sample of sixteen dress manufacturers in the Greater Los Angeles Region, a logit model (calibrated by regression methods) reveals the following quantitative relations between subcontracting activity and unit price:

$$CC_i = 1/[1 + 0.241\exp(0.016p_i)]$$
$$(n = 16; R^2 = 0.22; F = 3.95)$$

$$CS_i = 1/[1 + 0.002\exp(0.018p_i)]$$
$$(n = 16; R^2 = 0.54; F = 16.64).$$

The first equation is significant at the ninety-five percent level of confidence; the second is significant at the ninety-nine percent level. In these equations, the predicted values of CC_i and CS_i always lie between zero and unity, as they must if they are to be true proportions. The equations state that subcontracting activity is inversely related to unit price. Unfortunately, the equations are based on a very small sample size, and we have no way of telling how representative they are of the industry as a whole. Despite this note of caution, the equations are eminently reasonable from a theoretical point of view. They suggest to us in general that dress manufacturers producing high-quality outputs (usually in small batches) tend to internalize cutting and sewing functions, whereas plants that produce lower-quality outputs (in larger batches) tend to farm these tasks out. These remarks in turn imply that vertical organization in the dress industry is directly related to issues of the arrangement and control of labor processes, and we now scrutinize the substantive meaning of this implication.

A critical sign of the tendency toward vertical integration in the women's dress industry is the need for intensive managerial direction of the labor process. Disintegration follows in part from the absence of this need. Integration makes possible tight supervision and coordination of the labor process; disintegration makes these things impossible or difficult to achieve. But for labor-intensive plants producing high-quality, high-cost outputs of superior workmanship, control over the labor process is imperative. Without it, all the necessary detailed coordination between various manufacturing functions (designing, pattern making, cutting, sewing, finishing, and so on) would be compromised, and many important minutiae of the manufacturing process would undoubtedly be forfeited. Some confirmation of this idea is to be found in the observation (based on interviews with dress manufacturers) that producers of high-quality dresses in short runs generally organize the manufacturing process on making-through principles. This, by definition, reintegrates the labor process and reduces the opportunities for subcontracting activity. It also calls for skilled and attentive work requiring constant and careful supervision, so that the possibilities of efficient subcontracting are yet further reduced.

In contrast to this state of affairs, more capital-intensive plants producing relatively low-quality, low-cost dresses in long production runs require much less control over the details of the labor process as such. These plants are relatively less sensitive to the need for high standards of craftsmanship. They are, however, very much concerned with cost-effectiveness, especially in view of the intense competitiveness of the women's dress industry. At the more routinized and standardized end of the production spectrum, manufacturing processes are commonly broken down into a detailed division of labor (i.e., section work) in which unskilled and semiskilled employees work at a limited number of simplified operations. In this process, the quality of final outputs is directly traded off against extended and accelerated production runs, with the consequence that unit production prices are greatly reduced. At the same time, there is a concomitant diminution in the need for very detailed managerial intervention in the labor process, except, perhaps, for blunt policing of the work force, and even this is in part automatically secured where the piece-rate system is in effect, which is to say, almost universally. All of these circumstances encourage the vertical disintegration of production and the subcontracting out of specialized functions, and all the more so as subcontractors are typically locked into fierce competition so that their costs are slashed to the bone. Thus, for manufacturers producing cheap lines of dresses on a large scale, subcontracting represents a feasible and economically attractive option.

An echo of these same tendencies and relationships can be found in the observed differentials in the rates at which dress manufacturers contract out cutting and sewing. Cutting is a skilled operation, both because it calls for much manual dexterity and experience and because errors in the cutting process can be costly to the manufacturer in terms of wasted cloth. Hence, even when sewing is done on deskilled section-work principles, the preliminary cloth-cutting operations tend to call for definite labor skills. Sewing, by contrast, is usually at best a semiskilled occupation, and only rises above this level in special cases, as, for example, in plants producing high-quality outputs in a making-through process. Sewing, then, calls for considerably less managerial control than cutting; above all, interchanges between sewing-machine operators and their supervisors are at a less complex level than is typically the case with workers in the cutting room. This means that we should expect cutting to be much less vertically disintegrated than sewing, and to be sure, as indicated earlier, sampled plants put out 47.8 percent of their cutting but as much as 88.6 percent of their sewing.

Even after it has been demonstrated empirically that large routinized dress manufacturers producing standardized outputs tend actively to subcontract out much of their cutting and sewing, there still remains the question of how it comes about that subcontract shops have a comparative cost advantage in the performance of these functions. To answer this question fully and finally, we need to invoke some of the reasoning adduced in chapter 3, and in particular we need to deal with the interconnected issues of uncertainty and labor costs in the dress industry as a whole. Since these issues have already been dealt with in general at an earlier stage, only the briefest comments will be appended here.

First, then, subcontracting is a rational response to situations in which manufacturers face uncertain markets. This is especially the case in the dress industry, where the competitive conditions and the vagaries of fashion make it virtually impossible for manufacturers to predict with accuracy how well (or badly) a particular style or line will sell. Subcontracting is a strategy that allows manufacturers to pool their risks, and it permits a more efficient allocation of capital and labor than in the case where risks are fully internalized in each plant. By the same token, subcontracting allows manufacturers to raise or lower production quotas rapidly without undue strain or opportunity costs on installed productive capacity. This is especially important for low-quality producers making dresses for the mass market. Thus, on these grounds alone, subcontracting is highly cost-effective in the dress industry. Furthermore, the same uncertainty that encourages vertical disintegration of functions encourages independent contractors to seek out accessible (i.e., in this case, central) locations vis-à-vis the industry as a whole.

Second, subcontracting is also a powerful means of enforcing wages discipline. This is an especially urgent matter in the dress industry with its labor-intensive forms of production and, nowadays, its weaknesses in the face of cheap foreign imports. Subcontracting, however, helps to impose a ceiling on labor costs by externalizing what would be an internal labor market subject to endemic upward drift of wages and the development of potentially disruptive worker combinations within individual (and enlargened) manufacturing plants. The effect of a wage ceiling is achieved by the market intermediation of manufacturer-subcontractor relations. Competition for subcontract work imposes on contract shops a strong market discipline that forces them to keep a tight rein on wages, or else (if their costs rise relative to other contractors) eventually to go out of business. Indeed, so great is the pressure on dress contractors to keep costs down that they themselves sub-subcontract out work to homeworkers (generally, illegal immigrants) who are, in turn, competing among themselves for assignments. At the same time, all of this subcontracting activity balkanizes the labor force by dividing it into many small and fragmented units, and this further impedes the formation of worker solidarity.

In interviews with both dress manufacturers and contractors over the summer months of 1982, I found that there was virtually unanimous agreement that levels of subcontracting had increased sharply in the Los Angeles area over the previous few years. If the arguments presented here are in any sense valid, this increase can no doubt, in large part, be interpreted as being due to augmented cost pressures in the dress industry as a consequence of both strongly recessionary conditions and the insistent competition of foreign producers. A corollary of these remarks is the expectation that if economic conditions should become less competitive in the future, and if, in particular, the need for downward pressure on wages should slacken off, the process of vertical disintegration might be slowed down, or even, perhaps, reversed.

The Geographical Implications of Subcontracting:

To the extent that there is vertical disintegration of functions in the dress industry, to the same extent there will be a dense system of linkages tying manufacturers and their contractors into a network of reciprocal arrangements. This network is, first of all, a system of functional inter-actions, but it is also a definite geographical phenomenon. It leads directly to the spatial clumping of activities, for only in this way can the particularly onerous costs of externalized transactions in the dress industry be brought under control. Furthermore, in a system of subcontract relations, one of the special advantages that accrues from the geographical convergence of vertically disintegrated functions is that price signals are efficiently dissem-inated throughout the system and search costs are much curtailed (Stigler, 1961). There is, therefore, a clearly observable proclivity on the part of both manufacturers and contractors to gravitate to locations where max-imum mutual accessibility is ensured. As noted at an earlier stage, sewing contractors seem to be especially given to such convergence. Despite this dominating tendency toward spatial clustering, some (large) manufacturers and contractors actively shun the main garment district and take up lo-cations in peripheral areas, though, as indicated by figures 6.2 and 6.3, they do not in general move far from the core, and they still seem to be strongly connected to its various functional benefits.

THE PRINTED CIRCUIT INDUSTRY IN THE GREATER LOS ANGELES REGION

Production processes and location. The printed circuit industry is a highly specialized segment of the electronics industry. Manufacturers of printed circuits take various plastic laminates and chemical materials as basic inputs and transform these into finished outputs consisting of boards with elec-tronic circuitry etched onto them. The boards are made solely to the specifications of the buyer, and orders may range in size from single pro-totype boards to batches consisting of several thousand individual items. Many different kinds of industries consume printed circuit boards, but the general electronics and aerospace industries constitute the largest market by far. Consumers of printed circuit boards mount electronic components onto the boards, and these subassemblies are then inserted into various devices, such as calculating machines, computers, rocketry, television sets, and so on.

Printed circuit boards are of three main types, i.e., single-sided, double-sided, and multilayered, in ascending order of technological complexity and difficulty of fabrication. In all cases, the basic manufacturing process consists of two main sets of operations: (a) the physical cutting of the laminate material into boards and the drilling of complex patterns of holes into these boards; and (b) the chemical etching of circuitry onto the boards, which are then covered with a coating of protective material. In the case of multilayer production, there is the further problem of assembling different layers of drilled and etched laminates into a single composite board. All of these operations can be described in considerably more detail, and there are, of course, many other detailed operations involved in the manufacturing process in addition to those mentioned here. However, only these bare essentials need concern us in this analysis.

In general, the manufacture of printed circuit boards is carried out in small to medium-sized independent, single-plant firms. There is much vertical disintegration and internal specialization within the industry, as manifested in a fairly active pattern of interplant subcontracting. However, some printed circuit producers, especially the larger ones, are quite integrated. Occasionally, printed circuit plants themselves are vertically integrated as "captive plants" into downstream electronics assembly functions. Captive plants are to some degree sheltered from external competition, but in the independent sector of the industry competition is strong, and producers are under constant pressure to trim costs and root out inefficiencies. Producers also face much uncertainty. This is first of all because of sharp cyclical fluctuations in the markets served by printed circuit producers; and second of all because every individual order for printed circuit boards tends to be a special case calling for detailed design instructions so that sales linkages are constantly in the process of being re-created and renegotiated. Plants generally concentrate on production for a particular segment of the printed circuit market (e.g., small-batch versus large-batch production), and joint outputs are virtually unknown in the industry (if we exclude internal product differentiation involving different categories of boards). Labor used in the industry is predominantly unskilled and semiskilled, and, at least in the Greater Los Angeles Region, much of it is Asian and Latino. Total regional employment in the 150 plants that composed the industry in 1982 was 6,750, so average plant size was 45.0 workers.

In 1968, there were 69 printed circuit plants in the Greater Los Angeles Region. At this time, the industry was widely scattered across the whole region, though it was also predominantly attracted to suburban locations (fig. 6.6). There was a fairly strong concentration of plants in the northern part of the region in the San Fernando Valley, stretching from Burbank in the east to Chatsworth in the west. A diffuse cluster of plants was located in the Orange County area around Anaheim and Santa Ana. There

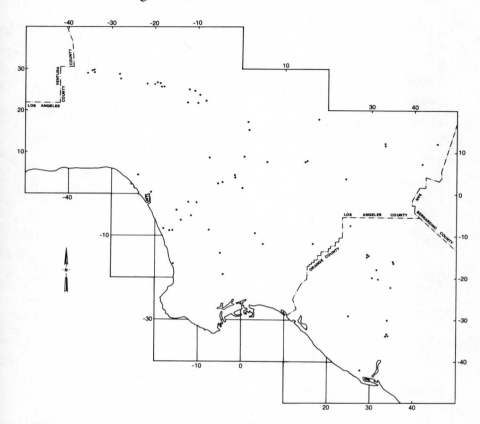

Figure 6.6. Printed circuits plants, 1968.

was also a small group of plants located in the El Segundo/Airport area in the central-western portion of the region. The overall geographical pattern of the industry in 1968 was, therefore, dominantly made up of subnuclei at decentralized suburban locations combined with subsidiary irregular scattering.

By 1975, much extension and infilling of the San Fernando Valley and Orange County clusters had taken place (fig. 6.7). There were now 120 printed circuit plants in the region. Notice in particular the growth in the number of plants at the southern end of the Orange County cluster in the Santa Ana and Irvine areas. At the same time, the small grouping of plants in the El Segundo/Airport area was now tending somewhat to fade away, presumably in part as a response to locational shifts in the aerospace industry away from the airport area and toward the suburbs.

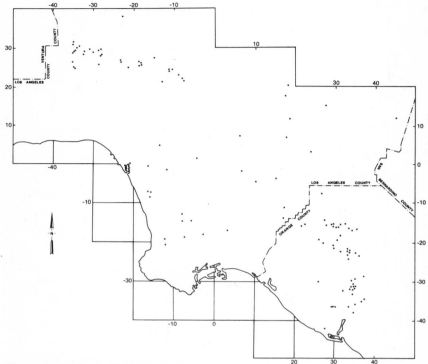

Figure 6.7. Printed circuits plants, 1975.

Further consolidation and outward spread of the San Fernando Valley and Orange County clusters is apparent in the map for 1982 (fig. 6.8). The Orange County cluster, above all, grew dramatically between 1975 and 1982, and, in comparison with the situation in 1975, a southward extension of the cluster into the area of Irvine is apparent. By 1982, few printed circuit plants remained in the central portion of the Greater Los Angeles Region, and suburbanization of the industry was by now virtually complete. Again, this suburbanization is dominantly marked by localized nucleation, but there is now also a definite pattern of dispersed, large, capital-intensive plants in the northeastern portion of region between El Monte and Pomona.

This overall pattern of locational evolution in the printed circuit industry in the Greater Los Angeles Region from 1968 to 1982 is part of a wider contemporary trend toward the decentralization and suburbanization of industry generally in large metropolitan areas. Decentralization has proceeded much further in the case of the printed circuit industry than it has

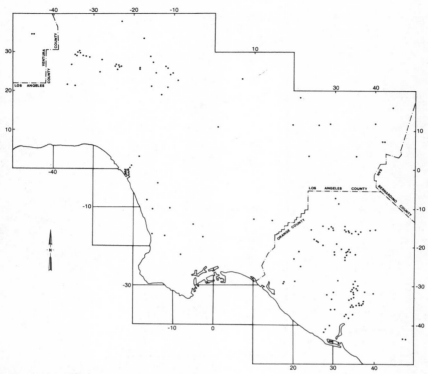

Figure 6.8. Printed circuits plants, 1982.

in the women's dress industry, which is still narrowly locked in to a central hub of activities. At the same time, the decentralization of the printed circuit industry has been something more than just a simple outward dispersal of individual establishments; for in both the southern part of the region, in Orange County, and in the north, in the San Fernando Valley, *two distinctive subclusters of producers have made their appearance,* both of them evidently organized around their own internal functional and spatial axes of transactional activity and associated local labor markets.

Linkage patterns 1: Materials inputs and outputs. Let us now consider some of these functional/spatial characteristics of the industry more closely. To begin with, we look at simple inputs and outputs.

Exclusive of fixed capital items, the main inputs to the printed circuit industry consist of different laminates and chemicals. In 1982, it was found that virtually all plants bought these inputs from within the region (Scott, 1983b). Figure 6.9 shows a sample of seventeen plants along with their main local suppliers of laminates and chemicals. A definite spatial associ-

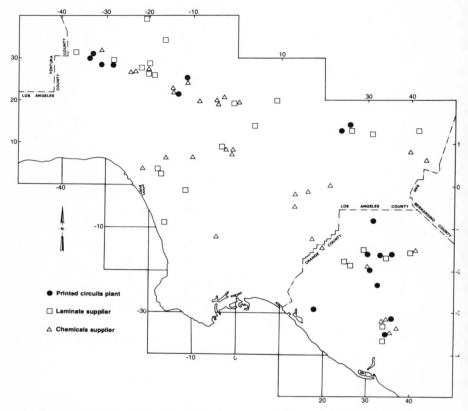

Figure 6.9. A sample of printed circuits plants and their main suppliers of laminates and chemicals.

ation exists between these different activities in the form of (a) locationally intercalated printed circuit plants and their suppliers in the fringes of the region, combined with (b) a centralized grouping of suppliers who are thus in a position to serve printed circuit plants in all the surrounding communities.

At the same time, printed circuit producers sell their outputs to a wide variety of other electronics firms both in and out of the Region. We can gather something of the spatial forces at work in this relation by a scrutiny of figure 6.10, which shows the locations of a sample of thirteen printed circuit plants along with those of their top five customers who are located in the region. In fact, some 49 percent of these customers lie outside of the region altogether. In spite of this dispersal of final destinations for

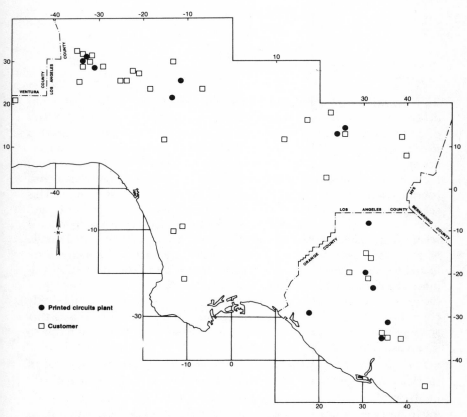

Figure 6.10. A sample of printed circuits plants and their main customers in the Greater Los Angeles Region.

printed circuit boards, there is an unmistakable spatial correlation between printed circuit plants and most of their major customers, suggesting that to some degree the industry's downstream linkages also exert a certain localizing effect on producers.

The geography of these linkages may be subject to more searching statistical analysis. We define two critical variables, $M1_i$ and $M2_i$, for this purpose. $M1_i$ is the proportion of the ith printed circuit plant's output that is marketed within a ten-mile radius of the plant. $M2_i$ is the proportion of the ith plant's output marketed within the Greater Los Angeles Region as a whole. A further variable, E_i, is defined as the total employment of the ith plant. The following logit models were then computed by means of regression methods:

$M1_i = 1/[1 + 0.256\exp(0.941\log E_i)]$
$(n = 19; R^2 = 0.37; F = 10.02)$

$M2_i = 1/[1 + 0.0004\exp(1.775\log E_i)]$
$(n = 21; R^2 = 0.47; F = 16.72)$.

Both equations are significant at the ninety-nine percent level of confidence. They signify that there is an inverse relationship between the size of any printed circuit plant and the proportion of its output marketed locally, which is roughly equivalent to a positive correlation between market area and plant size. As shown elsewhere (Scott, 1983b), plant size in the printed circuit industry is also strongly and positively correlated with routinization of labor processes and standardization of final outputs. This suggests in turn (via the interrelations between production processes and linkage structures) that (a) plants with small-scale and variable transactional relations are mainly linked to customers over a very narrow spatial range, whereas (b) plants with large-scale and stable transactional structures are linked to customers over a much wider spatial area. This particular conjuncture of plant characteristics and linkage relations was a definite prediction of chapter 4, and it is encouraging to note that it is at least modestly confirmed by these results. An immediate corollary of all of this is that small printed circuit plants are much more closely tied in spatial terms to their customers than are large plants.

Linkage patterns 2: Subcontracting relations. The subcontracting out of specific packets of tasks is a significant phenomenon in the printed circuit industry. Many plants subcontract out such specialized operations as drilling, multilayer laminating, solder fusing, plating, and the like. This is most especially the case where plants are small and where the operations involved call for relatively heavy expenditure on fixed capital items (such as numerically controlled drills or laminating presses). Subcontracting is then in part a means of collectivizing work tasks so as to avoid the heavy cost penalties incurred in the partial and inefficient use of capital. At the same time, as I argued in chapter 4, subcontracting can also be seen as a response to uncertainties in product markets, for it is a means of reducing the backward transmission of uncertainty through the relatively rigid institutional structure of the vertically integrated plant. Further, subcontracting (i.e., vertical disintegration) is encouraged where linkage costs are low, which is to say, where any plant has ready access to nearby specialized producers.

Surveyed printed circuit plants were asked to provide the addresses of their five main subcontractors (by value of work put out). Usable information on this matter was obtained from fourteen plants, and this infor-

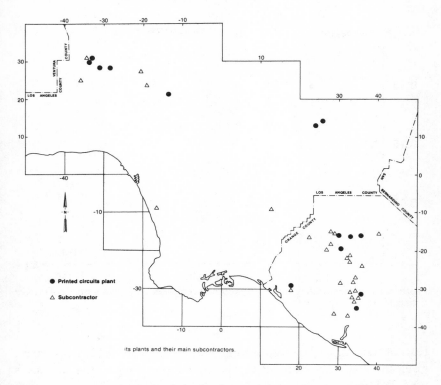

Figure 6.11. A sample of printed circuits plants and their main subcontractors.

mation is portrayed in figure 6.11. No distinctions were made here as to the kinds of work put out, so the subcontractors shown in figure 6.11 represent a heterogeneous variety of functions. In spite of this heterogeneity, the spatial pattern that emerges in figure 6.11 is unmistakably focused on the central Orange County complex with a minor subsidiary cluster in the San Fernando Valley. Even those printed circuit plants that lie outside of Orange County tend dominantly to look to Orange County subcontractors for any work that they may put out.

We may gain much further insight into these matters with the aid of a simple statistical test. This test runs parallel to the analysis of market linkages described above, and it consists of an attempt to correlate subcontracting activity (C_i) with total employment (E_i) for all plants, where C_i is defined as the value of all work put out as a proportion of the total revenue of the ith plant. The expectation is that there will be a negative correlation between these variables. This expectation is now tested on the

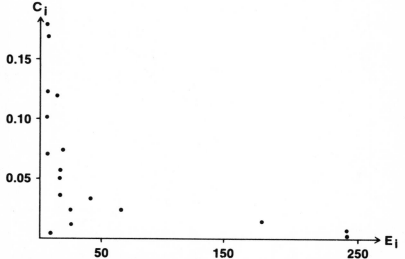

Figure 6.12. Subcontracting activity (C_i) relative to employment (E_i) for a sample of printed circuits plants.

basis of the sample data displayed graphically in figure 6.12. Once more, given the numerical shape of C_i, the logit form of regression analysis is used. We have

$$C_i = 1/[1 + 2.184\exp(0.855\log E_i)]$$
$$(n = 18; R^2 = 0.57; F = 20.96).$$

The regression is fully significant at the ninety-nine percent level of confidence, and as expected, the relationship between C_i and E_i is negative.

Notwithstanding the rather successful results of this test, it was decided to press forward and to attempt to develop a more elaborate statistical model of the subcontracting function. Thus, the variable AS_i (defined as average dollar sales per customer at the ith plant) is now introduced into the analysis. This variable is an approximate measure of levels of standardization and average batch size in any printed circuit plant (Scott, 1983b). We now have

$$C_i = 1/[1 + 1.815\exp(0.510\log E_i + 0.382\log AS_i)]$$
$$(n = 17; R^2 = 0.60 ; F = 10.63).$$

Unfortunately, with the variable AS_i in the equation, the significance of the individual regression coefficients falls in both cases to just below the ninety-five percent level, and the collinearity of the two variables further diminishes their joint explanatory interest. In spite of these deficiencies, this second equation still captures something of the logic of the subcontracting process in the printed circuit industry. It would seem, in short, that small plants producing many different small batches of work tend to move toward vertical disintegration of specific functions, whereas large plants producing large standardized batches are more prone to internalize those functions.

Résumé: industrial organization and intraurban location in the printed circuit industry. All of the above findings on input, output, and subcontracting linkages in the printed circuit industry are fully consonant with the theoretical ideas put forward earlier in this book. Two main points need to be made. In the first place, tightly convergent complexes of interrelated economic activity (as in the Orange County area) make it possible for relatively high levels of vertical disintegration to come about within those complexes by reason of the diminished spatial costs of transacting business within them. Something of this process is revealed in the data presented cartographically in figures 6.9, 6.10, 6.11. In the second place, as already noted, the putting out of work relative to total plant activity is most strongly developed among small and unstandardized producers of printed circuit boards. These types of producers presumably find it most difficult to make efficient use of large items of fixed capital, and hence they pool many of their specialized production requirements through the subcontracting mechanism. By contrast, standardized plants serving large customers can make use of fixed capital efficiently, and they accordingly opt for largeness of operational scale. In part, these relations between scale of production, capitalization, and subcontracting activity are functions of levels of certainty and uncertainty in final markets. Uncertain sales prospects and hence uncertain production schedules make it difficult to use capital efficiently, and this both limits the growth of plants and encourages vertical disintegration. Higher degrees of certainty enable plants to use fixed capital with considerable efficiency, and thus to expand and to integrate; this is especially the case if the segment of the market served is one that can be catered to by means of fairly routinized technologies.

These remarks may be further driven home by consideration of the case of captive printed circuit plants that are vertically integrated with downstream assembly functions. There are some sixteen captive printed circuit plants in the Greater Los Angeles Region, and each employs on average

98.8 workers. Independent plants employ on average 38.8 workers. Captive plants are geared to downstream functions whose demands for printed circuit boards are both massive and highly predictable. Captive plants have thus resolved, precisely, the problem of uncertainty; as a consequence, they are large and standardized, and they generate significant internal economies when vertically integrated with downstream activities. Integration is further encouraged by the managerial economies that accrue from joint supervisory and quality control when board manufacture is combined with assembly functions.

Thus, on the one hand, small printed circuit plants with irregular and unstandardized linkages (of whatever kind) will find it to their advantage to cluster together with their satellite functions in geographical space; this is because small-scale and unstable linkages are characterized by high unit costs, and clustering is a way of maintaining a ceiling on total linkage costs. On the other hand, large plants with the opposite linkage characteristics will be more free to form locationally dispersed patterns and hence may be expected to be found at more widely scattered locations than small plants.

CONCLUSION

These case studies of the women's dress industry and the printed circuit industry in the Greater Los Angeles Region reconfirm our expectations about the spatial structure of industrial activity in the large capitalist metropolis. They demonstrate once again the proclivity of industrial plants to gather closely together in specialized production spaces whose innermost cores are densely developed, and whose edges are zones of locational dissipation and dispersal. This pattern is further complicated by the tendency of small plants to gravitate to centralized locations and of large plants to drift to the periphery. By way of conclusion, let us examine some brief statistical synopses of these notions.

Tables 6.3 and 6.4 lay out data on the locational structure of the two industries relative to their major points of focus in the metropolitan region. Table 6.3 shows how the women's dress industry is arranged according to a series of zones radiating outward from the central garment district of Los Angeles. Table 6.4 provides data (also arranged by zones) for the printed circuit industry, though this time the zones are centered on the functional core of Orange County, and they extend outward only as far as the county boundaries. This restriction reflects the status of Orange

TABLE 6.3

SPATIAL ORGANIZATION OF THE WOMEN'S DRESS INDUSTRY IN THE GREATER
LOS ANGELES REGION

Ring number	Distance from California Mart (kilometers)	Number of plants	Average plant size	Employment density per square kilometer	Plants per square kilometer
1	0–1	72	40.2	921.3	22.9
2	1–2	13	58.5	80.7	1.4
3	2–3	5	69.8	22.2	0.3
4	3–4	10	72.1	32.8	0.5
5	4–5	3	110.0	11.7	0.1
6	5+	32	116.2	0.0	0.0

County as the current primary focus of the printed circuit industry in the
Greater Los Angeles Region. Note at once the contrasts in industrial land
use densities revealed by tables 6.3 and 6.4. Since women's dress manufacturers occupy much more centralized locations with respect to the whole
metropolitan region than printed circuit manufacturers, they show much
higher densities of both employment and plants per square kilometer than
the latter. More important, average plant size per zone increases markedly
and systematically from the center of each system outward. To be sure, in
both cases (but especially in the case of printed circuits) there are various
small plants scattered around the outer zones, though generally the correlations between average plant size and radial distance are unambiguously
positive.

TABLE 6.4

SPATIAL ORGANIZATION OF THE PRINTED CIRCUIT INDUSTRY IN ORANGE COUNTY

Ring number	Distance from functional center of county (kilometers)	Number of plants	Average plant size	Employment density per square kilometer	Plants per square kilometer
1	0–3	1	30.0	1.1	0.04
2	3–6	18	53.4	11.3	0.21
3	6–9	16	58.9	6.7	0.11
4	9–12	31	65.4	10.2	0.16
5	12–15	5	38.2	0.8	0.02
6	15–18	5	21.5	0.4	0.02
7	18+	5	19.6	0.1	0.00

Once more we may provisionally interpret these relationships in terms of transactional structures that tend to push small interdependent plants into focal locations, while the combined effects of land and labor costs help to keep larger plants in peripheral areas. It is to be stressed again, however, that we have no final analytical purchase on this critical problem, and much more research is needed before any definitive pronouncements can be possible. As already indicated, such research would undoubtedly offer the opportunity of recombining land-use theory and the problem of the spatial switching of techniques in significantly new ways. Meanwhile, we must now turn our attention to the equally critical problem of local labor markets in the metropolis and to the ways in which they respond to and restructure the locational impacts of the purely organizational dynamics of the production system.

SEVEN

Local Labor Markets in the Metropolis

INTRODUCTION: THE EMPLOYMENT RELATION

The manifest form of labor markets in capitalism is the exchange of labor-power for a wage. It is no doubt tempting to seek to interpret this sort of exchange as a straightforward market relation (like any other) involving nothing more than the transfer of a given set of use values for a given quantity of money. It is far from being straightforward, however. Whatever the quantitative interdependencies between labor supply, labor demand, and wages might be, they are always inscribed within and subsidiary to a many-faceted and politically volatile *employment relation*. This relation itself is an element of a wider class bargain in any community, and it consists of an ensemble of habits, norms, work rules, legal arrangements, and so on that define the conditions of work and the role of the worker in the labor process. It is thus a complex and relatively durable structure, and the form it takes at any given moment is pregnant with implications for the entire range of local labor market outcomes in the metropolis.

In any system of capitalist commodity production, wages and worker benefits confront employers as direct costs of production (see the equation system 3.2). Because of this, employers typically bear down wherever possible upon wages and benefits, just as they also constantly seek out transformations of labor processes in ways that allow them to undercut the discretionary powers of workers in the round of daily production and in the emergence of wider corporate strategies. These phenomena are

119

expressions of a constant political tension within the employment relation. To the degree that any one party to the relation maneuvers for advantages, collision and conflict are all the more likely. The employment relation is, therefore, a site of considerable strain and antagonism, whether overt or merely latent. By the same token, it is endemically subject to renegotiation and reconstruction through the sociopolitical action of the different agents bound together within it. As this occurs, dramatic transformations in the internal organization of local labor markets may come about and intra-metropolitan space itself may be significantly restructured as a consequence.

I propose to lead up to a concrete analysis of these issues by broaching at the outset a series of rather technical questions about the role of urban space in the formation of local labor markets. These questions concern the interconnections between commuting patterns, wage rates, and labor turnover phenomena in the large metropolis, all of which are important adjuncts of the employment relation in urban context and major points of interface between intraurban production space and social space. Then, in the next chapter, I shall consider (in the light of a further empirical case study) some of the deeply rooted political dynamics of the employment relation and their connections to the urban environment. A word of warning is in order at once, however. Of all the major problems that form part of the urban question in contemporary capitalism, the mechanisms of local labor market adjustment and their effects on intraurban location are assuredly among the most perplexing and underresearched. As a consequence, my remarks here will of necessity be highly speculative. With this proviso in mind, I now introduce the investigation via a simple description of commuting patterns in the metropolis.

COMMUTING PATTERNS IN THE METROPOLIS

A recurrent relationship underlying the structuring of intraurban space consists of (a) the establishment of employment activities at sites adjacent to suitable supplies of labor, and (b) the location of workers' residences near major places of work. The geographical manifestations of this (recursive) relationship become ever more complex as the metropolis grows and as different functions ramify with one another in urban space. Even so, these patterns of intraurban employment and housing remain continuously subject to their own locational interdependence, and this accounts for the persistent configuration of the modern metropolis as a bipartite system of production and social spaces tied geographically to one another through the commuting habits (by various transport modes) of workers.

It has been observed on many different occasions that the spatial structure of commuting patterns in the metropolis can be described in terms of a simple inverse function of distance (e.g., Evans, 1973; Lowry, 1964; Putman, 1983; Richardson, 1977). Thus, we can express E_{ij} (an index of the number of workers who live at i and work at j) in an equation of the form $E_{ij} = (d_{ij})$, where d_{ij} is the distance between i and j (see fig. 7.1). When this equation is empirically calibrated, it invariably identifies the lineaments of a commuting shed around a given workplace, j, such that nearby neighborhoods house a high proportion of the workers at j, and more distant neighborhoods house correspondingly smaller proportions. These relationships however, are much influenced by the socioeconomic status of commuters (Gera and Kuhn, 1978). In the case of female factory workers, for example, the commuting shed typically covers a comparatively restricted spatial area; but in the case of male managerial labor, it may range over the whole of the metropolitan region.

Figure 7.1 provides corroboration of these remarks. The figure gives empirical information on commuting patterns in Pittsburgh for four main occupational groups ranging from low socioeconomic status (laborers, domestic and service workers) to high (managerial and professional workers). In each case a logarithmic equation of the relative frequency of work trips against distance from homeplace to workplace is defined. The four equations trace out curves that are strongly convex to the origin. Two main points are worthy of note in regard to figure 7.1. First, observed work trips are remarkably short on the whole, and in all four cases over ninety percent of commuters reside within five miles of their places of work. Second, the spatial range of commuting activity in the metropolis is clearly related (as expected) to socioeconomic status. In order of ascending status, the coefficients attached to the distance terms in the four commuting equations are -1.850, -1.470, -1.125, and -1.080, respectively. These coefficients signify that the residences of lower socioeconomic status groups crowd much more closely in to their places of work than those of higher status groups.

These results demonstrate that employment centers and their surrounding residential areas are tied functionally together by spatially systematic commuting patterns whose form implies that workers make concerted efforts in their choice of residential location to secure high levels of accessibility to places of work. The same results are not inconsistent with

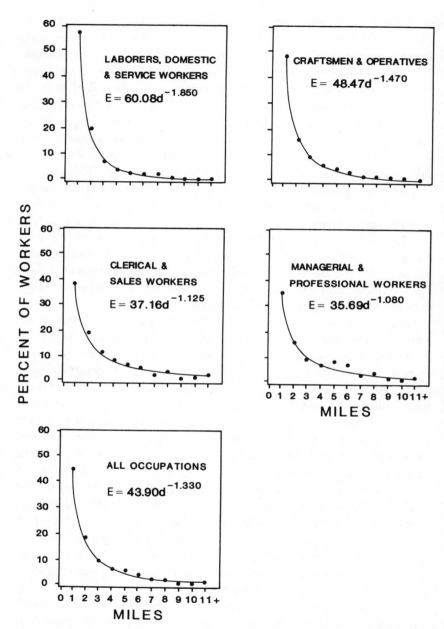

Figure 7.1. Empirical distribution of work trips by distance to workplace; redrawn from Lowry (1964, fig. 8).

the additional idea that employers, in their turn, search out locations that are as close as they possibly can be to suitable pools of labor. Before we can pronounce further on this latter issue, however, we must carry the investigation forward to an analysis of the effects of commuting patterns on wages as determined at place of work.

WAGE-SETTING MECHANISMS AND THE SPATIAL STRUCTURE OF INTRAMETROPOLITAN LABOR MARKETS

My intention here is to conduct a preliminary analysis of the formation of wage rates *at job site* relative to the given intraurban pattern of employment places and residential neighborhoods. Remark at once that I make no claims as to the finality of these spatial variables in the determination of intraurban wage rates. The wage system in capitalism is, in any case, shot through with the complexities of the employment relation, and there can be no possibility of accounting for wage levels simply and uniquely in terms of spatial conditions (Clark, 1983a, 1983b). Rather, I propose to show how spatial conditions (and, more specifically, commuting cost differentials) can intersect with the effects of the employment relation as a whole in a way that induces marginal variations in wage rates from one employment site to another. As I shall show, the evidence seems to suggest that these variations, marginal as they may be, have significant consequences for intraurban plant location.

Wage rates and commuting patterns. One of the few really coherent attempts to theorize the problem of the geography of intraurban wage rates was accomplished over two-and-a-half decades ago in a seminal paper by Moses (1962). Despite its erstwhile vintage, Moses's statement remains even today the cornerstone of most attempts to uncover the spatial logic of wage-rate differentials in the city, though it must be added that his analysis remains severely limited in its premises and range.

Moses begins with the simplifying assumption that all employment is concentrated at the center of the city while the working population is spread out in residential districts surrounding this central point. Let us define a basic weekly wage rate, w, as the standard level of remuneration available in the central employment cluster. We may call w the *reference wage*. The mechanisms underlying its determination remain unspecified, but there is nothing to stop us, if we wish, from defining it in purely institutional terms. Moses then shows how a *residual wage* (after discount-

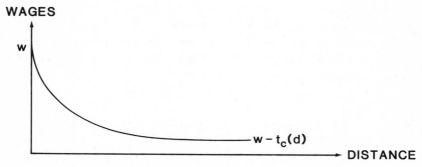

Figure 7.2. The reference wage, w, and the residual wage, $w - t_c(d)$, as a function of distance from the city center.

ing for commuting costs) can be defined for each commuter by place of residence. For a worker residing at d distance units from the center of the city, the residual wage can be specified as the basic reference wage less the cost, $t_c(d)$, that the worker would normally incur in traveling weekly to and from the center over the distance d. The corresponding function, $w - t_c(d)$ is graphed in figure 7.2, and of course this function declines steadily with increasing values of d. Any point on the surface $w\text{-}t_c(d)$ can be identified (in the context of the severely restrictive assumptions of this analysis) as the minimum wage that an employer would have to offer any prospective worker in order to induce that worker to accept equivalent employment at the homeplace rather than at the city center.

Thus, the function $w\text{-}t_c(d)$ can also be interpreted as a set of hypothetical spatially differentiated wage rates in a context where employment is geographically restricted either to firms clustered at the core of the city or to the residential locations of individual workers. But what, we may ask, will be the effect on noncentral wage rates if some plant employing not just one but a multiplicity of workers now locates away from the center? If we assume that the residences of workers are locationally fixed in the short to medium term, a simple answer to this question is forthcoming on the basis of Moses's model. Given that population densities in the metropolis customarily decline from the center outward, it can be argued that the further the new plant locates from the center, the more it will tend to drive offered wage rates above the local level $w\text{-}t_c(d)$. This upward pressure on wage rates at noncentral locations will be all the more intense the greater the plant's demand for labor. These propositions can be clarified by reference to figures 7.3 and 7.4.

Consider first figure 7.3. Suppose that the new plant locates at n distance

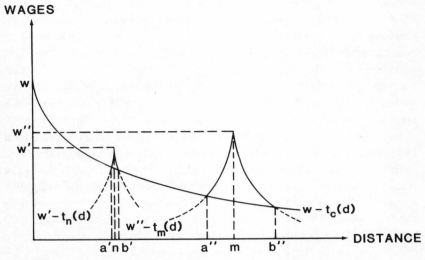

Figure 7.3. The effect on wage rates of outward movement of plant to locations n and m.

units from the central point. At this location, the plant must offer a competitive wage, w', that is large enough to entice a requisite number of workers away from centrally located employers and to take up jobs at the noncentral location n. Let $t_n(d')$ designate the weekly cost of the journey to work over the distance d' to n. Then, only workers residing at locations

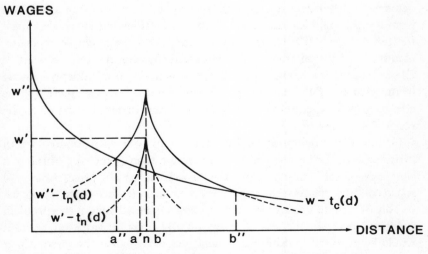

The effect on wage rates of increases in employment demand at peripheral plant.

such that $w' - t_n(d') \geq w - t_c(d)$ (where d is such that either $d + d' = n$ or $d - d' = n$) will be persuaded to give up employment at the center for employment at n. Obviously, the plant will want w' to be as small as possible while also ensuring that its employment needs are met. The plant will accomplish this wage-minimizing goal by fixing w' in such a way that the area over which $w' - t_n(d') \geq w - t_c(d)$ (an area represented by the spatial interval a' − b' in figure 7.3) yields a supply of labor (*given locally prevailing population densities*) that is just equal to the plant's demand.

Suppose now that the plant locates not at n but at the yet more peripheral location m. We take it that the plant's labor requirements remain the same as in the previous case. Given that population density in the vicinity of m is lower than population density in the vicinity of n, the firm must establish for itself a labor shed a″ − b″ that is more geographically extensive than the labor shed a' − b'. As a result, upward pressure on the offered wage rate at m will be correspondingly more intense, and, in fact, the wage rate must now rise to the level of w'', as shown in figure 7.3. Evidently, for any constant quantity of labor demand, this upward pressure will increase with increases of distance (i.e., decreases of population density) from the city center.

These simple principles relating wage rates to intraurban location are equally decipherable in the slightly different situation portrayed in figure 7.4. Here the plant's location is held constant at n while labor demand is now allowed to vary. Once more the strong propensity for noncentral wage rates to rise with increases in employment demand is apparent. As the demand for labor goes up, so wages increase from w' (drawing in workers from the geographical interval a' − b') to w'' (drawing in workers from the interval a″ − b″). Clearly, for any sufficiently large employment demand, the local wage rate may even exceed the central reference wage w. Observe too that so long as population densities do not suddenly increase in the vicinity of the new plant, local residents who work there will be able to earn for themselves a sort of excess wage or rent compared to the residual wage $w\text{-}t_c(d)$.

Certainly, the operation of any real system of local labor markets in urban space must be vastly more complicated than in the case of the two simple graphical examples worked out above. In the first place, the overall socioeconomic processes that fix the dominant reference wage, w, are assuredly of extreme complexity, and no determinate account of this problem is offered here. In the second place, in any practical situation, w itself would be expected to exhibit a tendency to rise or fall as the surrounding supply of labor goes down or up, respectively; moreover, in real urban situations with a multiplicity of employment foci, we would also clearly need to define the reference wage in some other manner than simply as the offered wage at the core of the metropolis. In the third place, population density cannot be considered fixed in the long run at all locations. Intensification of residential land uses and population increases will always tend to occur at those locations in the metropolitan system where comparatively lucrative residual wages (i.e., net of transport costs) can be earned; and local augmentation of the supply of labor will in turn have the effect of dampening or reversing upward shifts of local wage rates.

What all of the above discussion amounts to is a simple distillation of a few elementary ideas about wage fluctuations relative to commuting costs across urban space. The model suggests that increments to wages at job site will occur as local labor demand rises, thus imposing on firms the need to recruit from a wider labor shed. Conversely, decreases in wage rates are to be expected where available labor runs ahead of available jobs, for in this case, firms will be able to recruit adequate numbers of workers from a relatively smaller labor shed. As suggested by figures 7.3 and 7.4, these notions translate into the testable propositions that wage rates at any job site will be positively related to (a) the commuting cost of the marginal worker at that site, and (b) the average commuting cost of all workers at that site. It is of special interest and importance to note that groups of employers, all located in close proximity to one another, will tend via their collective labor demand to push·local wage rates upward, though the nearby presence of dense residential neighborhoods with abundant supplies of labor will help to counteract this effect.

In view of the above arguments, we might expect to observe marginal variations of wage rates in response to changing locational densities of jobs and workers even in situations where wage-setting mechanisms are clearly dominated by politico-institutional dynamics. Some workers, to be sure, will be more or less permanently sheltered from these sorts of wage variations, especially those who are highly skilled and organized and who are protected by relatively durable employment contracts. Others, however, such as secondary labor market participants who do not enjoy such protection, will be more directly affected. There remains the difficult task of assessing the quantitative importance of these spatial wage variations in practice.

Empirical observations on intraurban wage rates. Some concrete illustrations of the rough ideas presented above can be found in a body of data

TABLE 7.1

AVERAGE ANNUAL EARNINGS OF MANUFACTURING PRODUCTION WORKERS IN
ZONES OF THE NEW YORK METROPOLITAN REGION AS A PERCENTAGE OF WAGES
IN MANHATTAN, 1899–1954

Zone	1899	1919	1929	1939	1947	1954
Manhattan	100.0	100.0	100.0	100.0	100.0	100.0
Core (excluding Manhattan)	93.0	93.2	88.0	96.1	91.7	105.2
Inner ring	88.7	90.4	83.2	96.3	96.8	120.9
Outer ring	83.5	87.0	78.0	89.2	92.4	117.5

SOURCE: Hoover and Vernon (1959), p. 41.

assembled by Hoover and Vernon (1959) on the historical and geographical evolution of industrial wage rates in the New York Metropolitan
Region (see table 7.1).

Hoover and Vernon show that in 1899, when manufacturing industry
was overwhelmingly located at the core of the New York Metropolitan
Region, industrial wage rates (as paid at job site) declined steadily from
Manhattan outward. By 1939, wages still declined from the center outward, but now, in addition, a small subsidiary peak was beginning to appear
in the wage-rate surface in the inner suburban ring; and this subsidiary
peak can be seen (in part) as a response to the incipient decentralization
of industry from the core to the suburbs. With the full deployment of the
process of industrial decentralization in the 1950s, industrial wage rates
in the New York Metropolitan Region first of all now *increased* with
distance from the center out to the inner suburban ring, beyond which
they once more declined systematically with increasing distance from the
core. However, even in the outer suburban ring, realized industrial wage
rates by now exceeded those of Manhattan.

A pattern similar to the latter one is revealed by the data presented in
table 7.2, which shows wage rates at job site for manufacturing workers
in the Toronto Census Metropolitan Area in 1972. The data are categorized by two major employment groups, i.e., production and nonproduction workers in manufacturing industry. Both sets of data show a steady
increase in average wages from the center of Toronto out to the periphery,
except for the outermost fringe area (Zone IV in table 7.2), where they
begin to decrease again. In earlier research (Scott, 1981), I computed a
series of econometric equations that seemed to indicate that this pattern
of wages can indeed be correlated with (a) the comparatively high acces-
siblity of manufacturing establishments in central areas to the population

of the whole urban system and (b) the disproportionate piling up of manufacturing employment demands in suburban areas relative to the low population densities in surrounding communities. Even when the data were further broken down into seven different occupational groups, the same intraurban wage structures clearly emerged.

The data set forth in table 7.2 reveal a striking contrast in the spatial structure of wage rates for the two designated categories of workers. In both instances, the highest average wages are earned in Zone III. However, in the case of production workers, wages in Zone III are 18.8% above the corresponding value for Zone I, while in the case of nonproduction workers they are only 7.4% above the appropriate Zone I value. This outcome is consistent with the relatively greater decentralization of blue-collar jobs compared to white-collar jobs in most large metropolitan regions. In fact, it has often been observed that wage rates for many kinds of office and service functions characteristically *decline* from the center of the city outward (Evans, 1973), as might be expected given the continued overwhelmingly centralized pattern of these functions in the modern metropolis. In addition, Rees and Shultz (1970) have demonstrated in their study of local labor markets in Chicago that individual workers' wages are positively correlated with commuting distances. This latter finding may in part merely indicate that workers with high wages choose to commute over longer distances than workers with low wages. It is also, however, fully consistent with the hypothesis that wage rates as paid at job site fluctuate in relation to the spatial range of minimum necessary labor sheds.

In general, the observations marshaled above do suggest that wage rates in the metropolis are responsive in some degree to spatial variations of jobs and residences for at least some classes of workers, as predicted in the earlier theoretical discussion. It should be pointed out, however, that the data given in tables 7.1 and 7.2 are far from constituting unambiguous evidence in this regard, for they fail signally to hold constant a number of complicating effects. Thus, if high-wage industries have been selectively decentralizing, this in and of itself would account for the observed spatial pattern of wages. Note, however, that the data presented in table 7.2 do provide a very rough bipartite breakdown of wages by job type in manufacturing; and, as indicated, it was also found in earlier research that the hypothesized relationships hold for specific occupational groupings. A further significant finding of that earlier research was that each kilometer added to the commuting cost of the average worker at the average industrial plant in Toronto is accompanied by a $47.00 increase (in 1971 dollars) in annual remuneration levels at that plant. Since this is only an average tendency, it suggests that there are some occupations and some sectors whose wages are extremely sensitive to commuting costs, and these are therefore likely to be especially responsive in locational terms to intraurban distance relations.

Intraurban employment location again. As crude and provisional as the ideas and evidence worked out above may be, they do seem to be consonant with (and to illuminate) the actual locational behavior of factories and offices in the urban environment. Let us now review this problem in the light of the arguments developed here.

I argued in chapters 4 and 5 that disintegrated and tightly interlinked producers have strong incentives to move into close locational association with one another. Producers like this commonly face unstable and uncertain markets for their outputs (which is one of the main reasons why they are vertically disintegrated in the first place), and they therefore avoid investing heavily in durable capital equipment. Concomitantly, they tend to be labor-intensive, and their joint demand for workers may run into many tens (sometimes even hundreds) of thousands. Because of their inflated collective demand for labor and the direct impact this has on wage rates, such clusters of producers frequently locate as a body close to the geographical center of their main labor force. This locational strategy secures continued transactional efficiency while ensuring that upward pressures on wage rates are as restrained as they possibly can be.

Spatial aggregates of producers that have excessively large demands for labor will find locations near the core of the city especially attractive, for here accessibility to the entire urban pool of workers is maximized. Clothing manufacturers and office functions seem to exemplify this point in particularly striking ways. So great indeed is their joint demand for labor (with its concomitant tendency to push local wages rates upward) that they also characteristically try to keep labor costs under control by employing disproportionately large numbers of cheap ethnic and/or female workers in the production process. Workers, on their side, seek out housing locations that are readily accessible to places of work, and this leads to considerable intensification of residential land uses in the vicinity of major employment centers. This complementary process of residential land-use intensification reinforces the locational symbiosis between employment places and their dependent labor pools, and with the growth and diversification of the whole system of production and work, these twofold articulations of urban activity also expand and become more firmly inscribed on the landscape.

As these events proceed, some plants are able to break away from this

TABLE 7.2

AVERAGE MANUFACTURING EARNINGS AT JOB SITE BY ZONE, 1972, FOR THE
TORONTO CENSUS METROPOLITAN AREA

Zone	Annual earnings: production workers ($)	Average annual earnings: administrative, etc., employees ($)	Weighted averages of all earnings ($)
I	6,933 (100.0)	9,975 (100.0)	7,720 (100.0)
II	7,274 (104.9)	10,072 (101.0)	8,155 (105.6)
III	8,237 (118.8)	10,709 (107.4)	8,896 (115.2)
IV	6,856 (98.9)	10,395 (104.2)	7,890 (102.2)

SOURCE: Statistics Canada, *Manufacturing Industries of Canada: Sub-Provincial Areas,* Publication 31–209.
NOTE: Figures in parentheses translate data into percentages relative to Zone I.

system of interdependencies, which, as it grows, tends to become increasingly prone to crisis in the guise of rising wages, skyrocketing land prices, congestion, and so on. These are plants that find it possible to dispense with strongly developed local agglomeration economies, and they achieve this by such means as capital deepening, vertical integration, stabilization of production processes, standardization of outputs, or indeed any combination of these possibilities. Such plants are able to decentralize freely to peripheral zones, and those that arrive first in any given area may well find themselves enjoying the advantages of low local wage rates (table 7.1). As more and more plants shift into the same peripheral area, however, local wage rates will be likely to rise rapidly, and eventually they may attain to levels that even surpass those in other parts of the metropolitan region.

I want to advance the conjecture that the phenomenon of rising suburban/peripheral wage rates will reinforce the locational processes and patterns described above, for it will tend to make central and subcentral locations *more* advantageous for labor-intensive disintegrated clusters of industry, just as it will tend to make less accessible peripheral locations comparatively more advantageous for capital-intensive, routinized, standardized, and deskilled forms of production (Scott, 1980).

LABOR TURNOVER AND THE
METROPOLITAN ECONOMY

Labor-turnover activities intersect at many different levels with the wage system, and they inject an added measure of complexity into the whole problem of local labor-market analysis in the modern metropolis. Unfortunately, labor-turnover processes in intraurban space are, if anything, even less clearly understood than wage-setting mechanisms. Certainly, these processes hitherto have been largely ignored by urban theorists, and in the absence of any definite guidelines in the literature as to how to approach the problem, my discussion here will of necessity take the form only of some rough hypothetical sketches. I hope at least to be able to demonstrate that the problem of labor turnover in intrametropolitan labor markets is well worth taking more seriously as an important moment in the formation of urban space than it has been in the recent past.

Turnover, production, and location. Clark et al. (1986) have shown that labor-turnover adjustments are a significant mechanism whereby employers respond to short-run cyclical changes in the economy. This kind of response is a function of the relative short-run stickiness of wage contracts as compared to the apparently greater fluidity of physical accessions and separations. Thus, changes in the economic climate are frequently in the first instance reflected in changes in employment levels (and hours worked) and only in the second instance in wage rates. As a corollary, intraurban labor markets are presumably characterized by a comparatively stable wages system, spatially differentiated in the manner described earlier, and overlain by a more volatile process of short-run adjustments in the total quantity of labor employed.

This latter process is certainly much affected by the geographical structure of local labor markets, and above all by the degree of spatial accessibility of employers to workers and vice versa. The tempo and level of labor turnover are partly governed by this spatial relation. To begin with, plants that are located at the center of dense labor markets and thus enjoy immediate access to a large pool of workers are likely to attempt as much as possible to externalize the economic uncertainty that they face by means of frequent laying off and rehiring of workers. This phenomenon, however, is no doubt modulated by the degree of firm-specific capital embodied in any given class of workers, as Oi (1962) has suggested; this means, in practice, that we may expect those workers with the most standardized skills and those at the bottom of the employment ladder to be most susceptible to rapid turnover. Externalization is facilitated by the comparatively low costs of search and the reduced probability of extended job vacancies in large and dense labor markets. In this manner, firms can respond flexibly and efficiently to changing economic conditions while at the same time partially depoliticizing the intrafirm wage-profit frontier by denying to their least valuable workers long-term security of job tenure.

These options are especially important for subcontractors, who are thus able to pass on much of their own intrinsic instability to the labor force. Thus, in large and dense labor markets, a high proportion of workers may well find themselves at frequent intervals having to sit out slack periods of production within their communities, cushioned perhaps by unemployment insurance and the incomes of other family members.

Contrariwise, plants located in small and isolated labor markets may be expected to pursue more conservative labor-turnover strategies, and to internalize to a much greater extent their labor needs by hoarding workers over slack periods of production. This is because in smaller labor markets (for an equivalent level of unemployment) labor is more difficult to find when needed, and vacancies are likely to be lengthy (Mackay et al., 1971). In fact, according to Sirmans (1977) and Vipond (1974), smaller labor markets usually also have consistently lower unemployment rates than larger ones, and this would help to intensify contrasts between the kinds of turnover policies that prevail in the two cases, i.e., high turnover rates in large labor markets, low rates in small markets. Jayet (1983), Pencavel (1970), and Pettman (1975) have all remarked on the proclivity of turnover rates to increase with city size. Jayet has expressed this relation in terms of the principle that in densely populated urban areas short bouts of employment and unemployment tend to alternate at frequent intervals, whereas, in more sparsely populated nonurban areas, the periods of unemployment between jobs may be expected to be much more extended.

Because of these relationships, large metropolitan regions are undoubtedly a major locational attraction for production sectors that face very variable and competitive markets, as in the cases, for example, of segments of the clothing and electronics industries. These are also precisely the kinds of industries that are much given to vertical disintegration and spatial agglomeration; and they also have large demands for undifferentiated units of unskilled, low-wage labor. Within the metropolitan environment, plants in such sectors as these can externalize their labor markets to a high degree and thus can all the more effectively navigate (both individually and collectively) through various economic vicissitudes. Where market fluctuations have, in addition, a definite seasonal or short-run cyclical pattern, much of the community in the vicinity of these industries may be caught up in a rhythm of frequent temporary layoffs and recalls (Feldstein, 1975). I shall show in the succeeding chapter that this kind of rhythm sometimes becomes absorbed into local community culture and consciousness as an element of the overall phenomenon of the habituation of workers to the labor processes typical of given places. Workers themselves may respond in a variety of ways to these sorts of turnover dynamics. Many, especially new immigrants, are purely passive. By contrast, in the intriguing case of the Los Angeles film industry (an industry that is today highly disintegrated), a privileged group of core workers has managed through union roster systems to stabilize its hold on jobs, while other workers peripheral to this core are condemned to highly intermittent patterns of employment (Storper and Christopherson, 1986). This example illustrates the potential diversity of institutional and political responses to local production and labor-market characteristics.

At the same time, large secondary labor markets in which workers rotate rapidly through jobs would appear to act like magnets, drawing in yet more workers from other areas. This is evident in the case of the drift of secondary and immigrant ethnic workers to large metropolitan regions. Because secondary jobs come and go in large numbers and with great rapidity in these regions, there is always the prospect of at least some work over the course of the year for every worker actively engaged in job search. For those with low expectations to begin with, erratic alternations of periods of employment and unemployment are at least better than extended unemployment. In more stable labor markets with more security of job tenure, these workers might not in the first place be able to secure a suitable job, and in the second place, they might well find the waiting time before a job opening occurs to be intolerably long. If these arguments are correct, we may deduce that marginal unskilled workers will be drawn to centers with large stocks of unstable jobs proportionately more than they will be drawn to centers with small stocks of relatively stable jobs. This phenomenon may in part account for the observed positive correlation between city size and unemployment rates noted earlier.

Thus, many secondary workers are attracted to centers with unstable job prospects, just as unstable industries are attracted to centers with large pools of unemployed secondary workers. This mutual locational affinity is likely to lead recursively to further rounds of growth of secondary jobs and workers. And as the size of the entire local labor market increases, new agglomeration economies will be engendered in the form of reduced job search and recruitment costs (Stigler, 1961).

Manufacturing labor turnover in the New York SMSA. The above discussion suggests that disproportionately large numbers of job seekers, on the one hand, and unstable disintegrated forms of production, on the other hand, are likely to be found in juxtaposition within the metropolitan environment where they depend on one another in part via active turnover processes. It should be stressed that there is remarkably little published evidence and almost as little available empirical data that can be invoked to corroborate these ideas. However, I have assembled some data on manufacturing labor-turnover patterns in the New York SMSA that throw an encouraging (though less than definitive) light on the argument.

The data are presented in tables 7.3 and 7.4. They show total accessions (new hires and recalls) and total separations (quits and layoffs) in manufacturing industry in the SMSA broken down by two areas, i.e., New York City (the core) and the rest of the SMSA (the suburban ring). Table 7.3 gives turnover data on an annual basis for the period from 1973 to 1980; and Table 7.4 gives data on a monthly basis for 1980. These data need to be treated with considerable circumspection, for most of them were calculated from statistics that are already severely rounded, and hence numerical errors are likely to have crept in. What the tables reveal is the marked volatility (on both an annual and monthly basis) of labor turnover in the core area of New York as compared with turnover rates in the suburban ring. In the core, labor turnover (of all varieties) is on average 50% to 100% higher than in the ring, with the exception of quits, which are roughly equal in both cases. Observe that recall and layoff rates are particularly elevated in the core, and this, no doubt, is symptomatic of the short-run ebb and flow of the forms of manufacturing production to be found there.

These contrasts in labor-turnover patterns between the core and ring areas of the New York SMSA are certainly not simple unmediated reflections of pure spatial processes. On the contrary, there are also many differences between the core and the ring in such matters as occupation and the sectoral composition of industry, and these certainly have a direct effect on the core-ring contrasts revealed by tables 7.3 and 7.4. The manufacturing system of New York City is dominated above all by clothing and printing; in the suburbs we find a variety of chemical, metallurgical, machinery, and electrical industries. These different sectors are obviously likely to exhibit differential labor-turnover patterns simply by reason of their contrasting technologies, labor processes, and markets. In one sense, however, this is precisely the point that is at issue here, for producers set up at particular locations in part at least because those locations enable them to put into practice their preferred labor-turnover strategies. *Ceteris paribus,* relatively unstable industries will presumably be drawn to centralized locations in order to maximize their potential pool of job applicants, whereas more stable industries with smoothly ordered internal labor markets will be able to perform comfortably at more peripheral locations.

This latter proposition is advisedly hypothetical, and is, in any case, a

TABLE 7.3

LABOR TURNOVER RATES IN MANUFACTURING, NEW YORK CITY SMSA: NEW YORK CITY (NYC) AND SUBURBAN RING (SR), 1973–1980, AVERAGE MONTHLY RATES

Year	Total accessions		New hires		Recalls		Total separations		Quits		Layoffs		Total employment in manufacturing ('000)	
	NYC	SR	NYC	SR	NYC	SR	NYC	SR	NYC	SR	NYC	SR	NYC	SR
1980	4.6	2.7	2.5	1.9	2.0	0.7	5.0	3.1	1.2	1.2	3.0	1.1	498.7	92.0
1979	4.8	3.5	2.7	2.0	2.0	0.7	5.2	3.2	1.3	1.3	3.0	1.0	518.5	92.1
1978	4.8	3.4	2.7	2.0	2.1	0.0	4.9	2.8	1.2	1.2	2.9	1.5	532.1	88.3
1977	4.9	2.6	2.6	1.8	2.2	0.0	5.0	2.0	1.2	0.4	2.9	1.4	538.6	82.7
1976	4.9	3.3	2.7	1.9	2.1	0.5	5.1	3.5	1.2	1.2	3.1	0.7	541.1	79.0
1975	5.1	2.7	2.4	1.6	n.a.	n.a.	5.4	3.0	1.0	1.0	3.7	1.3	536.9	77.1
1974	4.9	4.1	2.7	3.5	n.a.	n.a.	6.2	2.8	1.5	2.3	3.9	0.0	607.2	82.1
1973	5.1	3.3	3.2	2.3	n.a.	n.a.	5.7	3.9	1.7	1.7	3.1	1.3	652.8	84.2

SOURCE: Computed from data in U.S. Department of Labor, Bureau of Labor Statistics, *Employment and Earnings.*

TABLE 7.4

LABOR TURNOVER IN MANUFACTURING, NEW YORK SMSA: NEW YORK CITY (NYC) AND SUBURBAN RING (SR), JANUARY-DECEMBER 1980, AVERAGE MONTHLY RATES

Month	Total accessions		New hires		Recalls		Total separations		Quits		Layoffs		Total employment in manufacturing ('000)	
	NYC	SR	NYC	SR	NYC	SR	NYC	SR	NYC	SR	NYC	SR	NYC	SR
December	3.1	1.8	1.4	1.4	1.6	0.3	5.5	2.3	0.7	0.7	4.0	0.0	489.6	92.2
November	3.1	1.8	1.8	1.8	1.2	0.6	4.7	2.1	0.9	0.9	3.1	0.5	508.4	94.4
October	5.1	1.9	2.8	1.5	2.1	0.2	3.9	2.6	1.1	1.1	1.9	0.6	510.8	94.6
September	4.9	3.0	2.9	2.2	2.0	0.7	4.4	2.5	1.3	1.3	2.1	0.8	508.9	94.7
August	5.7	3.1	2.5	1.6	2.8	0.2	4.7	3.4	1.5	1.5	2.3	1.0	505.7	93.9
July	4.7	2.8	2.6	1.9	2.1	0.8	6.6	2.8	1.3	0.7	4.5	1.4	493.2	93.8
June	4.6	2.7	2.7	2.0	1.9	0.6	5.3	2.7	1.1	1.1	3.3	1.4	510.3	94.6
May	5.8	1.9	2.1	1.4	2.9	0.3	5.2	3.3	1.4	0.8	3.1	1.2	501.6	91.5
April	3.5	1.6	2.7	1.5	1.3	0.0	6.6	2.8	1.3	0.7	4.5	1.3	493.2	91.7
March	4.7	2.1	2.7	2.0	1.8	0.5	3.8	2.5	1.2	1.2	1.8	1.1	509.1	92.1
February	5.0	2.4	2.8	1.5	2.2	0.3	4.0	2.7	1.1	1.1	2.1	0.8	503.9	92.2
January	5.5	1.7	2.6	4.5	2.2	0.3	5.2	4.6	1.4	2.7	2.9	1.0	492.7	91.9

SOURCE: Computed from data in U.S. Department of Labor, Bureau of Labor Statistics, *Employment and Earnings*.

very partial reflection of the locational forces and interdependencies that shape the configuration of intrametropolitan production space. Even so, and in combination with all the other factors that we have considered at previous stages in this book (the social division of labor, interindustrial transactions, and wage-setting mechanisms above all), labor-turnover processes can be seen as representing yet another level of socioeconomic intermediation of the recurrent geographical patterns that we find in the large contemporary metropolis. These patterns can be described above all in terms of the drift of internally focused production complexes to central and subcentral locations together with the outward diffusion of production units as resynthesis, capital deepening, and stabilization of output markets move forward.

CONCLUSION: THE GEOGRAPHICAL TRANSFORMATION OF LOCAL LABOR MARKETS

Centers of production and their associated communities of workers variously experience moments of turbulence and quiescence as crises come and go and as social contracts (both implicit and explicit) are dissolved or reconstituted. In many communities, durable bargains (sometimes overseen by the state) are struck, and for a time, the production system and communal life run their course in comparative harmony. At other times, employers, workers, and other participants in the urban scene may find that their expectations as to the daily ordering of work and life are no longer what they once were. This fragility can affect primary and secondary labor markets alike.

For example, as Clark (1986) has indicated, an extremely successful and intricate class bargain regulating the interrelations of management and unions in the Midwest car industry was put into place in the late 1940s and lasted down to the mid to late 1970s. In this bargain, both sides made large concessions. Workers acknowledged the legitimacy of temporary layoffs in times of recession, and management accepted limits on shop-floor controls and the pace of production lines. In return, both sides shared in the remarkable productivity gains that the industry managed to maintain over the 1950s and 1960s. However, as competition from foreign car manufacturers steadily intensified over the 1970s, and as American producers struggled to deal with changing structures of demand in a world of escalating petroleum prices, the bargain was strained to the breaking point. Resilient as it had been, it could no longer accommodate the stresses and conflicts of the new situation. Hence, in the late 1970s, after much intervening technical change in the industry, it started to break apart as permanent layoffs and high rates of unemployment throughout the industry in the Midwest sapped the power of the unions. In the early 1980s, an effort was made to reconstruct the contract, but now on the basis of significantly lowered expectations on the part of workers, particularly those without established seniority.

Thus, local class bargains may endure for a time, but even when they are partially codified in written contracts they are subject to reconfiguration when internally or externally induced crises make their appearance. In contemporary urban America, such crises have not infrequently been triggered by technological and organizational change brought on by management in its perpetual search, spurred by competition, for lower costs and higher profits. The peculiar forms that managerial initiatives like these take at any given time depend very much on the balance of political power and the alignment of class forces in the community and in society at large. As these initiatives are realized in concrete industrial change, the territorial organization of local labor markets is transformed, and the shape of the metropolis itself reordered.

Among the more persistent means by which local class bargains have been renegotiated to the benefit of employers in the post–World War II decades, three are of special significance in the present context. These are: (a) decentralization of industry to peripheral areas on the basis of capital deepening, resynthesis, and deskilling of units of production; (b) the initiation of new industrial growth centers in areas without any previous history of major industrialization or union organizing, as, for example, in the case of the new high-technology industrial complexes now springing up throughout the Sunbelt of the United States (and whose regressive labor relations are now being imported back into the older industrial areas); and (c) the more extensive use of politically disorganized segments of the labor force (such as women and minorities) in existing areas of large-scale industrial activity, either by *in situ* changes in employment structure or by means of long-distance and international subcontracting. In fact, diverse combinations of these strategies have been responsible for radical social and spatial transformations of virtually every major American metropolis in the recent past. In particular, as industries in some of the older regions of the country have restructured and relocated, large numbers of primary blue-collar jobs have also been destroyed. This has created a phenomenon of a "disappearing middle" in the labor markets of many large cities, and it has been accentuated by the countervailing growth of managerial and technical cadres at the top and unskilled, low-wage (often immigrant) workers at the bottom. Concomitantly, extremely segmented labor markets and social structures now increasingly characterize major U.S. metropolitan areas. The deepening cleavage between wealth and privilege on the one side and poverty and powerlessness on the other that is being produced in many American cities by the current round of economic restructuring and reorganization surely contains within itself the seeds of future urban social struggles and conflagrations.

EIGHT

Territorial Reproduction and Transformation in a Local Labor Market: The Animated Film Workers of Los Angeles

I have dealt so far with the problem of local labor markets and urban geography in highly generalized terms. In the present chapter, I illustrate, by means of a case study, several of the key ideas laid out above. This involves an empirical investigation of the sociospatial structure of the local labor market for animated film workers in Los Angeles. The case is, admittedly, rather unusual, but it turns out to be a remarkably revealing exemplar of local labor market dynamics in the large metropolis, and on this basis I shall extend a number of the conjectures proposed earlier. The discussion that now follows is based on a questionnaire survey carried out in the early summer of 1983, the detailed results of which have been published elsewhere (Scott, 1984b,1984c).

THE ANIMATED FILM INDUSTRY: A BRIEF DESCRIPTION

The animated film industry grew up in the United States in the 1920s and 1930s, and finally came to concentrate in Los Angeles soon after the Second World War. At the present time there are some thirty or forty animated film studios in Los Angeles. In the rest of the country there is at most only a handful of studios.

The structure of employment. Most animated film studios are extremely small in scale, though a select few may occasionally employ upwards of

141

400 to 500 workers. It is difficult to assess with accuracy the size of the total animators' labor force in Los Angeles, and all the more so as studios come and go at frequent intervals. Perhaps the best measure of employment in the industry is the membership of Local 839 of the International Alliance of Theatrical and Stage Employees (IATSE). Local 839 is the animated film workers' union in Los Angeles, and it has thus far managed to preserve closed-shop rules over much of the industry, at least insofar as the larger studios are concerned. Local 839 had 1,187 members in May 1983, down twenty-six percent from the peak membership of 1,610 in 1980, and membership is apparently still decreasing.

Animated film studios face extremely tight and uncertain markets, and competition is rampant throughout the industry. The biggest market for animated films is television. Because of the need to produce films in advance of the main television season, which runs from autumn to winter, studios have a strong seasonal rhythm of employment. Thus, work is anything but steady in the industry; it reaches a peak in spring and summer and then trails off throughout the rest of the year. Most workers fully expect to be employed on average only nine months out of twelve, and in fact many studios effectively close down for extended periods when the work dries up.

The membership of Local 839 of IATSE is highly variegated in terms of occupations and skills. Three main categories of workers can be defined, though each is in turn made up of many different individual job classifications. The three main categories are (a) creative workers, (b) rendering artists, and (c) technical workers, in descending order of skill and remuneration levels. These categories make up fourteen percent, thirty-eight percent, and forty percent, respectively, of the total membership of Local 839. *Creative workers* deal with the conceptualization, writing, and design of animated films; these are workers at a high level of professional attainment, and they are correspondingly highly paid. *Rendering artists* are skilled animators in the strict sense; their job is to give detailed visual expression to the general specifications produced by creative workers. *Technical workers* are unskilled or semiskilled workers (mainly female) who carry out routine labor tasks under intense supervision; by far the majority of these workers are engaged in so-called "ink-and-paint" operations, i.e., the detailed coloring in of the xeroxed celluloid overlays that constitute the raw material of any animated film. The ink-and-paint department of an animation studio is reminiscent in many ways of the sewing section of a typical clothing factory with its serried rows of female operatives sitting at their work tables and performing endless routine motions. However, in the animated film industry, even unskilled technical workers are (for the present at least) usually native-born U.S. citizens with a minimum of a high-school education.

No matter what their level in the job hierarchy, many workers acquire their main knowledge about and skills in animation techniques via on-the-job experience in different studios. Many of the more skilled creative workers and rendering artists also have some sort of formal education appropriate to the needs of the industry. In Los Angeles, there are several colleges and universities that offer educational programs suitable for prospective workers in the animated film industry. One of the sure signs of a mature local labor market and one of the conditions of its smooth internal reproduction is the public provision of specialized training in locally important trades.

The production process and industrial organization. The animated film industry is exceedingly labor-intensive. Even the most rudimentary forms of mechanization and automation have scarcely begun to penetrate the industry. There has been some experimentation on a small scale with the computerization of animation processes, but this has not yet reached the stage of major commerical viability. Certainly, the hardware and technical expertise necessary for successful automation of the industry are already available to a significant degree, but the great uncertainty of final markets evidently discourages the capital investment that would be required to transform the industry in this manner. The animated film industry is, if anything, even more archaic from a technological point of view than the clothing industry, which is usually held up as the prime example of an industry that has stubbornly resisted capital deepening and technical innovation. Techniques of production in the animated film industry have remained virtually unchanged since the 1930s, when the main forms and methods of organizing the labor process were introduced and when the internal division of labor and a limited form of Taylorism were first developed.

The industry is thus characterized by many different types and levels of labor tasks. The intrafirm organization of these tasks involves considerable expenditure of managerial effort, and where internal economies of scope and scale begin to break down, vertical disintegration of functions makes its appearance. Indeed, there is much vertical disintegration in the industry, and in Los Angeles, many specialized services are available as external economies. Among these are such activities as freelance scriptwriting, camera-equipment leasing services, photography and film development, musical composition, sound-studio rentals, dubbing, special effects, and so on. There are also specialized subcontractors who will take on tasks such as xerox processing or inking and painting, rather like the cutting and sewing contractors who occupy an analogous position in the clothing industry. As we shall see, there is now also considerable subcontracting of blocks of animation work to foreign countries, and this is one of the important recent changes that has started to bring in its train a wholesale transformation of the entire local labor market. In response to the deepening problems created by overseas subcontracting, Local 839 called a strike of its entire membership in 1979, and a further strike in 1982.

Toward an analysis. In sum, we can say that the animated film industry is highly competitive, volatile, and extremely labor-intensive. It is also heavily unionized and predominantly employs high-wage workers, many of whom are very skilled. These conditions create a basic predicament. On the one hand, the animation industry is characterized by great instability and rapid labor turnover. These are features that typify industries involved in secondary labor markets. On the other hand, the workers employed in the industry definitely constitute a primary labor force. The peculiarities and tensions of these apparently colliding circumstances have brought the industry today into an incipiently restructuring mode, and as will be made clear below, this is starting to manifest itself as a massive social and territorial transformation of the whole labor market. What has been happening recently in the animation industry is not unlike (give or take a number of special circumstances characteristic of the industry and its locale) what has been happening to many other U.S. industries. This includes the partial deskilling of the industry, the beginnings of labor market segmentation, and the reintegration of the industry into a new international division of labor.

THE GEOGRAPHICAL STRUCTURE OF THE ANIMATED FILM WORKERS' LOCAL LABOR MARKET

The animated film workers' local labor market in Los Angeles is largely defined in spatial terms by the shaded area depicted in figure 8.1. This area contains the residences of over 95% of all the members of Local 839 of IATSE. The residential locations of a sample of these workers (both employed and unemployed as of May 1983) are shown in figure 8.2. It may be noted that these locations are most heavily concentrated in the vicinity of the intersection of the Hollywood and Ventura Freeways, which

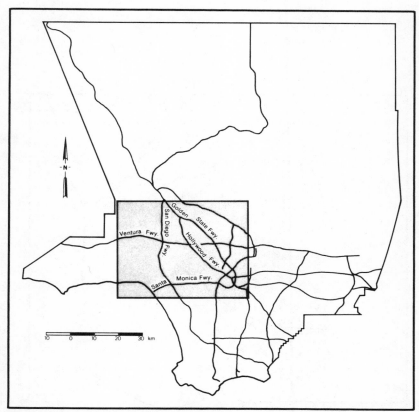

Figure 8.1. Los Angeles County showing main area covered by the animated film workers' local labor market.

is the geographical focus of the whole industry. Thus, even in Los Angeles, with its extensive freeway system and its unusually high levels of personal mobility, the local labor market is confined to a remarkably narrow area.

The locations of the studios where the members of Local 839 work are displayed in figure 8.3. The central focus of the Hollywood and Ventura Freeway intersection is again clearly evident, though studios also drift locationally out to the west along the San Fernando Valley, no doubt in search of comparatively inexpensive land, and also as a response to a parallel westward drift of animators' residences. The predominant spatial clustering of animation studios can be accounted for both in terms of their articulation within a complex system of interfirm linkages, and in terms of their reliance upon a specialized (indeed, unique) labor force that has been actively created and re-created in the northwestern area of Los Angeles as

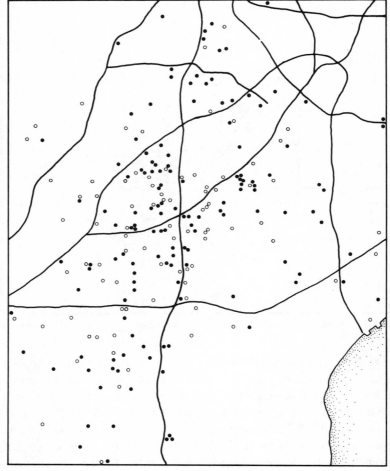

• Employed worker ○ Unemployed worker

Figure 8.2. Residential locations of a sample of employed and unemployed animated film workers.

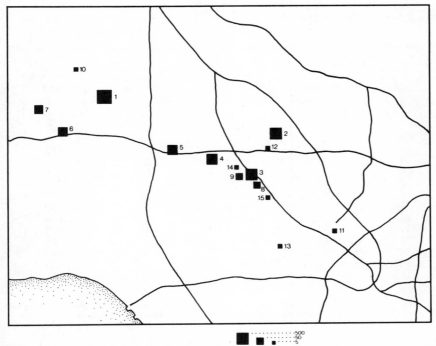

Figure 8.3. Location of animation studios.   Employment

part of the whole process of development of the industry. Studios occupy locations that are accessible to the available labor force in order to avoid having to offer premium wages as the only means of inducing workers to confront an extended journey to work. Workers, for their part, congregate around employment places in order to maximize their own accessibility to job opportunities.

These remarks may be imbued with further substance with the aid of some simple statistics. Let us consider in more detail the geographical structure of the locations of animators' residences. We begin by constructing a set of annuli centered on the intersection of the Hollywood and Ventura Freeways; each annulus has a band width of 1.5 miles. We now calculate the number of workers (in a sample of 270 employed and unemployed members of Local 839) who reside in each annulus. The residential density of workers in each annulus is then computed, and the results of this operation are laid out in table 8.1. Densities clearly decline with increasing distance from the center, and this is in conformity with the commuting patterns described in the previous chapter. If we now fit

TABLE 8.1

ANNULAR REPRESENTATION OF THE RESIDENTIAL PATTERN OF A SAMPLE OF
EMPLOYED AND UNEMPLOYED ANIMATION WORKERS

Ring	Inner and outer limits of ring (miles from center)[a]	Area of ring (square miles)	Number of workers residing in ring	Density of workers per square mile
1	0.0–1.5	7.07	15	2.12
2	1.5–3.0	21.21	44	2.07
3	3.0–4.5	35.34	33	0.93
4	4.5–6.0	49,48	32	0.65
5	6.0–7.5	63.62	23	0.36
6	7.5–9.0	77.75	28	0.36
7	9.0–10.5	91.89	19	0.21
8	10.5–12.0	106.03	13	0.12
9	12.0–13.5	120.17	9	0.07
10	13.5–15.0	134.30	6	0.04
11	15.0–16.5	144.44	5	0.03
12	16.5–18.0	162.58	1	0.01
13	18.0–19.5	176.71	3	0.02
14	19.5–21.0	190.85	6	0.03
15	21.0+	—	33	—
			270	

[a]The center is defined as the intersection of the Hollywood and Ventura Freeways.

a negative exponential function of distance to these density data we obtain $E^*_i = 3.22\exp(-0.48d_i)$, where E^*_i is the density of workers in the ith annulus and d_i is the median distance of that annulus from the central point as defined. The computed value of R^2 for this equation is 0.82. It is of some interest to remark that these statistical regularities exist even though the center of the local labor market is quite acentral to the geography of Los Angeles as a whole.

Disaggregation of these results into more refined spatial and social categories reveals that there is yet more detailed differentiation within the local labor market. In the first place, workers at any given studio are not drawn randomly from the set of all animated film workers; rather, workers tend to be drawn from residential locations that are relatively close to their place of work. This proposition is substantiated by figure 8.4, which suggests that there is a definite spatial bias (in the form of shorter rather than longer journey-to-work distances) in the labor shed of any particular studio. In the second place, the spatial relations between animators' homeplaces and workplaces are subject to variation according to occupational status. Table 8.2 illustrates this point. The table shows that, as we move up the occupational scale, the commuting distances of workers become

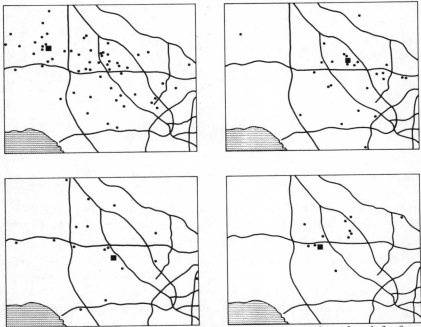

Figure 8.4. Residences of sampled animation workers relative to place of work for four major studios.

longer and longer. This, too, was a generalized proposition of the last chapter. In a previously published paper (Scott, 1984b), I have shown that these aspects of local labor market activity bear important relationships to wage-setting behavior at individual animation studios. In the case of low-wage animation workers, wages as paid at any studio were found to

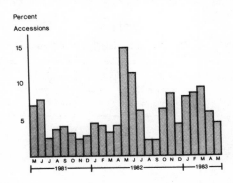

Figure 8.5. Accessions per 100 workers, May 1981–May 1983.

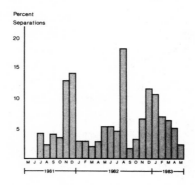

Figure 8.6. Separations per 100 workers, May 1981–May 1983.

be inversely related to the studio's overall accessibility to the labor force. In the case of high-wage workers, wage rates were found to be largely insensitive to accessibility differentials.

These findings suggest that the locations of animated film studios are especially attuned to the residential locations of the mass of unskilled workers in the industry. They also dispel forthwith any notion that metropolitan areas invariably constitute the minimum geographical level of local labor market differentiation. As we have seen, there is considerable locational friction in the animated film workers' labor market even at detailed intrametropolitan scales.

LABOR TURNOVER IN THE ANIMATED FILM INDUSTRY

We have ascertained that there are important connections between the locations of studios, residential activity, commuting patterns, job status,

TABLE 8.2

JOURNEY-TO-WORK PATTERNS OF EMPLOYED ANIMATION WORKERS

Type of worker	Average weekly wage	Average length of journey-to-work (miles)	Variance of journey-to-work lengths
Creative workers	$764.52	10.60	35.37
Rendering artists	$583.27	9.28	42.57
Technical workers	$448.82	7.08	28.45
All workers	$608.71	8.89	36.26

and wage rates in the animated film workers' local labor market in Los Angeles. These connections are profoundly modified by the action of labor-turnover processes, and it is now apposite to deal explicitly with this issue.

Consider figures 8.5 and 8.6, which show, respectively, accessions and separations of animated film workers in Los Angeles over the period from May 1981 to May 1983. General turnover trends over time among creative workers, rendering artists, and technical workers are broadly similar (though their magnitudes differ), so only aggregate data are presented in these figures. Notice at once the marked seasonality of these turnover patterns. Accessions tend to reach a peak in spring and early summer, whereas separations are at a maximum in the winter months. As already indicated, much of this seasonality can be ascribed to the exigencies of the annual cycle of television programming. However, the large and anomalous increase in separations which appears in figure 8.6 for the month of August 1982 was caused by the prolonged strike that began at that time.

These rhythms of accession and separation translate into a marked instability of employment for animated film workers (see table 8.3). On average, 36.6 percent of all animators were unemployed in May 1983, and most are unemployed on average for about three months in each year. Fully 59.7 percent of all animation workers experienced at least one period of unemployment between May 1981 and May 1983, and 39.4 percent changed their place of employment at least once during the same period of time. Thus, workers move with unusual rapidity in and out of periods of employment, and at the same time from one workplace to another. As might be expected, these average rates vary by detailed occupational category. On the one hand, susceptibility to unemployment increases as job status decreases. On the other hand, movement from workplace to workplace *decreases* as job status decreases. This latter finding requires some further comment, for on the face of it it seems to run counter to the argument set forth by Oi (1962)—and alluded to in the previous chapter—about skilled labor as a quasi-fixed factor of production.

Oi's argument suggests that firms will hoard their more skilled workers in order to protect themselves from critical labor shortages in times of need. Further consideration of the animated film workers' case, however, leads to the inference that we are dealing here with a labor market in which skills are more industry-specific than they are firm-specific. It appears that skilled workers are drawn from a pool shared in collectively by all studios. Thus, creative workers are typically taken on for relatively short periods of time determined by the amount of creative work needed to initiate and complete any given project; rendering artists enjoy a somewhat more stable relationship with their employers; and technical workers are largely tied to one particular studio, though note once again that technical workers also have the longest spells of unemployment of any type of worker in the animated film industry. At the top of the job ladder, then, workers move rapidly from studio to studio (and even in and out of the animated film industry) while avoiding lengthy intervals of unemployment; at the bottom of the job ladder, workers are affiliated with a given studio for comparatively long periods of time, though with intermittent and extensive intervals of unemployment as defined by a steady rhythm of temporary layoffs and recalls. These relationships are partially reflected in the journey-to-work patterns of animated film workers. Workers with high job status commute indifferently across the length and breadth of the entire territorial complex to wherever their current jobs may be located, whereas for those with low job status the journey to work is restricted to a relatively narrow spatial radius and is more insistently keyed in to one particular studio (see table 8.2).

I have already suggested that the geographical concentration of animated film studios in Los Angeles can be in part accounted for in terms of the externalized transactions that tie studios and ancillary functions together into a functioning industrial complex. In addition, the definite periodicity and volatility of the animators' local labor market certainly reinforce the spatial agglomeration of producers. No matter what particular kind of skill and experience may be in demand at any given moment of time, the strong locational association between animators' homeplaces and work-places means that job vacancies can usually be filled with some dispatch. This locational association also implies that studios can lay off workers with comparatively little risk of not being able to find replacements when needed, just as it implies that workers themselves are optimally positioned to move into appropriate job openings as and when they become available. Furthermore, the closed-shop rules that have hitherto prevailed through-out most of the labor market have served to protect laid-off workers from competitive raids by nonunion workers on the available stock of jobs.

The animated film workers of Los Angeles thus constitute an extremely fluid force that rotates rapidly in and out of periods of employment and (more selectively) through different places of work. Animators thus have a constantly changing experience of different job situations and fellow workers. As a consequence, they also have a powerful sense of their own collective identity as manifest in a close network of personal interconnec-tions and a rich fund of oral traditions. Hence, at least until recent times, there seems to have been a fair degree of social and political solidarity among animators at all gradations within the job hierarchy and a strong consciousness of their own peculiar position as a fraction of the total labor force. This solidarity, however, now seems to be on the point of breaking down, and this is one of the important symptoms of the radical transformation of the labor market that is now underway. This remark takes us at once into an examination of some of the political crosscurrents and tensions that run through the labor market at the present time.

POLITICO-GEOGRAPHICAL DYNAMICS OF THE ANIMATORS' LOCAL LABOR MARKET

Over the last couple of decades, the animated film workers of Los Angeles have been habituated to a labor market that has been imprinted with fairly durable rules of order. A social compromise was reached in which animated film workers of all kinds were allied within their union in the tasks of dealing with management and of securing regular improvements in remuneration levels and working conditions. Geographical consolidation of the whole territorial complex was secured over the postwar decades, and its temporal rhythms were assimilated into workers' consciousnesses as part of the normal character of workaday life. A pool of labor skills was built up, deployed, and shared among a constantly changing ensemble of employers. Job tenure was unstable, but a minimum of nine months' work a year at generous rates of pay seemed to be an irreversible norm. Many of the workers in the industry today refer to this former state of affairs as a sort of golden age that is now rapidly passing away; and, to be sure, the implicit and explicit social contracts which underlay this old way of things are now in the process of being reshaped on an entirely new basis, as it is, no doubt, in American industry at large.

How can we account for these transformations of the animators' local labor market? I shall describe, first, the development of overseas subcontracting and its impact on the employment relation, and second, some of the more long-run strategies that management seems likely to pursue as part of its currently successful attempts to restructure the local labor market.

Overseas subcontracting and its local effects. The current situation among members of Local 839 is one of high levels of unemployment, especially for technical workers (see table 8.3). Moreover, the prospects for relief of this situation are unpromising, even if there should be improved economic circumstances in the industry as a whole. There is also widespread disaf-

TABLE 8.3

UNEMPLOYMENT AND JOB-CHANGE PATTERNS FOR ANIMATED FILM WORKERS IN
LOS ANGELES

		For the period from May 1981 to May 1983		
Type of worker	Unemployment rate, May 1983 %	Average number of months unemployed	Workers experiencing at least one period of unemployment %	Workers who changed place of work at least once %
Creative workers	5.0	4.8	69.7	63.6
Rendering artists	33.6	5.6	65.0	47.8
Technical workers	56.8	7.6	55.0	25.3
All workers	36.6	6.0	59.7	39.4

fection within the membership toward the union itself, and an increasing sense of helplessness before the apparent inexorability of recent events. Above all, the old alliance between skilled and unskilled workers in the industry is evidently close to permanent rupture as the more skilled and highly paid workers seek to consolidate their more secure positions in the labor market and to align themselves more directly with management. These upheavals have as their proximate cause the development of overseas subcontracting of animation work, though their roots in fact go more deeply than this, and the basic predicaments that the animated film workers face are probably even more serious than they might at first appear.

Overseas subcontracting of blocks of animation work began in earnest sometime in the mid-1970s. Statistics on the quantities of work involved, their growth over time, and their directions of flow are quite impossible to come by. Studios themselves resolutely refuse to divulge such information. To judge by current rates of unemployment, the amount must be quite significant, and informal assessments among industry workers suggest, conservatively, that it now makes up well over fifty percent of all work. Only the large studios engage in such subcontracting, for only they have the necessary volume to make it commercially viable. Furthermore, the large studios are the ones most likely to have a heavy demand for routine unskilled technical work, and this is exactly the kind of work (especially inking and painting) that is most suitable for subcontracting abroad.

In conformity with the classical symptoms of the case as described by Fröbel et al. (1980), the emerging new international division of labor in the animated film industry involves the separation out of packets of tasks that can be economically performed at other locations. These are usually tasks that are highly standardized but quite labor-intensive. The work is initiated in Los Angeles by creative workers and rendering artists; it is then sent abroad for the technical stages of production; and it is brought back to Los Angeles for final editing and marketing. According to industry and union representatives, even some of the work of rendering artists is now also being sent overseas along with more technical work. However, no matter how routine the labor may be, effective supervision of work subcontracted to overseas studios remains a serious problem, and most studios have found it necessary to send managers and supervisors along with the work to ensure that it is performed to satisfactory standards. This obviously makes inroads into the cost-effectiveness of overseas subcontracting, though even so, according to rough estimates, the costs of an animated film can be halved by sending work abroad. It is to be stressed that even the most routine forms of animation work usually call for some sort of basic equipment and at least a margin of previous experience, and work is typically subcontracted out to countries with an already existing animation industry—to Australia, Spain, and Japan, in a first round of subcontracting operations, and more recently to Mexico, Taiwan, and, above all South Korea.

In response to the escalating problems caused by overseas subcontracting, Local 839 has called two strikes of its membership in the recent past. A first strike of two weeks' duration was organized in 1979. That strike produced a rather weak contractual concession from the studios to the effect that they would hire local workers up to their own installed production capacity before they would send work out of the country. The loophole in this agreement was that studios could (and did) simply reduce their production capacity and then send large amounts of work abroad. In 1982, therefore, Local 839 called a further strike that lasted nine-and-a-half weeks from August 5th to September 9th. Despite its length, the strike failed to secure an effective agreement with the studios on runaway production. The studios, correctly assessing that they were bargaining from a position of strength, held out against the strikers, and the union finally capitulated by accepting only the most anodyne contractual agreement on runaway production.

This period of political instability in the local labor market from 1979 to 1982 marks a time of transition in the form and structure of the animated film industry of Los Angeles. It also marks the start of a new spirit of militancy on the part of the studio managers against the union, and a growing sense of defeat and downward adjustment of expectations on the part of the workers. Evidently, the animated film industry of Los Angeles is undergoing a massive sociospatial transformation, and the local labor market is acquiring a new set of outlines quite different from those that have prevailed in the recent past. Overseas subcontracting of blocks of animation work is not only commerically attractive in the narrow sense, but it has also become de facto one of the instruments by which the breakup (or at least the reining in) of the animators' union seems likely to be brought about and the abolition of the closed shop secured. Already, the union is unable to marshal its members into an effective political force; it is unable to hammer out strong agreements with the studios; it is unable to impose union discipline on its members; and above all it seems quite incapable of developing an effective political strategy for dealing with the current conjuncture of events. This is all part of a wider and renewed attack on unions in the Los Angeles' motion picture industry at large (Storper and Christopherson, 1986). If we allow ourselves once more to speculate a little, we may perhaps see all of this as only the beginnings of an even more deeply rooted process of social and spatial transformation.

Long-run managerial options and the form of the local labor market. Like all firms in capitalism, animation studios search endlessly for ways of lowering their labor costs and of undercutting the power of the labor force to influence the shape of the employment relation. I shall briefly describe some of the strategies now opening up to the managements of animated film studios for the purposes of securing these ends. I shall evaluate the practicality of these strategies and their various likely impacts on the local labor market, and I shall attempt to indicate how they represent forms of extended political engagement between all participants in the market. I describe four principal strategies. These differ in certain significant respects though they are by no means mutually exclusive; all are fairly equally negative from the standpoint of the members of Local 839.

First, then, as we have noted, overseas subcontracting of blocks of animation work can—under the right circumstances—be an attractive means for studios to cut their labor costs. These circumstances include a high volume of work, standardized labor tasks, and liberal trade policies on the part of both sending and receiving countries. The disadvantage of overseas subcontracting is that it is associated with serious problems of supervision and coordination. These problems reduce the overall profitability of subcontracting strategies for animated film producers, though it is still possible for studios to secure dramatic cost savings by sending work overseas. A side effect of this subcontracting activity is that it helps to foster the growth of offshore producers who may eventually find themselves able to sell directly in final product markets in the United States. Already, indeed, some Asian subcontractors have established offices in the Hollywood area and are now starting to compete directly with local studios. In this sense, overseas subcontracting is a double-edged sword.

Second, large-scale technological innovation is a definite possibility in the animation industry, though it remains in a curiously retarded state. One of the major studios in Los Angeles is now developing a computerized video-synthesis process that can electronically color in outline forms. This process is likely to do away with traditional opaquing work, and it is said that it will eventually result in the displacement of four workers out of five. There are no doubt major opportunities for much further computerization of the industry, and not just of routine technical operations, but also of many sorts of low-grade rendering artists' work. Thus far, however, this sort of capital deepening in the industry has been quite slow (perhaps because of the overall instability of markets), and automation would appear to be more of a long-run than a short-run threat to workers.

Third, relocation of production facilities has been a traditional means in U.S. industry of cutting costs. Relocation is not at the present time a very attractive option for animated film producers, however. Producers are tied tightly into a system of interindustrial linkages, just as they remain bound to various specialized forms of labor (especially in the creative and rendering phases). It is virtually impossible to find these conditions of profitable production outside of Los Angeles, and even overseas subcontract work flows only to countries that have preexisting animation facilities with the necessary minimum conditions for effective production. Therefore, with the exception of possible further development of these extant overseas pockets of production capacity, significant relocation of the animated film industry seems unlikely. At least, it is unlikely unless and until there is considerable technological change in the industry with much further routinization, deskilling, and vertical integration.

Fourth and finally, if in fact the back of the union can be broken and closed-shop rules abolished, there would then be little to stop studios from simply filling their ink-and-paint and other unskilled technical labor needs with locally available immigrant Asian and Latino workers. Such a strategy could be developed in conjunction with the repatriation of at least some overseas production and the establishment of a piece-rate system of pay (hitherto stubbornly resisted by the union). This would in many ways be an ideal solution from the studios' standpoint. It would secure low-cost Third World labor services, but now under conditions fully controllable by the studios themselves and where problems of supervision could be resolved without heavy additional costs. If wages in the Los Angeles' women's dress and printed circuit industries are anything to go by (see chapter 6), it might conceivably be possible for studios to reduce their wage bills by up to forty or fifty percent by pursuing a strategy of *in situ* substitution of one type of labor for another. Should such a strategy be put into effect, there would be little to prevent the downgrading of displaced technical workers into interchangeable workers at the bottom of the employment ladder. These remarks are, of course, rather speculative. But in the event of the ultimate demise of union organization, there are reasonable grounds for supposing that such a scenario might rapidly be put into effect, just as it has already been implemented in so many other industries across the whole terrain of Southern California.

CONCLUSION

These arguments suggest that the social and territorial reproduction of local labor markets in the large metropolis is played out against a background of deeply rooted structural arrangements combined with many purely local and idiosyncratic circumstances. The precise ways in which these intersecting conditions manifest themselves depend very much on the consciousness and levels of political mobilization of the different participants involved in the local labor market. All of this is consistent with the recent asseverations of Clark (1983a, 1983b, 1986), who has argued strongly for a conception of local labor markets as systems of colliding social power. In the animators' labor market the employment relation is clearly embedded in a continuing political struggle over the long-run conditions under which the whole relation itself is defined. This struggle constitutes the basic social process through which the details of territorial reproduction and transformation in the local labor market are negotiated out.

At the present time, studio managements seem to have the upper hand in this struggle. Even if the animated film workers of Los Angeles were fully politically conscious and organizationally disciplined, there would still be little that they could do on their own to stem the tide of the social and spatial changes that are now so radically affecting their lives and expectations. These changes and the predicaments that they engender (unemployment, deskilling, labor-market segmentation, and all the rest) exist in the final analysis at a broad national level and call for broad national initiatives if they are at all to be decisively confronted. The labor market that has been forged around the animated film factories of Hollywood is a small but dramatic example of the peculiar problems and fortunes of local labor markets generally in capitalism. No matter what forms of production may be involved—consumer goods such as women's dresses, industrial components such as printed circuit boards, or ideological/cultural artifacts such as animated films—the logic of commodity production is the omnipresent and overarching condition of their territorial reproduction and transformation.

NINE

New Frontiers of Industrial-Urban Development: The Rise of the Orange County High-Technology Complex, 1955–1984

INTRODUCTION

Of all the currently growing industrial-urban centers in the United States, the most numerous by far are located in the Sunbelt. This region now contains many rapidly expanding growth centers, a high proportion of which are based on the resurgence of high-technology industry in the contemporary American economy. Centers such as Austin, Dallas-Fort Worth, Houston, Phoenix, San Diego, Santa Clara County, and so on all come immediately to mind in this context. Of all these emerging growth centers Orange County, California, is one of the most important and rapidly growing (though comparatively little-known), and it is, in addition, situated at the heart of the exploding macrourban region of Southern California. We may take Orange County as a paradigmatic example of the new patterns of industrialization and urbanization that are now being laid down on the American economic landscape. In particular, Orange County epitomizes with great clarity the basic geographical character of new growth centers in the Sunbelt, with their transaction-intensive economies, their deeply segmented local labor markets and regressive labor relations, and their high-technology production systems geared intimately to federal defense and space expenditures.

In the present chapter, I provide a simple empirical description of some of the more important economic and social changes that have occurred in

Orange County over the last few decades, and I then attempt to provide an analytical overview of these changes by bringing into play many of the basic theoretical ideas proposed in chapters 3, 4, and 7. We start out with a description of industrial growth in the county since the mid-1950s.

AN OVERVIEW OF THE ORANGE COUNTY HIGH-TECHNOLOGY COMPLEX

Orange County is situated in Southern California between Los Angeles County to the north and San Diego County to the south (fig. 9.1). At the present time, it is made up of some twenty-six incorporated municipalities, mainly in the more developed northern half of the county, together with a series of unincorporated communities and county lands (fig. 9.2).

The industrial base: Some definitions. Orange County began to emerge as a definite locus of industrial production sometime in the mid-1950s, and over the succeeding years its extraordinarily powerful engines of growth have driven it forward to become one of the most important and highly developed production centers in the American industrial system today (see, for example, table 9.1 and fig. 9.3). By far the greater proportion of the county's industrial activity is composed of high-technology enterprises producing aerospace and electronics outputs under federal contract. Around this basic core innumerable specialized input suppliers have converged.

For the purposes of this analysis, manufacturing industry in Orange County is divided into (a) a high-technology sector, and (b) all other manufacturing. The high-technology sector is further broken down into two subsectors designated *core* and *penumbra*. The core is defined in terms of four two-digit standard industrial categories, namely SIC 35 (machinery except electric), SIC 36 (electric and electronic equipment), SIC 37 (transportation equipment), and SIC 38 (instruments and related products). In Orange County these industries commonly make use of technically sophisticated manufacturing processes, and each has high proportions of engineers, scientists, and technicians in its labor force. Note that SIC 35 in the county is largely made up of the three-digit sector SIC 357 (office and computing machines). The penumbra is defined as an aggregation of three two-digit industries as follows, SIC 28 (chemicals and allied products), SIC 30 (rubber and miscellaneous plastics products), and SIC 34 (fabricated metal products). The penumbra consists of industries that are apparently somewhat less technically sophisticated than the core sectors,

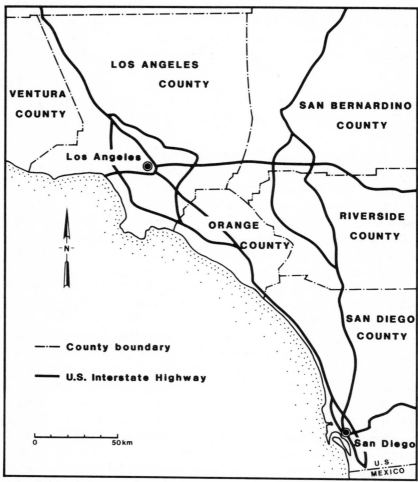

Figure 9.1. Orange County in the context of Southern California.

but they are closely identified with the core because they provide it with many critical inputs, and they are tied to it by strong locational affinities.

The pattern of growth. Let us reexamine the data given in in table 9.1 and figure 9.3. These data describe the growth of manufacturing in Orange County over the last three decades. They show that in the early 1950s manufacturing employment in the county was negligible; that growth accelerated rapidly in the 1960s and 1970s; and that by 1981 manufacturing enterprise had increased to the point where it was employing just

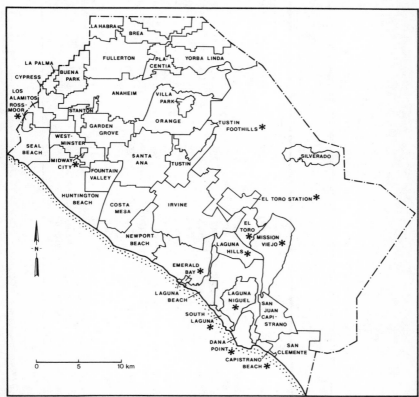

Figure 9.2. Orange County cities and communities; the asterisk designates unincorporated communities.

under a quarter-of-a-million workers. Of these latter workers, fifty-six percent were employed in the core high-technology sector and eighteen percent were employed in the penumbra.

From the very earliest days of the development of the complex, SIC 366 (communications equipment) has been the major employer and the central pole of economic activity. The fortunes of SIC 366 in Orange County have always been directly tied in to federal defense and space spending, and employment in the sector has consistently gone up and down as military and NASA appropriations have expanded and contracted (see fig. 9.4). In 1959, the sector employed 18.2 percent of the county's manufacturing workers, and it did so in just four large plants. By 1970, employment had increased to the point where it now accounted for fully 23.6 percent of all manufacturing workers in the county, again in pre-

TABLE 9.1

Manufacturing Employees and Establishments In Selected Industrial Sectors, Orange County[a]

Standard industrial category	1959 Employees	1959 Establishments	1970 Employees	1970 Establishments	1981 Employees	1981 Establishments
28 Chemicals and allied products	1160	34	3531	78	8057	128
283 Drugs	n.a.	2	n.a.	9	4719	26
30 Rubber and miscellaneous plastics products	1948	31	5288	108	13208	322
307 Miscellaneous plastics products	n.a.	21	3464	89	9532	288
34 Fabricated metal products	3727	93	8472	203	19964	493
35 Machinery except electrical	2412	119	9230	397	37388	973
357 Office and computing machines	n.a.	3	2498	28	18062	102
36 Electric and electronic equipment	10376	37	38725	197	55194	444
366 Communication equipment	7059	4	27995	30	25961	78
367 Electronic components and accessories	251	8	4696	67	19894	206
37 Transportation equipment	2477	70	6470	119	18627	206
372 Aircraft and parts	1164	19	3002	25	6836	49
376 Guided missiles, space vehicles, parts	—	—	—	—	7500*	7
38 Instruments and related products	2738	22	5445	65	14664	214
382 Measuring and controlling devices	n.a.	3	778	11	4422	62
384 Medical instruments and supplies	0	0	n.a.	25	5899	69
All other manufacturing	13835	410	41328	760	58292	1794
Total manufacturing	38673	816	118489	1927	225394	4574

Source: U.S. Department of Commerce, Bureau of the Census, *County Business Patterns.*
*Estimate
[a]This table uses the terminology of the current *Standard Industrial Classification Manual* (1972).

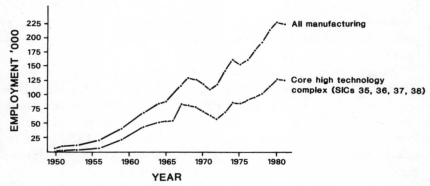

Figure 9.3. Manufacturing employment in Orange County, 1950–1981.

SOURCE OF DATA: U.S. Department of Commerce, Bureau of the Census, *County Business Patterns.*

dominantly large plants. However, federal defense and space spending (in real terms) was starting to dry up by the late 1960s and early 1970s, and SIC 366 then entered a long period of crisis and decline. By 1981 employment in the sector had fallen both absolutely and relatively to a level such that it now represented only 11.5 percent of the county's manufacturing labor force. Average plant size, too, had fallen sharply by 1981.

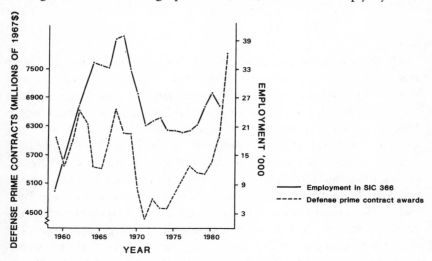

Figure 9.4. Total employment in SIC 366 (Communications Equipment) in Orange County compared with defense prime contract awards in the state of California.

SOURCES OF DATA: (a) U.S. Department of Commerce, Bureau of the Census, *County Business Patterns;* (b) Department of Defense, *Prime Contract Awards by State.*

Even so, the sector has remained to the present day the county's chief employer, and as defense expenditures have picked up again in the early 1980s, so the industry has begun noticeably to recover from its long period of crisis.

Thus, despite its many vicissitudes, the communications equipment sector (along with the aircraft and guided missile sectors, with which it is closely allied) has been one of the central conduits of growth in the Orange County industrial complex. Innumerable electronics, computer, and instrument industries have congregated around it in turn. These latter industries now constitute important poles of economic activity in their own right, and they are, in particular, very much linked in via upstream procurements to the penumbral industries of the complex. Into this vortex of economic activity a large and variegated labor force has been drawn. Concomitantly, population has grown apace, and an insistent process of urbanization has been set in motion. In short, Orange County has developed into a major growth center with a rapidly expanding train of secondary and tertiary effects. We may now inject more substantive detail into these propositions by attempting to identify and describe the stages of economic growth through which the county has evolved.

THE STAGES OF ORANGE COUNTY'S GROWTH

The origins of the complex, 1955–1960. In the mid-1950s, Orange County was in essence a quiet backwater given over to agricultural pursuits with some modest industrial production geared largely to local resources and needs. The population was small, and residential activity was mainly confined to a few communities in the northern half of the county and along the coast. Some suburban tract development was beginning to make itself evident, however, as the Los Angeles built-up area expanded southward. In fact, the geographical position of Orange County between Los Angeles and San Diego, together with its abundance of open space, cheap land, and excellent transport connections, made it a prime recipient of the overspill growth of the Los Angeles metropolis in the postwar years. The uncluttered landscape of the county, together with its abundant recreational facilities and varied natural environments, offered ideal living conditions for its rising middle-class population, and its conservative political inclinations (then as now) made it an attractive place for business.

The mid-1950s was a time when the aerospace and electronics industries in the United States generally were starting to boom under the stimulus of military procurements and the beginnings of space-program contracting. Los Angeles was already a major center of these kinds of industries, and local firms grew rapidly as the markets for aerospace and electronics outputs expanded. Concomitantly, many new branch plants were created at this time. These plants were invariably large in size, and they became prime candidates for locational decentralization as a means of escaping from the high land costs and congestion of Los Angeles. In this way, significant numbers of branch plants shifted to the suburban fringes of Los Angeles, and most especially to Orange County. Figure 9.5 captures the geographical expression of these developments just at a time (1960) when the county was beginning to consolidate its early growth as a focus of high technology industry.

A large proportion of the plants that located in Orange County in the second half of the 1950s were thus controlled from outside the local area. Most of them were big vertically integrated systems houses (as opposed to product houses making relatively standardized equipment) using large numbers of scientific and technical personnel in the development of custom-designed special-purpose outputs. Most of the more important of these systems houses (e.g., Babcock Radio Engineering, Hallamore Electronics, Hughes Ground Systems, Interstate Engineering) were classified under SIC 366, as mentioned earlier. Each employed several hundred workers in the assembly of highly specialized systems for ground support, space navigation, weapons guidance, aerial and submarine navigation, and so on. These systems houses formed the backbone of the industrial development of the county, and as they put increasingly deeper roots into the local area, so the county's industrial apparatus began palpably to evolve into an organized interdependent system.

The intermediate growth period, 1960–1975. Sometime in the 1960s, then, Orange County manufacturers began to draw together into a *complex* in the true sense, i.e., a congeries of interlinked industries sharing a common pool of labor and various infrastructural services. The number and variety of industrial establishments were increasing greatly at this time, and the whole complex was starting to give evidence of marked structural stratification. Above all, it now had taken on a dual aspect consisting of (a) a set of corporate branch plants representing the basic driving force of the complex, and (b) a set of small-scale entrepreneurial firms tied in to the massive purchasing power of the former group.

Total employment in the high-technology sector (core plus penumbra) increased from 24,838 in 1959 to 77,161 in 1970—an average rate of

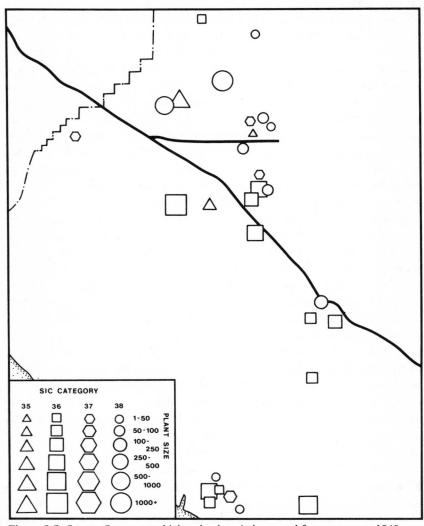

Figure 9.5. Orange County core high-technology industry and freeway system, 1960.
Source of Data: California Manufacturers' Association, *California Manufacturers Register,*
1960.

growth of 19.2 percent per annum (see table 9.1). Employment in SIC
366 was, of course, dominant, but other high-technology sectors were
now rapidly beginning to expand. The growth of SIC 367 (electronic
components and accessories) was especially strong in the 1960s, and SIC

357 (office and computing machines) was just coming out of its infancy. The high-technology penumbra was also now developing rapidly on the basis of its production of major inputs and subcontract services (in chemicals, rubber and plastics, and fabricated metals) for the core.

By the early 1970s, the high-technology complex had become as tightly organized in geographical space as it apparently was in economic space. The precise locational structure of the core complex in 1972 is depicted in figure 9.6. The level of spatial infilling revealed by figure 9.6 is rather remarkable compared to the situation for 1960 as shown in figure 9.5. The whole northern tier of the county is now covered with high-technology manufacturing establishments. Notice that two separate subsystems of industrial activity can be discerned. In the north, around Anaheim and Fullerton, there is a loose network of high-technology plants. Farther south, in and around Irvine, a dense major cluster of manufacturers has come into existence, most especially on the industrial park land owned and operated by the Irvine Company. We may take note, in passing, that figure 9.6 reveals the propensity of industrial establishments to avoid the central area of the county in Santa Ana with its relatively dense development of residential land use and its high property values.

The Recent Development of the Complex, 1975–1984. From 1970 to 1981, total employment in the core and its penumbra grew from 77,161 to 167,102, which represents an average growth rate of 10.6 percent per annum (see table 9.1). SIC 366 was still the major industrial employer in the late 1970s and early 1980s, though its relative weight in the county's economy was now much reduced. Otherwise, remarkable growth is evident in all the high-technology sectors over the 1970s. Nowhere is this growth more apparent than in the case of SIC 357 (office and computing machines), where employment increased at an annual average rate of 56.6 percent from 1970 to 1981. Strong growth is also observable in SIC 38 (instruments and related products), much of it accounted for by the three-digit subsectors SIC 382 (measuring and controlling devices) and SIC 384 (medical instruments and supplies). In 1981, too, there were seven large establishments in SIC 376 (guided missiles, space vehicles and parts), employing an estimated total of 7,500 workers. In spite of the limited number of establishments in this sector, it has been an extremely important element of the whole complex, and, through its many upstream linkages, one of the central motors of the county's growth.

The geographical outlines of the core high-technology complex in 1984 are shown in figure 9.7. The continuing intensification of industrial land use by comparison with the situation in 1972 is obvious. The loose sub-

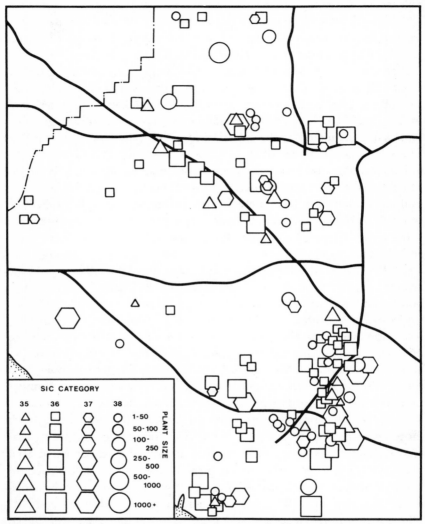

Figure 9.6. Orange County core high-technology industry and freeway system, 1972.
SOURCE OF DATA: California Manufacturers' Association, *California Manufacturers Register,*
1972.

system of plants around Anaheim and Fullerton remains a strong element
of the overall industrial pattern of the county. In addition, the subsystem
in and around Irvine has developed into an extraordinarily dense and
tightly knit assemblage of manufacturers. This latter subsystem is now the

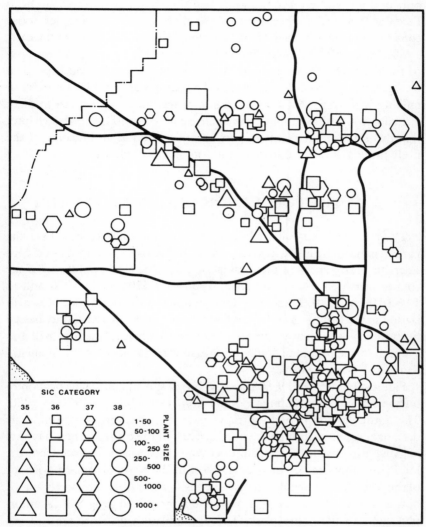

Figure 9.7. Orange County core high-technology industry and freeway system, 1984.
SOURCE OF DATA: California Manufacturers' Association, *California Manufacturers Register,*
1984.

dominant focus of the county's proliferating electronic components, computer, and instruments industries.

Outside the spatial confines defined by figure 9.7 there is even today
little industrial land use in the county. What development there is consists

only of a few scattered plants straggling southward along the San Diego Freeway. The major lineaments of the high-technology complex today conform quite closely to the main locational pattern laid down in the early 1960s. A reconsideration of figures 9.5, 9.6, and 9.7 reconfirms this view of things. Surprisingly, perhaps, development did not so much proceed by a gradual southward extension of the complex as it did by a process of infilling with respect to a spatial frame of reference that was set in place virtually from the beginning. We shall see at a later stage in this chapter that this state of affairs can in part be understood as an outcome of the lively internal locational logic of the complex as a whole.

THE POPULATION OF ORANGE COUNTY

The relentless expansion of Orange County's industrial base over the years has brought in its wake a massive influx of population and a considerable enlargement of the local labor pool. The total population of the county increased from 703,925 in 1960 to 1,420,386 in 1970 and to 1,932,709 in 1980. These data are testimony to the rapid pace of urbanization in the county over the last few decades. In 1963, the county passed from merely suburban to metropolitan status when it was designated as a standard metropolitan statistical area under the appellation Anaheim-Santa Ana-Garden Grove.

Figures 9.8, 9.9, and 9.10 trace the broad spread and intensification of human settlement in Orange County from 1960 through 1970 to 1980. The figures clearly depict the rapid pace of urbanization as well as its dominant concentration in the northern half of the county, where a typical negative exponential relationship between density and distance from the local core seems to be developing. Even in the more urbanized portions of the county, however, population is consistently rather extensively spread out, and this helps to create a pervasive sense of the geographical amorphousness of the entire place. Today, population densities are still not much higher than six or seven persons per acre over the greater part of the county, and only in the central area of Santa Ana (together with a small outlier in Anaheim) do they begin to rise even to the quite moderate level of twenty persons per acre and above.

Of all the persons residing in the county in 1980, 50.4 percent were actively employed, and of these, 72.1 percent worked in Orange County itself. Furthermore, just as the production system has attracted a large working population into the county, so also has it helped (via the division

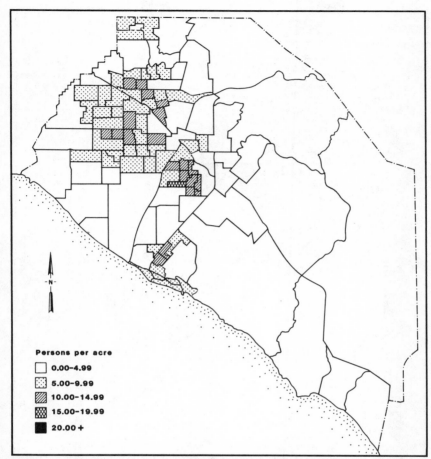

Figure 9.8. Orange County: Total persons per acre by census tract, 1960.
SOURCE OF DATA: U.S. Department of Commerce, Bureau of the Census, *Census of Population and Housing,* 1960.

of labor) to create different socioeconomic groups with contrasting residential characteristics. Two distinctive segments of the working population are especially in evidence both numerically and geographically, i.e., managerial and technical cadres on the one hand, and blue-collar manual workers on the other. Members of the former segment seek above all to live in the prime residential communities scattered along the coast, such as Seal Beach, Huntington Beach, Newport Beach, and places farther south. Members of the latter segment tend to occupy scattered neighborhoods at inland locations where house prices are more affordable.

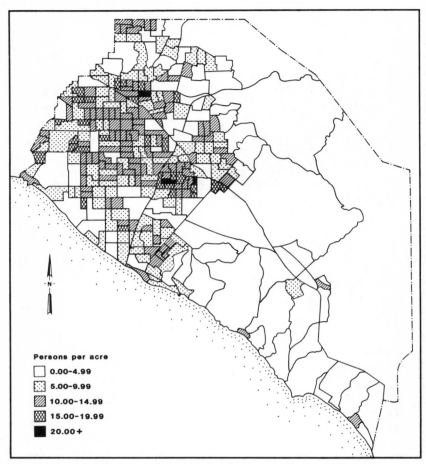

Figure 9.9. Orange County: Total persons per acre by census tract, 1970.
Source of Data: U.S. Department of Commerce, Bureau of the Census, *Census of Population and Housing,* 1970.

Increasing numbers of blue-collar manual workers in the County consist of new immigrants to the U.S., most especially Hispanics and, more recently, Asians. In 1980, Hispanics constituted 14.8 percent of the total population of the county and Asians 4.5 percent. As the local industrial system comes more and more to rely on low-paid unskilled and semiskilled workers, these percentages will surely increase. Figures 9.11, 9.12 and 9.13 outline the growth and distribution of the Hispanic population of the county for the years 1960, 1970 and 1980, respectively; these figures are based on census data, and it should be noted that the precise definitions

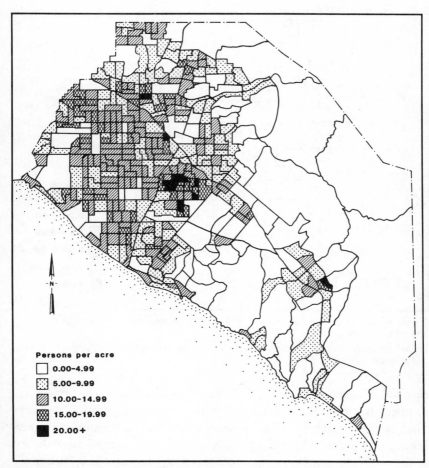

Figure 9.10. Orange County: Total persons per acre by census tract, 1980.
SOURCE OF DATA: U.S. Department of Commerce, Bureau of the Census, *Census of Population and Housing*, 1980.

of the Hispanic population have changed in each of the three census years. Figure 9.14 shows the distribution of Asians (or, to conform more strictly to the census designation, Asians and Pacific Islanders) in the county in 1980. Observe that the various population density maps running from Figure 9.8 to Figure 9.14 are constructed according to varying density scales so that direct visual comparisons between them are somewhat hazardous.

What is interesting about the patterns of Hispanic and Asian settlement

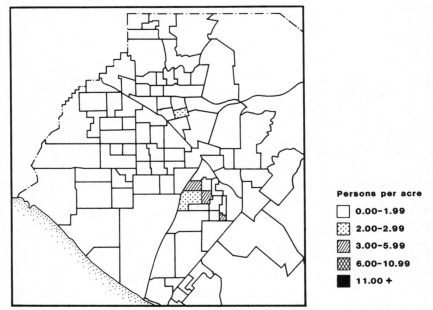

Figure 9.11. Orange County: Persons of Spanish surname, native and foreign born, per acre by census tract, 1960.

SOURCE OF DATA: U.S. Department of Commerce, Bureau of the Census, *Census of Population and Housing,* 1960.

revealed in figures 9.11, 9.12, 9.13, and 9.14 is not just that they evince, as might be expected, a strong proclivity to ethnic segregation, but also (and more surprisingly in this apparently formless community) a marked centripetal tendency. As in Burgess's long-standing concentric zone theory of the arrangement of intrametropolitan space (Burgess, 1924; Park *et al.*, 1925), the ethnic residents of Orange County gravitate toward the core of the whole urban system. This tendency is no doubt comprehensible in view of the pressures on such residents to maximize their overall access to employment opportunities; and in Orange County it is reinforced by the presence of many small manufacturing plants (whose preferred labor force consists of ethnic workers) close to the geographical center of the county.

It is of some interest to note that only 1.2 percent of the total population of Orange County is made up of Blacks. This seems to follow from the circumstance that Blacks are not especially sought after as employees, even by low-wage firms in Orange County. The reason for this may be that Blacks, despite their overwhelmingly marginal social position, have a le-

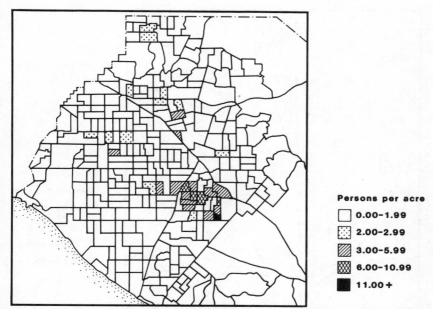

Persons per acre

☐	0.00–1.99
▦	2.00–2.99
▨	3.00–5.99
▩	6.00–10.99
■	11.00 +

Figure 9.12. Orange County: Persons of Spanish language plus other persons of Spanish surname per acre by census tract, 1970.

SOURCE OF DATA: U.S. Department of Commerce, Bureau of the Census, *Census of Population and Housing,* 1970.

gitimate legal and historical presence in American society. They therefore have at least latent potentialities of pressing employers for recognition of rights that many immigrant workers either cannot conceive of or feel unable to demand. Accordingly, Blacks have not participated in the burgeoning labor market opportunities of the county; nor does it seem likely (so long as cheap and malleable immigrant labor is available) that they will do so on a large scale in the foreseeable future.

THE LABOR FORCE

Occupational structure. Table 9.2 provides data on the resident labor force of Orange County by selected occupations for the year 1980. These data cover occupations in nonmanufacturing as well as manufacturing sectors. However, the selected occupations given in the table are thought to be especially representative of the employment structure of local man-

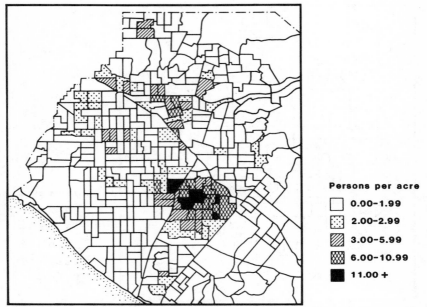

Figure 9.13. Orange County: Persons of Spanish/Hispanic origin per acre by census tract, 1980.

SOURCE OF DATA: U.S. Department of Commerce, Bureau of the Census, *Census of Population and Housing,* 1980.

ufacturers. For the purposes of comparison, occupational data for the whole of the United States are also given.

Table 9.2 reveals that the Orange County labor force is highly variegated yet is also top-heavy with managerial and technical workers. This latter observation is underpinned by data from the *Annual Survey of Manufactures,* which show that in Orange County manufacturing industry there are 6.1 nonproduction (white-collar) workers to every 10.0 production (blue-collar) workers, whereas in U.S. manufacturing as a whole this ratio falls to 3.5 to 10.0. On this criterion, Orange County is true to form as a center of high-technology industrial production. At the same time, however, blue-collar employment in the county has tended to grow rapidly in both absolute and relative terms over the last couple of decades. The trend is captured in figure 9.15, which shows production workers as a percentage of all workers in manufacturing for the period 1963–1978. Observe the contrast between Orange County and the United States highlighted by this figure. In Orange County the proportion of production workers in

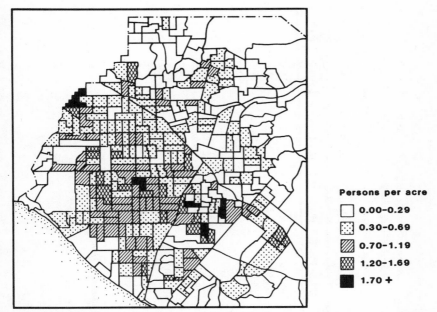

Persons per acre

☐ 0.00-0.29
▨ 0.30-0.69
▨ 0.70-1.19
▨ 1.20-1.69
■ 1.70 +

Figure 9.14. Orange County: Asians and Pacific Islanders per acre by census tract, 1980. SOURCE OF DATA: U.S. Department of Commerce, Bureau of the Census, *Census of Population and Housing*, 1980.

manufacturing employment has been increasing over the years, whereas in the U.S. generally the proportion has regularly declined.

As I shall argue below, this idiosyncratic trend in Orange County is to some significant degree the result of the susceptibility of local manufacturing plants to vertical disintegration of their productive functions. This has involved the systematic transfer of work from large plants to small plants, which signifies, in turn, a transfer of work from (a) plants with relatively highly unionized workers to plants with very low rates of worker unionization (see table 9.3), and (b) plants with overgrown bureaucracies to plants with proportionately smaller managements. The net outcome of this latter trend has evidently been rapid increases in the proportion of blue-collar workers in the manufacturing labor force. Large plants in Orange County also employ disproportionately large numbers of female workers (see table 9.4), and this may be a means perhaps by which they compensate for their comparatively high levels of unionization.

The production of skills. With the growth and internal differentiation of the Orange County complex has come a widening of the division of labor

TABLE 9.2

EMPLOYED PERSONS, 16 YEARS AND OVER IN SELECTED OCCUPATIONS, ORANGE COUNTY AND THE UNITED STATES, 1980

	Orange County		United States	
	Total	%	Total (000)	%
All occupations	974,845	100.0	104,450	100.0
Managerial and professional specialty occupations	281,642	28.9	22,654	21.7
Executive, administrative, and managerial occupations	148,720	15.3	10,379	9.9
Engineers and natural scientists	39,295	4.0	1,715	1.6
Technical, sales, and administrative support occupations	324,891	33.3	30,884	29.6
Technologists and technicians	25,645	2.6	2,074	2.0
Secretaries, stenographers, typists	44,179	4.5	4,827	4.6
Precision production, craft, and repair occupations	117,878	12.1	13,555	13.0
Mechanics and repairers	29,462	3.0	3,983	3.8
Precision production occupations	47,252	4.8	4,444	4.3
Operators, fabricators and laborers	131,207	13.5	19,988	19.1
Machine operators and tenders	38,232	3.9	6,544	6.3
Fabricators, assemblers, etc.	31,961	3.3	2,632	2.5
Handlers, equipment cvleaners, helpers, and laborers	32,951	3.4	5,086	4.9

SOURCE: U.S. Department of Commerce, Bureau of the Census, *Census of Population and Housing*, 1980.

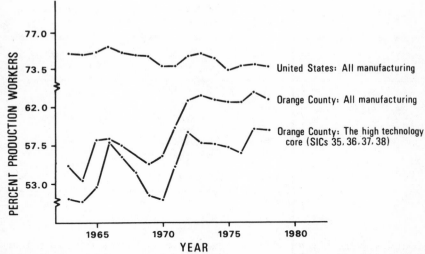

Figure 9.15. Production workers as a percentage of all workers in manufacturing, Orange County and United States.

SOURCE OF DATA: U.S. Department of Commerce, Bureau of the Census, *Census of Manufactures* and *Annual Survey of Manufactures*.

and the creation of a labor force in the very image of the complex itself. There has accumulated in the county an immense and polyvalent pool of labor with its various skills and attributes finely honed in the workplace and socially reproduced and sustained in the community at large.

As mentioned in chapter 8, one of the hallmarks of a mature industrial

TABLE 9.3

UNION AND NONUNION LABOR IN ORANGE COUNTY MANUFACTURING AS A
FUNCTION OF PLANT SIZE

Plant Size (employees)	Percent union labor	Percent nonunion labor	Number of plants surveyed
1–10	1.5	98.5	70
11–25	2.3	97.6	46
26–50	4.5	95.5	44
51–100	16.6	83.3	18
101–250	19.3	80.7	32
251–500	23.5	76.5	20
500+	20.0	80.0	17
Total	8.5	91.5	247

SOURCE: Buchner *et al.* (1981), p. 17.

TABLE 9.4

Male/Female Employment in Orange County Manufacturing as a
Function of Plant Size

Plant Size (employees)	Percent male	Percent female	Number of plants surveyed
1–10	79.2	20.7	70
11–25	74.1	25.9	46
26–50	69.4	30.5	44
51–100	59.5	40.4	18
101–250	64.3	36.6	32
251–500	54.3	45.6	20
500+	64.2	35.7	17
Total	63.1	36.9	247

Source: Buchner et al. (1981), p. 13.

complex is the development in adjacent areas of institutions of higher education offering courses and curricula suited to the needs of the local production system. In this way, moreover, a certain socialization of the tasks (and costs) of specialized worker training is secured. In Orange County there is a wide variety of such institutions, the most notable of all being the University of California at Irvine, which now offers advanced educational and research programs in many fields directly related to the high-technology complex. Among these fields we may mention electrical engineering, medical technology, and bioscience, the latter being a response to the recent local development of a significant industry producing medical and biotechnical products.

It should be added at once, however, that whereas the University of California at Irvine opened its doors in 1965, it has only lately begun in earnest to link its various programs to the needs of the local industrial apparatus. This remark runs counter to the notion that high-technology industry is drawn in the first instance to locations that are rich in appropriate educational resources (Oakey, 1981; Premus, 1982; Saxenian, 1983). In Orange County, the opposite is the case. Here, it is evidently the prior existence of high-technology industry that has brought about the internal transformation of the university. Now that the university is indeed beginning to respond to local demands for specialized manpower, it is likely to become an important element in the overall social and territorial reproduction of the high-technology complex. But equally, this importance is subjacent to and contained within (*not* prior to) the historical logic of the complex as a whole.

We must now turn to the central problem of how this complex is structured in terms of its inner logic of development.

VERTICAL DISINTEGRATION AND POLARIZATION

Orange County is a major growth center in the classical sense of the term. Its core is composed of dynamic propulsive (high-technology) industries around which a penumbra of dependent input suppliers has grown up. At the same time, the development of this system has been underpinned by the proliferation of a contingent labor force and associated urbanization phenomena. As the system has evolved, many new forms of production have made their appearance, and many new firms have moved into the county in a sort of import substitution process. In these ways, the organizational complexity of the whole system has tended to increase greatly with time.

Vertical disintegration. One particular aspect of these processes of growth and development is of critical importance. This concerns the evolutionary dynamic of the complex via the social division of labor and the vertical disintegration of production (see chap. 3.).

In the early phases of the industrialization of Orange County in the 1950s, producers were relatively self-sufficient. The large branch plants that moved from Los Angeles into the county at this time were typically vertically integrated and minimally interlinked. They were, for the most part, involved in the production of technologically contrived outputs (above all, sophisticated communications systems for military and space purposes) whose assembly posed innumerable scientific, engineering, and managerial problems. New technical problems had to be resolved, specialized equipment and production processes designed, and theoretical knowledge translated into workable and commercially viable practices. An informed guess, reinforced by recent interviews with local managers, is that there were significant internal economies of scope linking the various functions carried out in these branch plants at this time. These economies accrued from the advantages of keeping critical and often rapidly changing labor processes in-house and under the supervision of a single experienced team of managers and technicians. We may surmise, however, that many heavy costs were also incurred by this manner of proceeding, most especially the costs of maintaining a large internal bureaucracy and of massing together hundreds if not thousands of (unionized) production workers.

Thus, it seems likely that once it became technically and commercially feasible to farm out certain elements of the production process and to lower make/buy ratios, firms welcomed this opportunity as a means of raising profitability levels.

Again, on the basis of the informal interviews mentioned above, it would appear that vertical disintegration became more and more of a practical possibility as industrial technologies and procedures were stabilized so that progressive disarticulation of certain labor processes became economically feasible. These changes evidently involved two broad classes of events: (a) routinization of production processes to the point where reliance on the services of outside input suppliers was no longer especially problematical, and/or (b) the breaking apart of production processes in the sense that changes in procedures at one stage in the manufacturing system no longer had implications for procedures at other stages. At the same time, small and vertically disintegrated producers often have special advantages that under the right conditions (e.g., spatial concentration) make them attractive as subcontract partners. I have shown earlier that small plants are often endowed with the ability to carry out specialized functions; they are usually able to use their limited production capacities quite flexibly, whereas large plants are more frequently tied to cumbersome units of fixed capital; and small plants can invariably batten down heavily on labor costs (Friedman, 1977). It was apparently for such reasons as these that the large integrated high-technology plants in Orange County began rapidly in the 1960s and 1970s to experience vertical disintegration of their labor processes.

Spatial polarization. I have already shown in chapter 3 how vertical disintegration is associated with increasing levels of externalization of the transactional structure of production. Disintegration, then, results in producers becoming more functionally tied together within a network of interplant linkages. We may ask, to what degree does this functional association translate into a pattern of geographical association? We can answer this question by reconsidering some of the ideas about linkage costs proposed earlier in chapter 4.

At the outset, note that interlinkage activities always result in some pressure on producers to gravitate locationally toward their own center of gravity. However, this process does not invariably work itself out in a spatially uniform way. The inducements on producers to locate near one another will be strong where linkages incur high unit transport costs and where the expenses of face-to-face intermediation of inputs and outputs are great. Such is most especially the case where linkages are small in magnitude (so that transactional economies of scale cannot be obtained) and irregular in their spatio-temporal structure (so that linkage partnerships have to be continually rebuilt). Conversely, where linkages are large in scale and regularized in time and space, unit costs will tend to fall and linkage partners will be under less pressure to locate close to one another.

Thus, depending on linkage characteristics (which in their turn depend on the characteristics of production processes), we would expect to find varying spatial responses to the functional interrelationships between industries. And, indeed, in the case of the large aerospace and electronics producers in Orange County we may distinguish at least two main geographical tiers of disintegrated transactional activity. On the one hand, many producers are tied in to a far-flung national and even international network of linkages and subcontract relations involving flows of the order of millions of dollars in monetary value (Karaska, 1967). On the other hand, however, they are also clearly linked to a purely local system of detailed procurements and subcontract services. In the same way, Rees (1978) has shown for the case of the Dallas-Fort Worth growth region that as much as thirty-two percent of all backward linkages are directed to the local area. In the case of Orange County, such local backward linkages concern not just other aerospace and electronics producers but also throngs of relatively small-scale specialized firms in such detailed sectors as printed circuit fabrication, plastics molding, ferrous and nonferrous metal foundries, milling and lathing, sheet-metal work, contract drilling services, instrument manufacture, research and development, business services of all kinds, and so on. The general importance of these kinds of linkages in high-technology growth centers has recently been reemphasized by Oakey (1984).

As markets for final outputs grow, so the whole production system expands and so (via expansions of the division of labor) the process of vertical disintegration continues. Indeed, specialized disintegrated producers in their turn break up into yet more specialized fragments of economic activity. In this way, the whole complex becomes more and more finely differentiated in its internal configuration and more tightly organized in geographical space. With the unfolding of these intricately structured processes, ever more potent agglomeration economies are created so that costs of production tend to fall and profitability tends to rise everywhere in and around the complex. This then attracts further productive investments, leading to new growth impulses and the creation of new locational details within the complex.

PLANT SIZE AND THE EMPLOYMENT RELATION

In what now follows, I attempt to deepen and extend these remarks on industrial organization, vertical disintegration, and the development of the complex. Let us begin with a discussion of the interconnections between vertical disintegration on the one hand and plant size and the employment relation on the other.

The problem in general. I have alluded above to the process of vertical disintegration in Orange County as involving the transfer of work from large, often unionized plants with extended managements to small non-unionized plants with more restricted managerial inputs. If this pattern of reorganization is pervasive, we would expect it to be visible in two measurable indices of industrial activity, namely, (a) average plant size (which is expected to decrease) and (b) the average proportion of blue-collar workers in the labor force (which is expected to increase). These expectations will be reinforced where (as in the case of defense contractors in Orange County) actual or potential vagaries exist in final markets so that large plants will be tempted to disintegrate as a strategic measure to avoid the backward transmission of uncertainty through their internal vertical structure (Carlton, 1979).

We may add for future reference that if *horizontal* (as well as vertical) disintegration is occurring then these expectations are likely to be yet further intensified. Average plant size, in particular, will rapidly decrease with horizontal disintegration (i.e., as small plants "spin off" from more established enterprises). As Saxenian (1983) and others have shown, horizontal disintegration seems to be a typical mechanism of development in the early and competitive stages of the formation of new high-technology industries, and in Orange County it has recently been especially noticeable in the cases of the computer and medical technology industries.

Plant size. The proposition that vertical disintegration in Orange County has been associated with decreasing average plant size does not mean that some plants might not increase in size subsequent to disintegration. On the contrary, we know from the work of Stigler (1951) that there is at least a theoretical possibility that some plants may increase in size after disintegration. What *is* signified by the proposition is that vertical disintegration is likely to lead to either (a) given quantities of work being carried out by more and more individual enterprises or (b) given increments of growth engendering a correspondingly deeper social division of

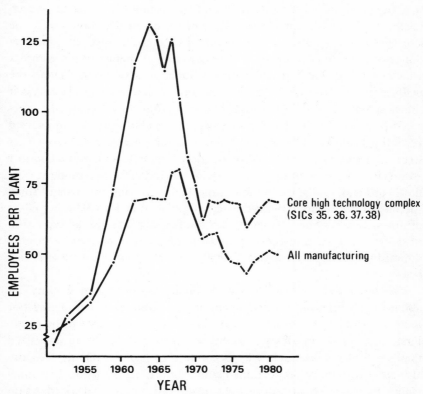

Figure 9.16. Average number of employees per plant, Orange County.
SOURCE OF DATA: U.S. Department of Commerce, Bureau of the Census, *County Business Patterns.*

labor. In either case, decreasing plant size will consist only of an *average* trend.

Consider now figure 9.16, which displays variations in average plant size in Orange County from the early 1950s to the early 1980s. The figure shows data for both manufacturing as a whole and for the core high-technology sector. Two distinct phases of development are distinguishable. From the early 1950s to the mid-1960s there is a phase of increasing average plant size corresponding to the steady decentralization of large capital-intensive and vertically integrated branch plants from Los Angeles. Then there is a phase from the mid-1960s and continuing irregularly down to the present day of dramatically *decreasing* average plant size. This second phase of development is in part related to the employment downswing that occurred after 1967–1968 in Orange County. It is also, however, related to the accelerating growth of small firms in the county over the late 1960s and the 1970s. The hypothesis is that this second phase predominantly represents a period of organizational change in the complex with much fragmentation of productive functions. By the mid-1960s the main industrial base of the county had been securely set in place, and it was now poised on the threshold of further advances via internally structured processes of the division of labor, the establishment of specialized vertically disintegrated plants, and industrial innovation. These tendencies were no doubt partly triggered by the deep cuts in federal prime contract awards that occurred in the late 1960s and early 1970s. Accordingly, over the 1960s and 1970s, the complex absorbed increasing numbers of small specialized producers serving the central polar industries. The net effect of this incursion of ever-widening circles of small plants was an expansion of the externalized transactional structure of the complex, and a steadily diminishing average plant size. I shall elaborate further on these points below.

The employment relation. Vertical disintegration in Orange County has also evidently involved a reassignment of work from plants with high labor costs to plants with low labor costs. Two main points need to be made. First, large plants in Orange County are demonstrably more unionized than small plants (see table 9.3). Second, large plants in Orange County also seem to require proportionately more bureaucratic labor than small plants, for they face proportionately greater tasks of internal coordination of production activities. Hence, the shift of work from large to small units of production is at once a way of replacing unionized with nonunionized labor and of shedding white-collar workers in favor of blue-collar workers. These changes are intensified by the circumstance that nonunionized blue-collar workers in Orange County are increasingly composed of low-wage Latino and Asian immigrants, many of them undocumented. All this is achieved by the externalization of transactional structures, so that what was once accomplished by an internal hierarchy of control is now secured by market and quasi-market relations between plants. We might say, then, that in addition to all of its other functions, vertical disintegration is a way of substituting markets for hierarchies (Williamson, 1975, 1985).

If the above arguments are correct, we would expect to observe, among other things, both tangible decreases in union membership and tangible increases in the ratio of blue-collar to white-collar workers in Orange County manufacturing industry over the last couple of decades. Let us deal with these two points in turn. First, as Table 9.5 indicates, union

TABLE 9.5

UNION MEMBERS IN MANUFACTURING INDUSTRY, ORANGE COUNTY, 1964–1981

	Union members in manufacturing	
Year	Total	As % of manufacturing employment
1965	27,300	28.9
1966	31,800	31.5
1967	34,000	29.4
1968	35,000	26.9
1969	34,900	27.6
1970	32,300	27.3
1971	30,100	27.4
1973	31,100	22.2
1975	29,400	19.5
1977	22,400	12.6
1979	22,600	10.5
1981	27,200	12.1

SOURCES: State of California, Department of Industrial Relations, Division of Labor Statistics and Research, *Union Labor in California* (published biennially after 1971); U.S. Department of Commerce, Bureau of the Census, *County Business Patterns*.

membership among Orange County manufacturing workers has indeed decreased dramatically (in both relative and absolute terms) since the mid to late 1960s. Orange County now has the lowest rate of worker unionization of any county in the state of California. We must exercise considerable caution, however, in attributing the trends revealed in table 9.5 uniquely to local vertical disintegration, for they are also part of an overall nationwide tendency toward lower levels of unionization. Unfortunately, the available data do not allow us effectively to decide what part of declining union membership in Orange County may be due specifically to vertical disintegration and what part may be simply a reflection of the national trend. Second, if we now turn back to figure 9.15, we may note that the proportional representation of blue-collar workers in the manufacturing labor force has increased steadily since the late 1960s, as expected. This finding is all the more emphatically underlined by the fact that what has been happening in Orange County manufacturing in this respect runs absolutely counter to the trend for the United States as a whole. At the same time, a third important point can be adduced on the basis of these remarks. It seems reasonable to infer that the observed changes in the employment relation in Orange County have been at least in part responses to labor-cost pressures, and we should no doubt therefore also expect to

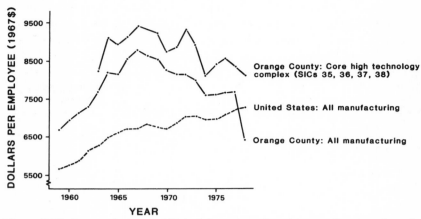

Figure 9.17. Orange County and United States manufacturing payroll per employee in constant 1967 dollars.

Source of Data: U.S. Department of Commerce, Bureau of the Census, *Census of Manufactures* and *Annual Survey of Manufactures*.

detect some slowing down of wage increases as vertical disintegration has proceeded. In fact, average remuneration levels (in constant dollars) have actually *decreased* in Orange County manufacturing establishments since the late 1960s (fig. 9.17). This is the case, moreover, no matter whether we measure the trend in terms of average payroll costs per employee or in terms of the average wages of production workers. Thus, while the complex has grown at a rapid rate, it has nevertheless managed to head off any sort of upward wage spiral over the last decade or so. This is, to say the least, remarkable in view of both the upward trend in wages in the U.S. as a whole and the persistent labor shortages that seem to have plagued Orange County employers over the years.

ORGANIZATIONAL STRUCTURES AND INDUSTRIAL LOCATION IN ORANGE COUNTY: SOME EMPIRICAL DETAILS

We proceed now by looking at some specific empirical expressions of vertical disintegration and locational activity in the Orange County industrial system.

The temporal course of vertical disintegration. A rough index of the vertical disintegration of manufacturing production in any sector or group of sectors can be defined as the ratio of aggregate materials costs to the value

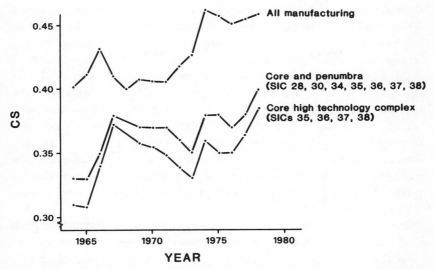

Figure 9.18. The index of vertical disintegration (cost of materials ÷ value of shipments) for Orange County industries.

of shipments. The basic notion behind the index is that vertical disintegration will be accompanied by rises in outside purchases of inputs relative to total sales, and this will then be manifest as an increase in the magnitude of the index. Unfortunately, the index suffers from several deficiencies (see below), though it is a tempting measure to use precisely because it can be easily computed from official statistics published in the *Census of Manufactures* and the *Annual Survey of Manufactures*. Furthermore, on the basis of these statistics, the index picks up vertical disintegration over aggregates of establishments (rather than over aggregates of firms), and this is exactly the principle of aggregation that is most appropriate for the purposes of the present exercise.

Figure 9.18 shows numerical values of the index for (a) all manufacturing, (b) the core high-technology complex, and (c) the core plus penumbra in Orange County between 1964 and 1978. In all three cases, the trend of the index is broadly upward, signifying that vertical disintegration has indeed tended to increase with the passage of time among Orange County manufacturers. I have shown in other work (Scott, 1986) that there is a modest but definite statistical association between the index and two relevant measures of industrial organization in Orange County, namely, average plant size and the ratio of blue-collar to white-collar workers. The former measure is on the whole negatively correlated with the index of vertical disintegration and the latter is positively correlated. These results are broadly consistent with the analysis set forward in the previous section of this chapter, though they are open to criticism on a number of grounds. In particular, the index of vertical disintegration, as defined, is subject to extraneous perturbations resulting from differential changes in production technologies, prices, profits, and wages. It is also susceptible to statistical bias, since in the present instance it is constructed out of a composite of several rather heterogenous sectors of production with widely varying technologies and rates of growth. Finally, the index does not allow us to discriminate between forms of vertical disintegration that give rise to purely local industrial linkages and those forms that engender nonlocal linkages. For all of these reasons, the testimony of figure 9.18 must be treated with due caution.

In view of these difficulties, we turn now to a more direct description of the intertwined processes of disintegration and location. Here, we consider three representative industries: (a) the injection-molded plastics industry, (b) the printed circuit industry, and (c) the surgical and medical instrument industry. The first two cases exemplify very clearly the phenomenon of vertical disintegration and spatial clustering. The third case is a dramatic recent example of local industrial development by means of spinoff and the horizontal disintegration of functions.

Injection-molded plastics. Injection-molded plastics are a crucial input to Orange County aerospace and electronics producers. Some of these producers maintain an in-house "captive" (i.e., vertically integrated) molding facility, but they are relatively few in number. For the most part, injection-molded plastics are manufactured in vertically disintegrated plants in response to the demands and specifications of the buyer (Angel, 1984). Thus, as the complex has grown, so also has this symbiotic industry multiplied.

Figure 9.19 outlines the recent spatial distribution of injection-molded plastics plants in Orange County. Observe the tendency for plants to gravitate toward the main foci of production. Here, they can cut back to the maximum on spatially determinate transaction costs just as they can, in effect, pool the many specialized demands of individual customers, thereby helping to even out the flow of work. Occasionally, injection-molded plastics plants are vertically integrated with a mold-making shop, especially in cases where molds are changed frequently and the shop can be run close to full capacity. However, it was found by Angel (1984) that 58 percent of a sample of injection-molded plastics producers in the greater Los Angeles Region subcontract out the mold-making function. Figure

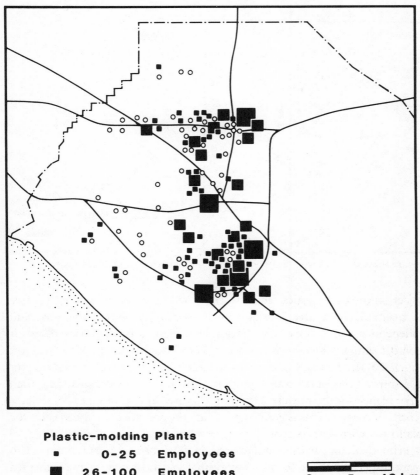

Figure 9.19. Plastic injection molding plants and moldmakers in Orange County. Redrawn from Angel (1984).

9.19 shows specialized vertically disintegrated mold makers in Orange County, and, once more, the proclivity of such plants to congregate close to their main markets is strongly evident.

Printed circuit boards. As pointed out in chapter 6, printed circuit boards constitute an essential input to the electronics industry. As in the case of

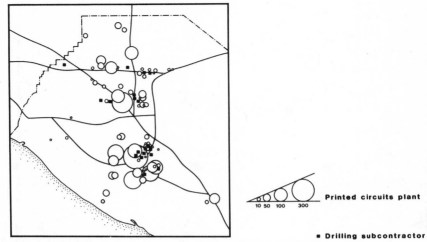

Figure 9.20. Printed circuit plants and drilling subcontractors in Orange County.

injection-molded plastics facilities, many circuit board shops are captive to major manufacturers, though most form vertically disintegrated and independent units. Like injection-molded plastics plants, printed circuit board manufacturers are prone to cluster close to their major customers (fig. 9.20). In the study of the printed circuit industry developed in chapter 6, I showed that small plants are more susceptible to such clustering than large plants, for their external linkage costs are generally higher per dollar's worth of output. This is equivalent to the proposition that the smaller the plant, the narrower its spatial circle of customers.

Printed circuit board manufacturers in their turn subcontract out much work, especially those forms of work that are most efficiently performed on the basis of large indivisible units of fixed capital equipment such as numerically controlled drilling machines or laminating presses. In figure 9.20 the locational pattern of drilling shops serving the printed circuit industry in Orange County is superimposed on the map of circuit board manufacturers. These drilling shops are small in size, and on average they employ no more than four or five workers each. They are clearly located in close proximity to the geographical center of the whole complex. Of the twenty-four drilling shops located in the Greater Los Angeles Region in 1982, no fewer than nineteen (i.e., 79 percent) were concentrated in Orange County.

Surgical and medical instruments. In 1984, there were some seventy-five plants in Orange County classified under the four-digit SIC category 3841 (surgical and medical instruments). This industry has only very recently made its appearance as an important element of the industrial fabric of Orange County; indeed, it is a more recent development even than the burgeoning computer industry. All the indications are that it will continue to grow strongly in the future. The industry has evidently been attracted to the area by reason of the county's sophisticated modern industrial base with its many and varied support services and its highly trained technical labor force. Much of the development of the industry has apparently occurred by a process of horizontal disintegration (spinoff) and specialization. One of the more recent offshoots of the industry has been a group of plants producing cardiopulmonary equipment in the Irvine area. In fact, the industry as a whole is overwhelmingly concentrated in and around Irvine (fig. 9.21), and there is currently a major effort underway to build connections between the industry and the nearby medical school at the University of California, Irvine.

In addition to surgical and medical instruments there is much local production capacity in such related fields as dental equipment, optical products, hospital supplies, pharmaceuticals, and most recently in biotechnology, the latter fueled by local venture capital. This constitutes an elaborate foundation on which a major subcomplex of medical industries seems to be rising. As this subcomplex grows it will undoubtedly evolve, like the rest of the high-technology complex, through a series of evolutionary stages marked by much further horizontal and vertical disintegration of functions.

THE SPATIAL STRUCTURE OF THE COMPLEX

Toward an analysis. On the basis of the three case studies described above, it would seem that there is a powerful positive interrelationship in Orange County between the fragmentation of labor processes and the locational clustering of units of production. More generally, there appears to be an intricate logic that runs from the organization to the location of industry and back again. This logic is intermediated above all by the external transactional structure of the production system, and it helps to push units of production into various forms of locational association with one another. Additionally, producers also presumably try to find locations that ensure their accessibility to an adequate supply of labor without their having to offer premium wages (see chapter 7). This latter locational impulse com-

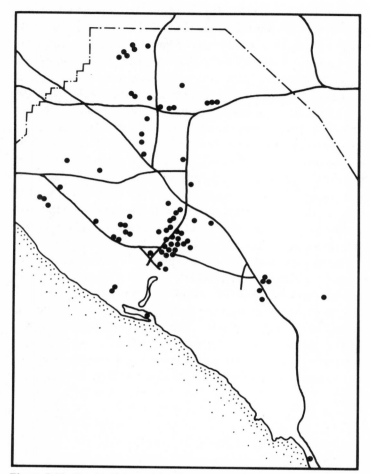

Figure 9.21. Orange County: Manufacturers of surgical and medical instruments.
SOURCE OF DATA: Contacts Influential, *Commerce and Industry Directory, North Orange County Firms 1983–1984* and *South Orange County Firms 1983–1984*.

bines with the former to give rise to subtle spatial patterns of industrial development. Let us inquire a little more closely into these relationships.

It was shown above that small plants have an especially strong tendency to cluster together compared to large plants, for they frequently face much higher unit transaction costs. Simultaneously, interlinked clusters of small plants are quite likely to be extremely labor-intensive, with joint employment levels rising to many tens of thousands of workers. These clusters are therefore also under much inducement to gravitate (as collective bodies of producers) toward the spatial center of their main areas of labor supply, and in this way to reduce upward pressure on (spatially determinate) wage rates. By contrast, the linkage costs of large plants are often relatively low in unit terms by reason of the economies of scale that come with enlarged transactional activity. Thus, the linkage structures of large plants are usually less geographically restrictive than those of small plants, and large plants are accordingly more able to select from a wider set of locations. The fact that large plants tend to use up great quantities of space means that they are also subject to some pressure to shift to peripheral locations where land prices are comparatively low.

All of these remarks are, of course, speculative, and the question of the operative locational tendencies within major industrial complexes remains very much a matter for future research. Even so, the discussion above suggests at once that any large industrial complex will almost certainly exhibit distinctive patterns of internal locational differentiation. These patterns will be likely at a minimum to consist of (a) a spatially dominant network of small plants in selected central areas of the complex, overlain by (b) a more dispersed distribution of large plants, the latter becoming dominant in peripheral zones. We can scrutinize these propositions further on the basis of a statistical test involving the data underlying figures 9.5, 9.6, and 9.7. The test proceeds in two main stages.

Concentration versus dispersal. To begin with, we subject the data to a simple quadrat analysis. Orange County is gridded into 271 quadrats, each of which is 7.5 square kilometers in area. Industrial plants in the core high-technology complex are then divided into three main size categories, i.e., small (1–100 employees), medium (100–500 employees) and large (500+ employees). For each of the years 1960, 1972, and 1984, we compute the average number of plants (μ_k) per quadrat in the kth size category (see table 9.6). We now calculate the theoretical probability, under assumptions of complete locational randomness, that any given quadrat will have at least one plant in the kth size category. This probability is defined by a Poisson process. If $p_k(0) = e^{-\mu_k}$ is the probability that any given quadrat has *no* plants of size k, then $1 - p_k(0) = 1 - e^{-\mu_k}$ is the probability that the same quadrat has *at least one* plant of size k. From this latter expression we may calculate the expected number of quadrats with at least one plant of size k. This expectation is equal to $271(1 - p_k(0)) = 271(1 - e^{-\mu_k})$. We now compare this expectation against the observed number of quadrats with one or more plants of size k. The comparison is carried out in column g of table 9.6, where the observed number of such quadrats is expressed as a ratio of the expected. Remark that by

TABLE 9.6

Quadrat Analysis of Plants in the Core High-Technology Complex (SICs 35, 36, 37, 38)

a) Employment-size class	b) Number of plants in size class	c) Average plants per quadrat (μ_k)	d) $1 - e^{-\mu_k}$	e) $271(1 - e^{-\mu_k})$	f) Observed number of quadrats with at least one plant	g) $f \div e$ as %
1960						
1–100	18	0.066	0.064	17.42	14	80.37
100–500	7	0.026	0.025	6.91	6	86.83
500+	4	0.015	0.015	3.97	4	100.76
1972						
1–100	96	0.354	0.298	80.83	54	66.80
100–500	29	0.107	0.101	27.37	21	76.73
500+	16	0.059	0.057	15.54	15	96.53
1984						
1–100	199	0.734	0.520	140.92	96	68.12
100–500	62	0.255	0.225	60.98	43	70.51
500+	29	0.107	0.101	27.37	22	80.38

TABLE 9.7

ANNULAR STRUCTURE OF THE HIGH-TECHNOLOGY CORE COMPLEX

		1960		1972		1984	
Ring	Distance band (kms)	Number of plants	Average size of plant	Number of plants	Average size of plant	Number of plants	Average size of plant
1	0–3	1	90	2	78	2	35
2	3–6	3	128	24	76	48	118
3	6–9	1	375	51	186	110	232
4	9–12	11	220	15	233	42	270
5	12–15	10	180	32	817	63	415
6	15–18	7	3507	9	731	14	1094
7	18+	3	10	13	644	24	80

means of this latter operation we abstract away from differences in the number of plants in each size category. Clearly, as shown in table 9.6, the smaller the employment size class, the more concentrated is the corresponding locational pattern of plants; and the larger the employment size class, the closer to random is the locational pattern of plants. It may further be noted that degrees of locational concentration tend to increase over time, and this may perhaps be interpreted as an additional sign of the increasing vertical disintegration of the complex.

Annular structure of the complex. We may ask if there are not yet further levels of spatial structure in the locational pattern of the Orange County core high-technology complex. To be sure, it is possible to discern a certain amount of spatial segregation according to sector, but this is not the important issue at the present moment. More pertinent for immediate purposes is the circumstance that after suitable statistical manipulation, we can find a definite annular gradation in plant size. This effect is observable in relation to the system of concentric rings (drawn at 3 km. intervals) displayed in figure 9.22. This is actually the same system of rings that underlies table 6.4 in chapter 6. The point of origin of this system coincides with the center of gravity of the whole northern half of the county in Santa Ana. Computation of average plant size for each ring for each of the years 1960, 1972, and 1984 yields the data presented in table 9.7. For the year 1960, the overall pattern is rather shapeless, as indeed it ought to be, given that this was a time when the complex had not yet really begun to form itself into an organized system. By 1972, there is a definite tendency to increasing average plant size from the center outward.

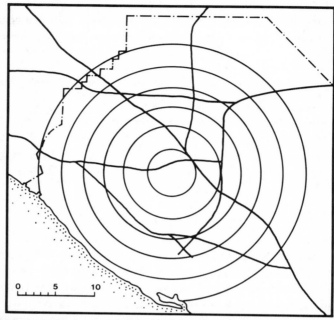

Figure 9.22. Basic annular structure of the industrial geography of Orange County; rings drawn at 3 km intervals.

And by 1984, the tendency is fully confirmed, though note that in the far periphery of the whole system average plant size drops rapidly again. This latter phenomenon may well be due to the existence of specialized market and locational niches beyond the geographical confines of the complex proper. Finally, note that the two subsystems of plants in the Anaheim-Fullerton area and in and around the Irvine area are also internally structured according to a very finely grained annular pattern of increasing average plant size from their centers outward, though I have made no effort to report upon this latter issue in greater detail.

CONCLUSION

The development of Orange County has involved the historical convergence of three major lines of force. First, the central axis of the county's growth has always resided in the production system with its strong organizational dynamics, as discussed above. Second, this system has steadily drawn into its orbit a large labor force containing many different skills and attributes necessary to the efficient functioning of the industrial base. Third, there then came into existence a whole series of urbanization phenomena (infrastructure, transport networks, housing facilities, educational establishments, etc.), which ensured the successful social and territorial reproduction of the entire complex. These intertwined events have come to represent a vigorous process of industrialization and urbanization in Orange County today. The more the complex has expanded, the more it has produced, by its own internal momentum, a wider pool of agglomeration economies, and thus it has expanded farther still.

In fact, the effective putting together in Orange County of an entire industrial complex in which capitalistic forms of production can proceed at an accelerated pace has now turned the county into one of the foremost industrial regions of the United States. In this sense alone, the county is at the other end of the spectrum from the old declining industrial regions of the Frostbelt. Yet both kinds of region have been made within a similar overarching set of capitalist social and property relations. They are testimony to the extraordinary unevenness and disparity that characterize all forms of capitalist development. They are also potent testimony to the genius of capitalism for constructing and deconstructing the social and geographical conditions of its own existence as each new regime of accumulation and mode of social regulation comes and goes. Within the context of the broad capital-labor relation, the cycle of territorial development, reproduction, and transformation proceeds endlessly; it assumes different forms and different modulations at different times and in different places, but its basic underlying logic remains unchanged: production for accumulation. In Orange County, local history is, as it were, being replayed anew. Significantly, it is being replayed in an area where communal historical experience of the capital-labor relation in industrial contexts hitherto has been partial and shallow.

In all of the above, I have tried to show how a high-technology industrial complex and some of its associated social appendages grew up on the tabula rasa of Orange County. I have sought to achieve this goal both by empirical description and by theoretical investigation. Certainly, the research reported upon here is extremely provisional, and almost all of the basic analytical problems to which it alludes remain unresolved. Orange County and other places like it obviously pose many puzzling questions to social theorists. We need at this stage much more research into the processes governing the origins and trajectory of such places. In particular, we really know surprisingly little about their fundamental mechanisms of growth and internal spatial differentiation. Once we have gone beyond the self-evident observation that the Orange County high-technology complex owes its initial forward drive and momentum to federal defense and space contracting, we are left with surprisingly little by way of further analytical windows on the county's growth. Four questions seem to be of particular pertinence in this regard. First, how precisely (on a sector-by-sector basis) do processes of industrial fragmentation and recomposition structure such multifaceted phenomena as the Orange County industrial complex? Second, how and to what extent are the internal order and logic of these phenomena determined by a system of local labor-market processes? Third, to what degree is their development sustained by the kinds of urban environments that ramify throughout their territorial extent? And fourth, what kinds of internal politics develop around such complexes, and how do these politics sustain or impede local industrial growth? In spite of encounters with these questions throughout this book, they remain open to further probing. Their eventual resolution will no doubt depend to a large extent both on the persistence of economic geographers in exploring the detailed empirical conditions underlying the emergence of new growth centers in the Sunbelt and elsewhere, and on the degree to which theoreticians can put together generalized analyses of the essential central mechanisms of production, work, and territorial development in late capitalist society.

Orange County is a foretaste of a novel and still only dimly apprehended pattern of industrial development and urban growth. It is part of a new landscape of capitalism within a newly emerging regime of accumulation and mode of social regulation. Concomitantly, we stand in urgent need of a refashioned theoretical human geography that is equal to the tasks of dealing with these issues and conscious of their central political meaning.

Urbanization and the New Spatial Division of Labor

DECENTRALIZATION PROCESSES

Identification of the problem. Thus far in this book, the argument has concentrated on processes of centralized growth and the locational convergence of units of production. Such processes, however, are in reality almost always accompanied by countervailing trends to the decentralization of production. Indeed, one of the most spectacular developments in the urban and economic geography of the United States and the world system over the last four or five decades has been a pervasive locational dispersal of much industrial capacity. This outcome has been associated with and in large degree mediated by an increasing *functional* centralization of industrial capital and the rise of the multiestablishment and multinational corporation; and it has been driven forward to a high pitch of development by the crisis conditions that afflicted international capitalism as the long postwar boom came to an end sometime in the late 1960s and early 1970s.

The boom itself was a period when large metropolitan regions in the United States continued to grow, even though increasing quantities of productive capacity were already being pushed out into peripheral areas. With the dissipation of the boom and the onset of crisis, many of these formerly growing metropolitan regions started to lose both jobs and population while favored parts of the periphery started, for a time at least, to grow. One manifestation of this process was the celebrated "nonmetropolitan population turnaround" of the 1970s. Many cities were beset by epidemics of plant closures and attendant social ills ranging from stubborn

203

unemployment to severe fiscal crisis. These problems were exacerbated by wholesale industrial restructuring brought on by the crisis and underpinned by various forms of merger, rationalization, and technical change (Bluestone and Harrison, 1982; Massey and Meegan, 1979. The old unionized mass-production industries that had previously formed the basis of the prosperity of the cities of the Manufacturing Belt were deeply affected by these events. Industries such as steel, shipbuilding, machinery, cars, rubber, domestic appliances, and so on were each in turn subject to radical transformation and relocation, with devastating consequences for many traditional industrial areas. Thus, much of the old industrial plant in the North and East of the United States was abandoned or destroyed, and in its place, new and more efficient units of capital were established in various hinterland regions. The improved competitive position on world markets of many of the newly industrializing countries added to the woes of the older industrial centers, and influxes of cheap manufactured imports intensified levels of plant closure and unemployment in core areas. The various oil shocks of the 1970s helped to deepen and extend the crisis. Even a steadily falling dollar on international exchange markets and an expanding reserve army of the unemployed seemed to do little to stem the tide of domestic economic crisis and foreign competition.

The 1970s thus represents a period of dramatic transformation of American cities and regions. This was a time when the whole space-economy of the United States was undergoing reorganization within a new spatial and international division of labor in which increasing amounts of routine blue-collar work were being transferred to dispersed peripheral sites. At the same time, many locations in the Sunbelt and elsewhere were starting to mushroom in the form of new centers of concentrated industrial growth. While these trends most certainly represent a unique conjuncture of events, some of their underlying structural dynamics seem to have been operative at previous times in the development of American capitalism. Indeed, from the very beginnings of modern industrialization, both decentralization and the geographical reconcentration of production at new locations have worked their effects on the economic landscape. The pervasiveness and significance of decentralization processes may be exemplified in four brief empirical vignettes.

First, as indicated in chapter 5, the early gun industry in Birmingham was almost wholly reconstructed organizationally and spatially after the introduction of integrated mechanized technologies in the 1850s and 1860s (Allen, 1929). This caused severe erosion of the old central gun quarter of the city, while at the same time standardized (military) gun production became concentrated in large production units located in the suburbs.

Second, Lichtenburg (1960) has shown that in the 1920s and 1930s the U.S. radio industry was largely a small-scale labor-intensive sector of production heavily dependent on external subcontracting services and locationally focused on New York and other cities of the eastern seaboard. After the Second World War, the industry was transformed into a capital-intensive sector, and production was thereafter embodied in a relatively small number of large routinized branch plants located in small towns in the Midwest.

Third, as Steed (1971) has observed, the Ulster linen industry was originally organized into an elaborate complex of small vertically disintegrated plants concentrated in Belfast. In the 1950s and 1960s, this complex dissolved almost entirely away as the industry was penetrated by international capital and production was reorganized within a few major integrated producers using largely synthetic fibers.

Fourth, and finally, over the 1960s, 1970s and 1980s, assembly operations in the semiconductor industry were effectively routinized and their scale of operation greatly expanded. As a result, specialized assembly branch plants broke away from the heartland of the industry in Silicon Valley with its rich stock of agglomeration economies and many ancillary industries (Scott and Angel, 1987). These branch plants located in various parts of the world periphery, but above all in the large metropolitan regions of East and Southeast Asia, with their abundant supplies of cheap female labor. It is of interest to note that in recent years, significant backward linkage from these branch plants to local input suppliers in Asia has started to occur, and in some favored regions the beginnings of industrial complex formation are actually discernible (Scott, 1987).

These examples might be multiplied a hundredfold. They are all testimony to the powerful decentralizing forces that have been as much a part of modern capitalist spatial development as the countervailing trend toward centralization and agglomeration. We have already spent considerable time investigating the latter trend; let us now consider the obverse side of the problem. Why and how does the locational dispersal of production occur? What effects does this have on metropolis-hinterland relations and on developmental trajectories in the periphery? By way of a preliminary treatment of these questions, I shall first of all criticize, and then seek to go beyond, some standard theoretical responses in the literature.

Incubation, the product cycle, and hierarchical filtering theory. The data presented in chapter 2 provide ample evidence of the ravages that the crisis conditions of the 1970s have wrought on large numbers of American cities. Many urban centers—above all in the Manufacturing Belt—entered sometime in the late 1960s into what has appeared to be a chronic syndrome of economic stagnation and demise, as revealed by one of its most serious symptoms, i.e., plant closure and decentralization. In this context, by the way, the term *decentralization* is meant to refer not just to the actual physical migration of industrial plants from core to peripheral regions, but also, and more significantly, to the decline (relatively or absolutely) of the core and the growth of the periphery as a result of (a) closures and *in situ* employment declines in the former area, and (b) new openings and *in situ* employment increases in the latter. Actually, as both Birch (1979) and Schmenner (1982) have demonstrated, only a very small proportion (less than four or five percent a year) of industrial plants in the United States do actually physically shift location.

A great deal has been written about the aggressive decentralization of industrial activities that has occurred over the last couple of decades. Much of the research that has been published on the problem in the recent past can be summarized in terms of a composite story that I shall designate here (for want of a better term) *incubation, product cycle, and hierarchical filtering theory.* This story proceeds on the basis of a threefold account of (a) the presumed locational needs of small new firms, (b) the evolution of industrial technologies and products through time, and (c) the diffusion of units of productive capital down the urban hierarchy. I shall briefly describe and criticize this story (extracting from it some of its useful insights) and I shall then attempt to move forward into what I take to be a more satisfactory analysis of the problem of decentralization via an account of the formation of a new spatial division of labor. This account will be based on and fully consistent with the theoretical analysis of industrial organization and location already completed in chapters 3 and 4 above.

The story begins with the idea that small new firms require "incubation" if they are to survive. Such firms are said to be extremely fragile, and they therefore seek out for themselves an economic environment that can provide them with supportive facilities and services (i.e., positive agglomeration effects). Many theorists have taken it for granted that environments like this occur above all in the vicinity of the core of the city. Thus, the core is said to function as an incubator or seedbed in the sense that small new firms can maximize their chances of survival if they are attached (umbilically?) to it (Hoover and Vernon, 1959; Struyk and James, 1975). Of course, we can at once see in this part of the story something of the *real* process of the division of labor and the endogenous creation of external economies of scale. But this allusion to the real is analytically deformed in incubation theory by an unfortunate biologistic metaphor that invites us to view the process as something akin to the hatching of eggs. We know, moreover, that the process (i.e., disintegration and locational convergence) is not at all necessarily tied to central-city areas, but that, on the contrary, it may proceed at diverse types of locations. The incubator hypothesis goes on to claim that many seedbed firms will grow and expand within the nurturing environment of the central city, and as they do so, they will increasingly be able to provide internally for themselves the economies of scale that they formerly consumed as pure externalities. They thus become steadily more self-sufficient, and they may in fact eventually be able to dispense entirely with their initial incubator location. Accordingly, once they have outgrown their original premises, they are likely to start to abandon the central city for the cheaper land of the urban fringe.

In an attempt to broaden the bases of this theory and to make it rather more realistic, some analysts proceeded in the 1960s and 1970s to graft onto it the notion of the product cycle, which had hitherto been developed as a largely aspatial concept (Norton and Rees, 1979; Thompson, 1969; Vernon, 1966). This part of the story revolves around the proposition that technological change in any sector can be defined in terms of nonreversible "learning curve" economies. In the early phase of the cycle, producers are alleged to be small and labor-intensive and to face uncertain markets. This phase essentially coincides with the incubator process and is associated with centralized locational development. Then, as markets expand, technologies are stabilized and routinized, and producers grow in size. They become more capital-intensive, more given to production of large standardized batches of output, and ever more ready to relocate in noncentral areas. Finally, a stage is reached in which fully routinized, mass-production technologies (using largely unskilled labor) are installed. This stage corresponds to the upper reaches of the producer's learning curve, and in product-cycle terms it represents full industrial maturation. By the time this stage is attained, production is concentrated in large branch plants organized within oligopolistic corporations (Markusen, 1985). This final phase in the product cycle is also associated with considerable dispersal of units of production. These locate primarily in medium-sized or small towns in peripheral areas where adequate supplies of cheap, unskilled (frequently female) labor are available.

The latter locational process also comprises the hierarchical filtering component of the story. The claim is that as process and product technologies evolve, according to the cycle, so industrial plants are repelled from large metropolitan regions and diffuse steadily downward and outward through the urban system. The unfolding of this trend has been characterized by Thompson (1969, p. 8) as the movement of plants "from places of greater to lesser industrial sophistication."

This composite story about industrial change and locational readjustment contains several informative insights. If only in a formalistic way, the story synthesizes complex empirical relata that have been observed recurrently for many different sectors of production. And yet, at the same time, it is a demonstrably restricted account of how production systems evolve over time and how their geographies change. I have already criticized the disastrous biologistic metaphor with which the story begins. In addition, the story seizes upon the abstracted surface manifestations of change in particular industrial sectors in the recent historical past and mistakenly proclaims them to be universal. Because the story is insensitive to the complex inner mechanisms of production systems as both technical and social organizations in capitalism (and instead fixates on the assumption of asymptotic capital deepening and routinization), it is committed to an unduly narrow set of theoretical predictions. It does not and cannot deal analytically with reversals of the so-called cycle (Storper and Christopherson, 1985), or with radical ruptures in the pattern of technological change (as in the case of the new flexible technologies discussed by Piore and Sabel, 1984), or with alternative political and locational responses to continuing technological change (Clark, 1986; Morgan and Sayer, 1985). The story fails, in short, to grasp the historical and sociological fullness of the problem of production in capitalism, and hence its strictly location-theoretic advocacies are of limited interest and value.

We might say that this story has successfully captured a certain number of trends that have been especially characteristic of the era of mass production and mass consumption of the recent past, but that it has restricted meaning outside of this particular historical episode. Notwithstanding this criticism, the combined effects of technological maturation and decentralization have indeed had marked impacts on the landscape of international capitalism in the postwar decades, and I shall now deal explicitly with this issue. As I do this, I shall seek to reassimilate at least some of the testimony of product-cycle theory into the transactional analysis of industrial organization and location outlined at an earlier stage in this book, and thus to resituate the whole idea of industrial maturation within a wider concept of the production system and the division of labor.

THE MAINSPRINGS OF INDUSTRIAL DECENTRALIZATION IN THE POSTWAR YEARS

Capital intensification and resynthesis. Recall the obvious but central point that technological and organizational change in production systems is endemic in capitalism. The pressures of competitive profit seeking result in the constant reinvestment of the economic surplus back into the broad sphere of production, leading in turn to irregular but perennial economic expansion. Sometimes, and in some sectors, these pressures give rise to a widening social division of labor, the fragmentation of production processes, and a vast extension of the external transactional structure of production. At other times and in other sectors, they lead to a narrowing of the social division of labor together with the resynthesis and reintegration of production processes. I have illustrated this latter point earlier in chapter 3 by reference to the hypothetical case of a composite pin-making machine that boosts labor productivity by means of technical resynthesis of the tasks otherwise performed by a series of detail workers. This latter kind of technological/organizational change is commonly expressed in the form of capital deepening, i.e., increasing capital-labor ratios, and it frequently induces both vertical integration (since resynthesis reduces the number and variety of tasks) and horizontal integration (since increasing capital-labor ratios tend to enlarge the domain of internal economies of scale so that a given quantity of output can now be produced efficiently by a smaller number of plants). It was just this sort of capital deepening that paved the way for the large-scale, deskilled, mass-production branch plants (owned by oligopolistic firms) that first began to emerge in a major way in the 1920s and 1930s and then proliferated widely in the postwar decades. This is the classical phenomenon of industrial maturation as posited by product-cycle theory; it is one of many alternative actual and potential tendencies.

In two recent books on the dynamics of industrial technology, some of the factors underlying this tendency have been discussed at length (Abernathy *et al.*, 1983; Piore and Sabel, 1984). The authors of these books suggest that manufacturers in certain basic sectors of production have been able to cultivate stable mass markets, thus making possible the installation of routinized large-batch line-flow production processes with immense internal economies of scale and scope. This development was typically accompanied by a shift from relatively flexible to relatively inflexible production apparatuses as represented by large units of fixed and dedicated capital, for such capital can be used extremely efficiently where uncertainties in the matter of market demand are reduced or eliminated. Coincidentally, the increasing mechanization of production helps (sometimes) to deskill sections of the labor force in the sense described by Braverman (1974), and enables producers to make increasing use of undifferentiated low-wage labor at the bottom of the employment ladder. Furthermore, increases in the scale and stability of production are likely to result in increases in the volume and predictability of external linkages, which means, in turn, that external transaction costs will tend to fall per unit of output.

Geographical transformations. Any sector of production that is undergoing changes of these sorts is likely also to be susceptible to major locational readjustment. Two main points must be made here.

In the first place, where significant deskilling of production processes has occurred, manufacturers are likely actively to seek out depots of cheap labor in peripheral areas wherever historical and geographical circumstances may have created them. Manufacturers will be all the more ready to relocate in the vicinity of these depots where the labor force is in addition politically passive and lacking in historical experience of the capital-labor relation. That is to say, decentralization frequently is an attempt both to escape from organized high-wage labor and to redefine labor relations in ways that significantly reduce workers' discretion, influence, and autonomy in the labor process (Storper and Walker, 1984). Among the observable signs of this process are the movement of deskilled units of production into such local labor-market niches as: (a) suburban communities with large reserves of underemployed females; (b) the small towns and rural areas (with their passive and industrially inexperienced populations) outside of the main manufacturing regions of the United States; (c) the old market towns of France, Italy and Spain; (d) the Intermediate Areas of Britain with their chronically unemployed workers; and (e) the dense and overcrowded cities of selected parts of the Third World. Locational niches such as these have all been extensively penetrated by routinized deskilled branch plants in recent decades. However, it is to be stressed that before units of production can move to cheap labor sites in the periphery, certain other conditions must also usually have been satisfied at the outset. This brings us to our next main point.

In the second place, then, producers must also be able to free themselves from dependence on centralized agglomeration economies in the form of clusters of specialized input suppliers and ancillary service industries. This can be accomplished by means of vertical integration and resynthesis combined with a switch to production techniques that generate simplified, bulk, and low-cost linkage structures. Moreover, localized industrial complexes invariably generate many kinds of external *dis*economies in addition to their positive agglomeration effects, and these diseconomies accentuate the tendency to decentralization. The same tendency is further reinforced by the secular improvements in transport and communications infrastructures that have occurred as the world's major capitalist economies have expanded. In these connections, it is of considerable interest to speculate as to what degree the emerging disamenities of growth centers actually shape the direction of technological change by encouraging the development and application of those particular kinds of innovations that facilitate locational decentralization. This proposition is equivalent to a call for a specifically geographical approach to the problem of technical change.

It should be added that decentralization also usually makes it possible for producers to obtain cheap land inputs (whether in the suburbs or further afield) and thus to adopt lavish plant layout strategies that would be quite uneconomical at more central sites. I make this point because, contrary to ideas widely favored in an older industrial location theory, the development of horizontal plant layouts (together with truck transport in some versions of the theory) cannot simply be insinuated into the role of independent variable in the process of industrial decentralization. Rather, it must be seen as a contained and subjacent moment within the system of technological and spatial transformations in industrial capitalism as a whole (see Scott, 1982). This means that in any prospective analytical model, the firm's inputs of land, labor, capital and location must be dealt with in their full interdependence. But we must also continue to keep in mind the warnings of Sayer (1986) to the effect that locational processes (like all other social processes) are remarkably open-ended and contingent, and they are therefore always at least latently liable to reconfiguration within new systemic arrangements.

THE MULTIESTABLISHMENT FIRM AND
THE NEW SPATIAL DIVISION OF LABOR

The spatial dynamics of the multiestablishment firm. The technological and organizational tendencies alluded to in the previous section have frequently been part and parcel of an even wider set of changes involving the transformation of the firm itself from a single-establishment entity into a spatially variegated multiestablishment organization. In particular, with continued increases in capital-labor ratios and widening rounds of restructuring, firms generally grow in size as they find it possible to realize significant internal economies of scale and scope (Penrose, 1959). Such growth brings with it opportunities for the firm to split up into different units, each of which can be assigned to a peculiar kind of location. This phenomenon, in brief, involves increasing functional integration (vertical, horizontal, conglomerate) on the one side, and geographical disintegration on the other. A special case of this type of firm is the *multinational enterprise*, which is in fact no more than a multiestablishment firm with the additional characteristic that some of its internal parts are located in different political jurisdictions.

However we may designate them, such firms are invariably organized around firm-specific know-how (economies of scope) that can be transferred to geographically specialized operating units (see panel B of fig. 3.3). Thus, in spite of its spatial dispersal, the multiestablishment firm is able profitably to internalize critical transactions that would otherwise be subject to market failure of one sort or another. Almost all the modern theoretical statements on the subject insist upon this interpretation (Buckley and Casson, 1985; Caves, 1982; Dunning, 1981; Rugman, 1982; Teece, 1985). As Chen (1983, p. 209) has written, such firms rely on "ownership-specific advantages to exploit the location-specific advantages of the host country [or region]."

The emergence of the multiestablishment firm has depended greatly on the enhancement of managerial capacities, the increased efficiency and growth of production units, and a deepening division of labor between the tasks of conception and execution in production. As the number of such firms has multiplied, much economic rearranging of the economic landscape has also occurred, and a new spatial and international division of labor has begun to be set in place. The role of the modern industrial corporation in all of this is defined by the locational predilections of its different internal functions, three of which would seem to be of special interest in the present context, namely, (a) the management and control function, (b) skilled manufacturing tasks requiring qualified workers, and (c) deskilled process and assembly work (Lipietz, 1986). The first case is typified by high-level office activities that tend to locate in disintegrated (and currently expanding) business complexes in large cities where they are able to engage in intricate business transactions with one another and to draw on many different kinds of services. The second case involves labor processes that commonly depend on very specialized material and labor inputs, and which therefore gravitate to particular kinds of growth centers with particular kinds of externalities (witness the corporate high-technology branch plants that proliferate throughout the Orange County industrial complex). The third case refers to integrated, deskilled, mass-production branch plants, and this is the case that is of primary interest in the present instance.

As we have noted, the latter type of plant tends often to seek out scattered peripheral locations where labor is abundant, wages are low, and traditions of worker resistance to managerial initiatives are weak or nonexistent. The very organizational form of the large multiestablishment corporation has certainly hastened whatever endemic tendencies there may be to industrial restructuring and decentralization in modern capitalist societies. The large corporation is a mechanism for achieving more coordinated forms of production over a wide range of activities, and it aggressively pursues mass-marketing goals in order to underpin this advantage. By the same token, (and on the basis of its significant R&D resources) it is one of the principal conduits through which routinization of process technologies and standardization of outputs are brought about in practice (Malecki, 1986). Simultaneously, by securing for itself a multiple locational presence, it greatly increases its operating flexibility. Thus, multiple sourcing and parallel production strategies enable corporations to avoid crippling bottlenecks (such as strikes, shortages, or political disturbances) in one area simply by stepping up production at other plants in other areas. In addition, the geographical extension of the corporation allows it to engage in widely varying practices in the matter of production methods, labor relations, subcontracting activity, and so on at different locations. And because of its wide range of locational choices, it is able to play off various governmental jurisdictions against one another as they compete among themselves for new investments by offering such inducements to prospective locators as tax holidays, subsidies, infrastructural services, and the like. The net effect is that in the postwar years many different sectors of production have been restructured under the aegis of the large multiestablishment multinational corporation, and this in turn has had major consequences for metropolis-hinterland relations.

Metropolis and hinterland. One of the important geographical consequences of these developments has been the emergence of a new spatial and international division of labor. The single most important expression of this phenomenon is the spatial disaggregation of the internal functions of the firm and their dispersal over different regional and national terrains, though it is also increasingly manifest in much long-distance subcontracting activity (Fröbel *et al.*, 1980). Concomitantly, the new spatial division of labor is also strongly marked by the circulation of semifinished manufactures from one geographically distinct workstation to the next. In this process, skilled white-collar and blue-collar labor tasks are commonly assigned to the core regions and countries of the international capitalist system, whereas unskilled, routine tasks (especially those that consume large quantities of labor) tend to be shifted out to selected parts of the periphery.

In a very crude and schematic way, this spatial-*cum*-international division of labor reappears as a division between the large metropolis and its dependent hinterland. Thus, the metropolis is to an ever-increasing degree a focus of centralized managerial and administrative activities caught up in webs of vertically disintegrated business service functions. Further, as the economy has become more and more international in scope, so the whole urban system has been reconstituted as a hierarchy of national and subnational control centers dominated by a handful of global cities (Cohen, 1981; Friedman and Wolff, 1982; Hymer, 1972). This system forms the central coordinating apparatus for subordinate hinterland areas functioning as sites of dependent unskilled process, assembly, and resource extraction activities. This distinctive spatial arrangement of production is increasingly evident in the modern world, though it is not necessarily either ubiquitous or even dominant in any given instance. Indeed, it coexists alongside an older spatial division of labor in which different regions specialize in their comparative locational advantages and then trade among one another through markets on an interfirm (as opposed to an intrafirm) basis. A number of additional qualifying remarks on the metropolis-hinterland relation under the new spatial/international division of labor are apposite.

Thus, it would be a major error to suppose that the large metropolitan regions of the core capitalist countries are now becoming uniquely specialized in the production of white-collar services. Such services are certainly a rapidly expanding and in many cases dominant component of the modern metropolitan economy, but many centers continue to function as major and even growing foci of manufacturing employment. With the recent development of new flexible production technologies, often in combination with just-in-time production systems, there has been some actual recentralization of industrial sectors (e.g., transportation equipment) that had earlier tended to disperse. There is also currently much expansion in many of the large metropolitan areas of the United States of small sweatshop industries and subcontract shops employing low-wage immigrant labor. Conversely, white-collar office and service functions are themselves susceptible to capital deepening and routinization, and some of these functions are now actually starting to move out of core areas and into suburban and other fringe locations where land is cheap and abundant supplies of low-wage female clerical labor are available (Nelson, 1986). This latter trend has been accentuated by steady improvements in electronics communications technologies, which have made contact between dispersed back offices and managerial nerve centers in the core increasingly easy. In fact, as shown in chapter 2, even some head-office functions are now decentralizing from larger to smaller urban centers.

In addition, the so-called periphery is no longer (if it ever was) simply a receptacle for routinized, self-contained branch plants moving out to the extensive margins of industrialization in order to make use of an undifferentiated mass of unskilled workers. On the contrary, the periphery is composed of a highly variegated set of regions and productive activities, and many of these regions are now beginning to develop as important foci of economic growth. For example, innumerable large cities in the newly industrializing countries are currently experiencing major rounds of industrial expansion, as illustrated most dramatically by such places as Hong Kong, Mexico City, Sao Paulo, Seoul, and Singapore. Contrary to the stagnationist theses of some versions of dependency theory (see, in particular, Frank, 1979), it has indeed been possible for some parts of the world periphery to take off into advanced industrialization. What is more, in parts of North America and western Europe outside of the traditional industrial regions, major new industrial-urban complexes are springing into existence on terrain that was formerly largely cut off from the principal circuits of international capitalism. The emerging new high-technology growth centers of the American Sunbelt are the paramount example of this phenomenon.

CONCLUSION

In the new zones of industrial production that have begun to sprout in peripheral (and formerly peripheral) areas of the world system, alternative kinds of industrial technologies, organizational structures, and employment practices are being experimentally tried out and put into effect. These experiments take on such forms as the speeding up of production lines, the reassertion of managerial authority in the labor process, expanded local subcontracting, selective reskilling and deskilling of workers in the context of new social environments (often described in purely ideological terms as possessing a high "quality of life"), and so on. The net effect of these experiments is that older established industries in traditional core regions are to an augmenting degree being forced, via the pressures of economic competition, to conform to production and labor market norms now being hammered out at both isolated production sites and new growth centers in the periphery. This is evident, for example, in the current rounds of union contract negotiation going on throughout the old Manufacturing Belt, where a formerly privileged working class is finding that it must make significant concessions to management if local jobs are to be retained. This threatens the many economic and social gains (in both the workplace and the community) painstakingly won by workers in older industrial regions over the course of the present century.

The landscape of capitalism is nowadays indeed a seamless garment, and we can only understand its individual parts in relation to the dynamics of the whole. This means that political efforts to deal with local and specific problems such as plant closings, union give-backs, or the widespread reemergence of the sweatshop economy are likely to be stillborn so long as they remain confined within individual communities. For these problems are all elements of a wider national—indeed, international—structure of locational relations that needs to be comprehended and politically confronted as a whole.

ELEVEN

The Social Space of the Metropolis

INTRODUCTION

The modern metropolis is not just an important focus of production and work but also of residential behavior and social life. It is a geographical composite made up of both production space (industrial and commercial land use) and social space (a congeries of residential communities). As I suggested in chapter 1, most conventional accounts of urban geography strongly accentuate the latter while relegating the former to a secondary and even negligible level of significance. Here, in the interest of what I take to be a more disciplined order of theoretical discussion, I have resituated the question of social space by dealing with it only after an elaborate analysis of the structure and dynamics of production space has been accomplished. This maneuver is *not* intended in any way to depreciate the question of social space, or to insinuate that it is only of minor importance in comparison to production space. Much less is it intended to consign the question to the oblivion of mere superstructural status in a sort of social clockwork governed by the forces and relations of production. It does, however, suggest that before we can understand the specifically *geographical* emergence of the modern metropolis in capitalism, we must first of all seek to comprehend it in its primary function as a focus of production and work projected through a regime of agglomeration economies and polarization effects.

Thus, the functional core of the city is made up of those interdependent economic activities that secure the material reproduction of urban life at the outset. These activities are also the basis of the formation of pools of workers who are housed in residential districts located within ready access of employment places. The residential districts called into being in this

217

manner are the bases of the social space of the city, and within them extremely subtle processes of social reproduction and political activity go on. To repeat, I do not propose to argue in what follows that social reproduction in the urban environment is fixed uniquely in response to the needs of the production system. I shall certainly argue strongly for a view of intraurban social space as being deeply marked in both its locational and functional characteristics by the operation of the division of labor and local labor markets. But I also want to affirm both the historical open-endedness of the configurations of social space and their very real suscep-tibility to change by political renegotiation and social action. Indeed, it is not possible to understand the course of urban development in either the United States or Western Europe over the entire history of capitalist ur-banization without keeping such change fully and consistently in view.

DIVISION OF LABOR AND NEIGHBORHOOD FORMATION IN THE METROPOLIS

The employment-residence relation. In contemporary capitalism there is typically a pervasive and deeply rooted split between place of work and place of residence. The labor force that is called into existence in the vicinity of any complex of productive activity must be housed at sites within feasible commuting distance of employment locations. Accordingly, the residential locations of workers are arranged in tightly organized tiers of land use around major clusters of job opportunities. In chapter 7 I suggested that this process involves a twofold locational interdependence. On the one hand, workers choose residential locations that are accessible to employ-ment; on the other hand, employers tend to favor locations close to the center of gravity of their main labor force. As a result, employment activ-ities in the city tend to concentrate at central and subcentral sites that are invariably surrounded by spatially extended residential areas. This char-acteristic pattern of centrality and encirclement in the city is sustained by the complex interrelations between commuting costs, wage rates as paid at job site, and land rent.

A closer scrutiny of this problem reveals that the spatial pattern of urban population usually breaks down into an elaborate mosaic of socially dif-ferentiated neighborhoods and communities. Any attempt to address this issue strains current theory virtually to breaking point, and I certainly make no claims about providing definitive answers here. I do hope in what follows to be able to suggest a few guidelines as to fruitful directions of inquiry, while at the same time laying down some foundations for a decisive rupture with both the neoclassical and ecological theories that have so far dominated theoretical analyses of the social space of the city. The argument proceeds on the hypothesis that the broad outlines of urban social space can most adequately be analyzed in relation to the problem of the reproduction of the different strata of urban society as given by the occupational division of labor, employment activity and job status.

Production space in the city is the domain of work. Social or residential space is the domain of family life and communal being. The former brings contrasting social fractions together in one place; the latter tends to separate them again. We have already seen that these two kinds of space interpenetrate with one another in a diversity of ways. I propose to develop an argument here to the effect that (a) the sociospatial differentiation of the metropolis is a mediated outcome of the employment structures generated by the production system, while (b) this same differentiation (expressed above all in the formation of socially distinct neighborhoods) helps to streamline the social reproduction of selected occupational fractions of the labor force and thereby constitutes a significant public good in the urban environment. This public good is engendered both by the spontaneous choices and actions of individual households and by direct political intervention, and as it is brought forth in these ways, so the total stock of agglomeration economies in the city is expanded.

Urban analysts such as Duncan and Duncan (1955), Uyeki (1984), Wheeler (1968), and others have shown repeatedly by means of statistical induction that the occupational status of urban residents accounts for a major proportion of all variation in urban social space. There are, of course, many other important dimensions of intraurban social differentiation (e.g., ethnicity, age, family status, lifestyle, and so on), and these need to be taken very seriously indeed (see below). Occupation, however, seems to be of principal importance, and on the basis of the purely empirical testimony of factorial ecologists (Schwirian, 1974) the relevant occupational groups in urban space can evidently be defined in terms of a primary bipartite split between white-collar and blue-collar social groups and neighborhoods. In this connection, Marchand (1986) has provided a very useful discussion of occupational segregation in Los Angeles from 1940 to 1970. His analysis indicates that for each of the years 1940, 1950, 1960, and 1970, a dominant and extraordinarily stable spatial split existed between the residences of white-collar groups (i.e., professionals, managers, and clerks and salesworkers) and those of blue-collar groups (i.e., craftsmen,

TABLE 11.1

LINEAR CORRELATIONS OF THE SPATIAL RELATIONS BETWEEN OCCUPATIONAL
CATEGORIES IN LOS ANGELES

		P	M	CS	C	O	SW	L
1940	Professionals	1.00	0.49	0.53	−0.53	−0.71	−0.18	−0.43
	Managers		1.00	0.36	−0.47	−0.62	−0.42	−0.10
	Clerks, Salesworkers			1.00	−0.31	−0.59	−0.30	−0.65
	Craftsmen				1.00	0.67	−0.27	−0.09
	Operatives					1.00	0.02	0.11
	Service workers						1.00	0.04
	Laborers							1.00
1950	Professionals	1.00	0.56	0.43	0.38	−0.54	−0.71	0.39
	Managers		1.00	0.30	0.59	−0.35	−0.64	−0.53
	Clerks, Salesworkers			1.00	0.45	−0.27	−0.62	−0.37
	Craftsmen				1.00	−0.17	−0.64	−0.47
	Operatives					1.00	0.44	−0.13
	Service workers						1.00	0.38
	Laborers							1.00
1960	Professionals	1.00	0.48	0.36	−0.38	−0.72	−0.46	−0.58
	Managers		1.00	0.54	−0.37	−0.70	−0.52	−0.55
	Clerks, Salesworkers			1.00	−0.21	−0.78	−0.50	−0.77
	Craftsmen				1.00	0.37	−0.18	0.04
	Operatives					1.00	0.35	0.69
	Service workers						1.00	0.56
	Laborers							1.00
1970	Professionals	1.00	0.68	0.51	−0.45	−0.70	−0.47	−0.58
	Managers		1.00	0.51	−0.45	−0.62	−0.49	−0.52
	Clerks, Salesworkers			1.00	−0.18	−0.75	−0.40	−0.53
	Craftsmen				1.00	0.33	−0.06	0.16
	Operatives					1.00	0.16	0.43
	Service workers						1.00	0.43
	Laborers							1.00

SOURCE: Marchand (1986), table 4.7.

operatives, service workers, and laborers; see table 11.1). The correlations
of the intragroup spatial relations for these two broad occupational categories are markedly positive, whereas the intergroup correlations are
uniformly negative. As the correlation coefficients laid out in table 11.1
plainly indicate, the spatial split is never perfectly realized, though it is
constantly present as an enduring feature of the social space of the metropolis.

This broad pattern of residential segregation by occupation is replicated
in every large city in all the advanced capitalist societies. Note, however,
that the very terms in which the split is identified do not in any sense

refer directly to housing or family life but to the occupational division of labor. If this identification can be theoretically sustained, it poses at once a major puzzle: that is, how does it come to pass that an occupational division of labor that is established in the first instance in the workplace is thrown out as it were into urban social space where it reappears imperfectly but definitely as a division of resideı ial neighborhoods? In the succeeding discussion, I attempt to provide the groundwork of a response to this question by focusing on the role of spatial segregation in the reproduction of the urban labor force. The discussion proceeds on the basis of a speculative enumeration of those factors that seem to encourage workers to select residential locations close to other similar types of workers. As the argument moves forward, I am at pains to steer a hazardous course between two methodological pitfalls. On the one hand, I keep my distance from purely behavioristic modes of analysis, and I attempt instead to root the problem of individual locational choice in the context of a logic of social relations. On the other hand, I also seek to avoid the sort of functionalism that simply invokes a presumption of social necessity as a means of explaining given outcomes. Rather, I want to insist on the notion that individuals are able to recognize where their own self-interests lie (however mediated and unselfconscious the recognition may be in any given instance) and that they therefore actively attempt to secure corresponding advantages for themselves (Giddens, 1984). It should be added that as the social space of the metropolis breaks up into segregated (or, rather, quasi-segregated) neighborhoods, many emergent social and political effects make their definite historical appearance, and these too must be dealt with in any thoroughgoing account of residential activity.

Urban neighborhoods. As we saw in chapter 2, there is a strong and deepening occupational division of labor in capitalist society between white-collar workers and blue-collar workers. This division is itself a reflection of the deep split (in terms of organizational structure and requisite human attributes) between the tasks of administration and physical production in the total economic system. Over the course of the present century, this division has also come to represent one of the most significant lines of cleavage in patterns of sociospatial segregation in the city.

There can be little doubt that simple income differentials play a major role in the emergence of these patterns. Many blue-collar workers are much more financially restrained in their journey-to-work habits than white-collar workers, and they are concomitantly less willing to commute over long distances (Gera and Kuhn, 1978). One consequence of this is that blue-collar workers cluster rather more clearly than white-collar workers in identifiable pockets of housing around their main foci of employment. In the past, this seems to have given rise (à la Park et al., 1925) to an inner residential zone in the metropolis given over to working-class habitations, surrounded by an outer zone of expanding white-collar suburbs. With the suburbanization of much manufacturing after the Second World War, however, the phenomenon of the working-class suburb became increasingly common. Concomitantly, the typical zonal pattern of social segregation in the American city gave way in part to a roughly sectoral arrangement comprising alternating radial segments of white-collar and blue-collar housing. Furthermore, as white-collar jobs have progressively displaced blue-collar jobs at the core of the city, many white-collar workers have started to colonize inner-city neighborhoods formerly occupied by blue-collar workers. This latter process has given rise to pervasive gentrification near the centers of many large American cities.

These brief comments suggest that accessibility and transport costs play an important and enduring role in the structuring of urban residential space. Even so, as Tilly (1961) has indicated, actual levels of intraurban social segregation are certainly greater by far than those that would be observable if commuting distances were the only variable involved. This is because, as I shall argue, individuals also make critical decisions about residential location as a function of the match between their own socioeconomic characteristics and those of the neighborhood in which they choose to live. As a matter of fact, levels of residential segregation in the American city surpass even those that may be expected as a result of the combined effects of commuting cost differentials and individual market-mediated preferences about housing and neighborhoods. This is because intraurban social segregation is also in part sustained by direct political intervention. It is common practice in American cities to reinforce the social homogeneity of higher-status neighborhoods by erecting barriers to entry. Thus, zoning for large lots, limitations on multifamily dwellings, building codes that enforce lavish standards of construction and maintenance, restrictive convenants, and so on, all help to prevent the incursion of incompatible and disruptive elements into such neighborhoods. Then, when these barriers to entry fail or are counterattacked, the result is invariably plummeting property values and the outward flight of former residents who attempt to find requisite levels of social segregation elsewhere. These remarks only raise with new urgency the question posed above. Why do families in the modern metropolis seek out peculiar kinds of neighborhood homogeneity? In particular, what is there in the quality of one's occupational status and commitments that might give rise to strong inclinations for living among individuals with a similar background? And how do residential preferences that relate to occupation and work intersect with preferences that have their roots in other principles of social organization (ethnicity above all)?

The broad thrust of an answer to these questions can be derived from the observation that neighborhoods are the privileged locales within which social reproduction of the determinate forms of life engendered in the capitalist city goes on. An alternative way of saying the same thing is to suggest that the reproductive potential of urban space can only be fully realized when it is also socially divided. Here, I use the term *reproduction* in its double sense to mean both generational replacement and the maintenance of stable subjective/ideological accommodations with workaday life. The hypothesis is, in short, that neighborhoods are places of both biological and social revivification via their central behavioral unit, the family. Three major aspects of this proposition call for detailed attention.

First, the social characteristics of neighborhoods are of crucial concern to families by reason of their significance as centers of child rearing and socialization. The life of urban children is focused with especial intensity on the local residential community through peer groups, schools, and environmental cues. These features of neighborhoods affect in important ways the specific patterns of behavior, attitude, and speech that children acquire. Kohn (1969), among others, has suggested that white-collar and blue-collar parents differ subtly but significantly from one another in their child-rearing habits and in their conceptions of effective education. These differences reemerge in preferences about pedagogy and children's peer groups. These are especially important matters in the present context because in American cities the local school is one of the most important institutions within the neighborhood. Kohn further advances the hypothesis that parents' preferences about child rearing and schooling are rooted in the norms and values that they internalize in the workplace: in the case of white-collar workers, ability to work cooperatively with others in open-ended situations; in the case of blue-collar workers, practicality and authority. White-collar parents are generally especially anxious to secure for their children an environment that ensures successful reproduction of their own socioeconomic characteristics, namely, the acquisition of those personal attributes that will eventually enable their children to lay claim to an occupational rank that is at least equal to their own and that will help to block downward social mobility.

Second, neighborhoods constitute important signifiers of social status and labor market capacity. In all social life there is a theatrics of self-presentation, as we know so well from the writings of commentators such as Goffman (1954) and Sennett (1974), in which speech, dress, gestures, and so on all combine to demarcate and to consolidate claims about social and economic position. In many ways, what separates white-collar from blue-collar workers is not so much income (though at the extremes there are certainly great income differences between the two groups) as their subtle but detectable behavioral and cultural traits. White-collar workers actively reproduce their niche in society and demonstrate their command of the personal attributes necessary for successful fulfillment of the generalized roles associated with that niche by conspicuous displays of the requisite semiological codes. Living arrangements in the form of a house, neighborhood, and communal associates are integral elements of these codes. They represent important and concrete cues about lifestyle, participation in socially sanctioned forms of domestic life, and the legitimacy of claims to occupational status and performance.

Third, neighborhoods are also places in which useful interfamily social networks develop. Both Ley (1983) and Timms (1971) have suggested that this process is potentiated by the social homogeneity of neighborhoods and above all by the circumstances that they bring together within narrow geographical confines people with similar practical experiences of life and work. The networks that then come into being function as important communal resources, especially in working-class and ethnic neighborhoods. They form the basis of a mutual support system involving both the transmission of socially significant information (e.g., about job opportunities or civil obligations) and the reconfirmation of conventional viewpoints and forms of consciousness. In working-class and ethnic neighborhoods, these networks constitute important buffers against the vagaries of urban life. Recent immigrants to the city are especially reliant on them. Such immigrants are often unfamiliar with the language and customs of the host society, and it is crucial for them to have a supportive means of navigating through the social and labor market complexities that they face. As a corollary, some of the most tightly clustered neighborhood groups in the American metropolis today are composed of particular ethnic populations who form not only a distinctive fraction of the labor force (see next section) but a very distinctive spatial entity too.

Each of these three main principles of neighborhood organization represents one facet of the problem of social and spatial reproduction in capitalist cities. These principles are contingently related to occupational differentiation and to the contrasting forms of consciousness that various fractions of the labor force internalize as part of their active engagement in the daily tasks of life. That said, we must be careful not to exaggerate claims about the underlying structural role of the occupational division of labor in the emergence of urban neighborhoods. There are, as already noted, many additional levels of social segregation in the modern metropolis, and these intersect in complex and often contradictory ways with the effects of occupational stratification. One of the most important expressions of this interweaving of different social logics in the formation of intraurban residential space is provided by the phenomenon of ethnic neighborhoods.

ETHNICITY, LOCAL LABOR MARKETS, AND NEIGHBORHOOD FORMATION.

There is in urban social geography a long tradition of concern with ethnic neighborhoods (see, for example, Peach, 1975; Ward, 1971). This tradition has produced an important harvest of insights about the texture of life in the ghettos and barrios of American cities. It has tended, however, to fall back on explanatory frameworks that rely heavily on ecological concepts. Concomitantly, it has been peculiarly remiss in providing reasoned accounts of, first, the urban dynamics that engender inflows of immigrants into the city, and, second, how immigrants set about the business of earning a living. Some of the more "culturalist" accounts of ethnic communities in the American city provide glimpses of how and where people sleep, eat, raise their families, and socialize with their neighbors (all of which are admittedly serious issues), but seem to be incurious about the central problems of work and livelihood. These accounts, in brief, are lacking in any concept of ethnicity as an emergent effect that is negotiated out as new arrivals to the city encounter the labor-market conditions and employment possibilities of modern industrial capitalism.

In simple empirical terms, one of the most familiar aspects of the growth of large industrial cities in the United States over the last century has been their reception of wave after wave of ethnic immigrants drawn in to their expanding employment base. The low-wage labor needs of the large metropolis have continually been replenished in this manner. Wherever, in the world at large, historical and geographical circumstances have created local instabilities (as a result of poverty, famine, political repression, war, and so on), the resulting streams of migrants have time and again been caught up in the functional orbit of industrial urban capitalism. In this way, over the years, migrant populations have moved in—and continue to move in—to the sweatshops, factories, and unskilled service industries of urban America. Irish, Germans, Poles, eastern European Jews, Italians, southern Blacks, and other groups have all severally made up these migration streams. And now, most recently of all, Latinos and Asians have begun to move en masse into large American cities, and most especially into the burgeoning growth centers of the Sunbelt (see, for example, Soja *et al.*, 1983). As these populations become, each in turn, embroiled in the daily activity patterns of the city, their ethnicity is socially transacted out as it were on new terms. Typically, these ethnic groups form dense segregated neighborhoods close to centers of employment where unskilled low-wage jobs abound. Such centers have generally been found within inner-city areas, but now, with the growth of suburban industrial complexes, they are also increasingly located in the urban periphery. These neighborhoods are held together as geographical units by the tight social networks (built up around idiosyncrasies of language and culture) that develop within them. In such neighborhoods, immigrants tend to remain socially and politically isolated from the broader working class of which they constitute an important segment.

Ethnicity in the American metropolis is thus preeminently a contingent outcome of local labor market pressures and needs. This involves the continual recreation of pools of cheap and malleable labor (including women and adolescents) suitable for employment in the disintegrated complexes of labor-intensive manufacturing and service industries that cluster within the metropolis. In this specific sense, urban ethnicity is at once a durable phenomenon, and yet it is also largely transient insofar as any particular group is concerned. With the notable stubborn exception of Blacks, groups with subordinate cultural identities in the American city have fairly consistently been assimilated over the course of three or four generations into the mainstream of urban life (Rodgers, 1981; Zunz, 1981). Thus, the socialization processes and upward mobility characteristic of American society have continually undercut the conditions under which cheap exploitable labor at the bottom of the employment ladder can be internally reproduced. The concomitant vacuum has invariably been filled by new rounds of immigration, new rounds of ethnic neighborhood formation, and new rounds of social and political fragmentation.

This is a far cry indeed from the purely ecological theories of moral order and social solidarity that have so far seemed to dominate the literature on urban ethnicity.

CLASS, COMMUNITY, LOCALE

In previous chapters of this book we have learned that the modern metropolis, by its very nature, comprises an extraordinary variety of productive activities. In the present chapter, we have seen that this diversity is matched by an equal richness in forms of urban social life. A structural commonality running through this entire gamut of urban phenomena is the capital-labor relation as expressed in a variety of local class bargains, compromises, and practices. I use the term *local* advisedly here in order to emphasize the point that each individual metropolis is not just a re-petitive re-creation in microcosm of a set of macrosocial structures, but is, in addition, a unique configuration of past history and current circumstances. Indeed even at the level of *intra*urban space we can observe much idiosyncrasy in the ways in which commmunities operate as social and political alliances. Thus, the overarching capital-labor relation—whose social point of origin is the workplace—becomes fragmented and reconstituted in innumerable different ways as individuals are recombined in the social space of the city with its peculiar associations, predicaments, and political conflicts. Castells (1984) and Harvey (1958a, 1985b) have written at length and with great insight about these matters, and they have shown us how urban social movements are often not in the very least posited on work-related issues, but on problems whose origins are more proximately tied to housing conditions, community planning, and the so-called secondary circuits of capital.

These remarks bring us at once to what is surely one of the central puzzles of social history and urban geography. Does the communal life of the metropolis drive wedges between different social groups and fractions and thus impede the formation of class consciousness, as Katznelson (1981) has argued? Or is community in some sense a prelude to the formation of class consciousness, as Calhoun (1982) has averred in his dense study of popular agitations in England at the time of the Industrial Revolution? I see no way of answering these questions as a straighforward matter of abstract principle. Undoubtedly, we will find that the answers depend very much on the specifics of conjuncture and place, and we know from the empirical investigations of historians and sociologists such as Bodnar (1982), Chorney (1981), Dawley (1976), Hershberg (1981), Kornblum (1974), Pollard (1959), Zunz (1981), and others, these specifics vary widely from case to case. I suggest that in a situation of overall massive depoliticization of class relations, as in the case of American society in the 1980s, there is much in urban life that helps further to reinforce political fragmentation and political demobilization.

Perhaps the last great broadly based urban alliance of workers in America existed in the cities of the Manufacturing Belt in the decades immediately following the Second World War. Unionization was widespread, especially in the large assembly industries of the region where tens of thousands of workers were brought together in daily labor. Coincidentally, workers' consciousness and class capacity were sustained in cities such as Boston, Chicago, Cleveland, Detroit, Philadelphia, and so on, by rising confrontations over housing issues and municipal politics. Even here, however, class action across a wide front was rarely, if ever, fully achieved. Rather, in each city, in each industrial sector, and in each neighborhood, localized problems and counteraction continually deflected energies away from the more remote and global issue of class politics. Moreover, in many cities, as Hill (1984) has shown concretely for the case of Detroit, stabilizing social contracts were worked out on a tripartite basis between management, unions, and municipal administrations. These social contracts tended to hold local social formations in loose but durable order via accommodating agreements among the principal agents in metropolitan society.

In spite of the more-or-less successful containment of worker unrest in the cities of the Manufacturing Belt over much of the 1940s, 1950s, and 1960s, producers were still caught in what was coming to be seen as a deepening locational trap. Over the course of many years, workers in these cities had developed organized frameworks of response to managerial actions, just as they had also established significant rights and entitlements in both the workplace and the municipal environment. In the first place, a class bargain had been set in place such that workers participated directly in industrial productivity gains (Bluestone and Harrison, 1982). In the second place, workers also had definite leverage via union representatives in decisions about work conditions, shop floor management, factory rules, and so on. In the third place, by bringing pressure to bear on local governments, workers were also to some degree able to impose indirect costs on producers via taxes, zoning regulations, building codes, pollution controls, and so on. Capitalist industrialization has always required for its successful deployment the formation of dense agglomerations of capital and labor. But this same agglomeration brings with it both a buildup of working-class political experience and a rising tide of external diseconomies. Small wonder, then, that much industrial capital has sought in recent decades to make an exit from the older cities of the Manufacturing

Belt and thus to escape from the very problems that its own logic of accumulation and agglomeration has created in the first place. By the same token, much new industrialization and urbanization in the United States is now taking place at locations (such as Orange County) without any significant prior experience of traditional working-class politics.

As a result of all the industrial restructuring that has gone on over the last few decades, relations of class, community, and locale have taken on some surprisingly new colors in both the United States and the world at large. Two issues stand out as being especially pertinent in the present context. First, in the large global cities of contemporary capitalism a peculiar pattern of social and labor market segmentation has begun to appear as more and more middle-level jobs are being restructured or destroyed. As noted in chapter 10, this segmentation is starting increasingly to take on the extreme form of a cleavage between high-level managerial cadres on the one hand and low-wage immigrant workers on the other hand, so that cities such as New York, Los Angeles, and Chicago display to an ever-increasing degree the incongruous spectacle of great economic power and social status juxtaposed against pervasive poverty and social marginality (Soja and Scott, 1986). This situation would seem to be pregnant with latent social conflicts and collisions. Second, and by extension of the argument in the previous paragraph, many of the new growth centers of the Sunbelt and elsewhere represent places where the capital-labor relation in the metropolitan environment is being reforged anew. This phenomenon provides examples to and pressures upon those production units that remain within longer-established industrial communities, and, as a corollary, the various practices now developing within these new growth centers are beginning to diffuse back to older regions. In this way, geographical differences within the national space-economy come to be important further factors in the reproduction of class relations, and hence in the evolution of social and spatial inequality generally.

What further social, cultural, and political tendencies will emerge within both old and new metropolitan complexes in the advanced captialist economies as the current conjuncture unfolds remains very much an open question. On the basis of the discussion presented here, it seems reasonable to claim that these tendencies are likely to be intimately bound up with the development and transformation of cities as agglomerations of capital and human labor. But we must also remain fully alert to the circumstances that cities are implicated in the reproduction of class relations in capitalist society in complicated, contradictory, and historically evolving ways. This means that we can never simply make a tally of current trends and forces and then project them unproblematically into the future. For this very reason, indeed, the urban question itself seems to change its colors every few decades and periodically to reemerge within new theoretical syntheses.

TWELVE

Conclusion

In all of the above discussion I have been at pains systematically to unravel some of the critical relationships between the logic of production, the formation of local labor markets, and the dynamics of community in the modern metropolis. This has involved nothing less than an attempt to reconstruct large segments of urban theory on the basis of a conception of the organizational and locational rationality of industrialization processes in capitalism.

My point of departure in the unfolding of this theoretical exercise consisted in a description of the macroeconomics of commodity production under capitalist rules of order. I showed how industries subject to these rules are organized and how in turn the principles of industrial organization can be fruitfully conceptualized in terms of the dynamic interface between the internal and external transactional structures of production. On this basis, I indicated how external economies (in the narrow sense, a set of aspatial phenomena) and derivative agglomeration economies (a specifically *spatial* set of phenomena) come into existence, and how the latter give rise to localized production complexes in the space-economy. The discussion moved on to scrutinize the manner in which these complexes develop and grow through progressive fragmentation of production activities and widening rounds of the division of labor. My argument then demonstrated how the agglomeration economies that lie at the center of these events are complemented and intensified by the local labor market phenomena that come into being around the focal employment opportunities of the emergent metropolis. I further pointed out how the growth of metropolitan industrial complexes is sometimes halted or reversed in cases where technological change evolves down the path of increasing internal economies of scale and scope in the context of deepening diseconomies of agglomeration, and I showed how the metropolis then becomes ever more closely intertwined with a wider territorial system that today, via the new spatial and international divisions of labor, is nothing less than the world itself. I finally attempted to sketch out a few notions about residential activity and social existence in the large metropolis and about the highly mediated but definite connections between these phenomena and the production system. I should hasten to add that I am all too aware of the inadequacy of these latter formulations. They are highly preliminary and most certainly too laconic. At the same time, I am conscious of the fact that most accounts of urban geography tend to place overwhelming emphasis on the residential and the social (at the expense of the production system), and my own reticence in these matters may perhaps be excused as a corrective to this discursive imbalance. That said, I acknowledge that one of the most important and challenging tasks that urban geographers must face in the future is to deepen and enrich our understanding of the dynamics of the social space of the metropolitan community as it takes shape around concentrated hubs of economic production and work.

The entire argument of this book represents both an analytical agenda for future research into the systematic dynamics of city-forming processes, and, as a corollary, a set of conceptual coordinates for thinking about the historical geography of industrialization and urbanization in capitalist society. In all of the above I have concentrated primarily on certain theoretical underpinnings of this agenda (illustrated in part by reference to a series of critical empirical case studies) while refraining from any attempt to be comprehensive in the matter of a historical geography. The realization of this latter project in scholarly form remains as yet no more than a distant prospect, though the terrain in view would seem to offer some exceptionally rich and rewarding prospects for substantive research. In this book, I have, in particular, glossed over a number of important contextual details of history and geography that inevitably condition patterns of industrialization and their expression in urban form. Two matters are of special significance here. First, despite my emphasis on the abstracted logics of production, labor markets, and communal development, social processes are in fact emphatically *not* abstracted from time; they are embedded in a complex temporal matrix made up of cycles of different amplitudes, episodic shifts from one conjuncture to another, and the long flow of history. Second, at any given moment, social processes have a tendency to work themselves out in sometimes surprisingly different ways from place to place as they come into contact with diverse preexisting conditions. All of this temporal and geographical variability helps to account for the enormous variety of forms of economic organization and urban experience that occur in reality. Consider, as examples of this proposition, such contrasting modes of industrial development as represented by craft communities, the classical factory system, mass production, or modern high-technology industry; this variety is further compounded when we take into account the (approximate) respective urban analogues of these phenomena in the form of Birmingham at the beginning of the Industrial Revolution, Manchester in the mid–nineteenth century, Detroit in the interwar period, or the great megalopolis of Southern California today. We must also acknowledge that each country in the capitalist system is marked by its own peculiar space-time trajectory of industrialization and urbanization.

In spite of all this substantive complexity, the rough analytical scenarios sketched out in previous chapters of this book would seem to describe patterns of events that are endemic to capitalist society. These patterns have been variously inscribed on the landscape of capitalism from its very historical beginnings, though, as pointed out, they take on different specific forms in different times and in different places. The landscape is continually being structured and restructured as localized territorial complexes of human labor and social life are created, transformed, and then dissolved again in conformity with what Schumpeter (1950) called the creative destruction of capitalism. The modern metropolis is central to these processes, both as their basic spatial point of reference and as their most intense concrete expression. It is my hope in this book to have provided at least some of the elements of a coherent view as to how the metropolis emerges (via the division of labor) out of the specific rationality of capitalist industrialization, and how in turn it has come to be the preeminent spatial focus of modern society.

One final point needs to be made regarding the wider significance of this investigation. An understanding of the problems dealt with in this book is essential if we are to deal in political terms with the changes that are now working their effects on the whole of the North American and Western European space-economies. These changes derive in large part from the dissolution of many of the central sociopolitical accommodations put in place during the Keynesian welfare-statist era of social regulation stretching roughly from the 1930s to the late 1970s, and their replacement by more competitive and very much more highly privatized forms of economic organization. This has been associated with incipient but potentially revolutionary shifts in the core capitalist economies away from fordist mass production in its most rigid forms of expression, and toward more flexible systems of manufacturing combined with massive expansion of the service sector. These events have also typically been associated with large-scale changes in the geographical distribution of productive activity and urban population, as represented most dramatically by the decline of the U.S. Frostbelt and the rise of the Sunbelt. Concomitantly, over the last couple of decades a marked proliferation of new industrial/urban regions and spaces has come about in many different parts of the world.

These new developments suggest that we will certainly have to continue to sharpen our tools of analysis as the regime of accumulation and its associated mode of social regulation unleashed by the restructuring of the 1970s unfolds before us, and enters in the 1980s and 1990s into a phase of intensive development and normalization. If recent changes in the older cities of the United States, as well as contemporary patterns of growth in many new Sunbelt centers (such as Orange County) are a sign of things to come, then we do need radically to rethink many of our central notions of economic and urban geography. I propose that the lines of theoretical investigation developed here are likely to prove useful in dealing not only with familiar forms of industrial and urban development but also with many of the qualitatively new forms that now seem to be making their irreversible historical and geographical appearance on the landscape of capitalist society.

References

Abernathy, W. J., K. B. Clark, and A. M. Kantrow (1983). *Industrial Renaissance: Producing a Competitive Future for America*. New York: Basic Books.

Alchian, A. A., and H. Demsetz (1972). "Production, information costs and economic organization." *American Economic Review* 62: 777–795.

Allen, G. C. (1929). *The Industrial Development of Birmingham and the Black Country, 1860–1907*. Hemel Hempstead, Herts.: Allen and Unwin.

Alonso, W. (1965). *Location and Land Use*. Cambridge, Mass.: Harvard University Press.

Angel, D. (1984). "The organization and location of the Los Angeles plastic injection molding industry." M.A. thesis, Department of Geography, University of California, Los Angeles.

Armour, H. O., and D. J. Teece (1980). "Vertical integration and technological innovation." *Review of Economics and Statistics* 62: 470–474.

Barnes, T., and E. Sheppard (1984). "Technical choice and reswitching in space economies." *Regional Science and Urban Economics* 14: 345–362.

Bater, J. H., and D. F. Walker (1970). "Further comments on industrial location and linkage." *Area* 4: 59–63.

Bell, D. (1973). *The Coming of Post-Industrial Society*. New York: Basic Books.

Berger, S., and M. J. Piore (1980). *Dualism and Discontinuity in Industrial Societies*. Cambridge: Cambridge University Press.

Birch D. L. (1979). *The Job Generation Process*. Cambridge, Mass.: Program on Neighborhood and Regional Change, Massachusetts Institute of Technology

Blackaby, F., ed. (1978). *De-industrialisation*. London: Heinemann.

Bluestone, B., and B. Harrison (1982). *The Deindustrialization of America*. New York: Basic Books.

Bodnar, J. (1982). *Workers' World: Kinship, Community, and Protest in an Industrial Society, 1900–1940*. Baltimore: Johns Hopkins University Press.

Braverman, H. (1974). *Labor and Monopoly Capital*. New York: Monthly Review Press.

Buchner, J., J. Curley, J. Everly, and J. Perez (1981). *A Survey of Orange County Manufacturing Employers*. Orange County, California: Economic Development Corporation of Orange County.

Buckley, P. J., and M. Casson (1985). *The Economic Theory of the Multinational Enterprise*. New York: St. Martin's Press.

Burgess, E. W. (1924). "The growth of the city: an introduction to a research project." *Publications of the American Sociological Society* 21: 178–184.

Calhoun, C. (1982). *The Question of Class Struggle: Social Foundations of Popular Radicalism during the Industrial Revolution*. Chicago: University of Chicago Press.

Cameron, G. C. (1973). "Intra-urban location and the new plant." *Papers of the Regional Science Association* 31: 125–143.

Carlton, D. W. (1979). "Vertical Integration in competitive markets under uncertainty." *Journal of Industrial Economics* 27: 189–209.

Castells, M. (1973). *La Question Urbaine*. Paris: François Maspéro.

———. (1984). *The City and the Grassroots*. London: Edward Arnold.

Caves, R. E . (1982). *Multinational Enterprise and Economic Analysis*. Cambridge: Cambridge University Press.

Chapman, S. J., and T. S. Ashton (1914). "The sizes of businesses mainly in the textile industries." *Journal of the Royal Statistical Society* 77: 469–555.

Chen, E. K. Y. (1983). *Multinational Corporations, Technology and Employment*. New York: St. Martin's Press.

Chorney, H. (1981). "Amnesia, integration and repression: the roots of Canadian urban political culture," pp. 535–563 in M. Dear and A. J. Scott, eds. *Urbanization and Urban Planning in Capitalist Society*. New York: Methuen.

Clark, C. (1951). "Urban population densities." *Journal of the Royal Statistical Society*, Series A 114: 490–496.

Clark, G. L. (1983a), "Fluctuations and rigidities in local labor markets. Part 1: theory and evidence." *Environment and Planning A* 15: 165–185.

———. (1983b). "Fluctuations and rigidities in local labor markets. Part 2: reinterpreting contracts." *Environment and Planning A* 15: 365–377.

———. (1986). "The crisis of the Midwest auto industry," pp. 127–148 in A. J. Scott and M. Storper, eds. *Production, Work, Territory: The Geographical Anatomy of Industrial Capitalism*. Boston: Allen and Unwin.

———. M. S. Gertler, and J. Whiteman (1986). *Regional Dynamics: Studies in Adjustment Theory*. Boston: Allen and Unwin.

Coase, R. H. (1937). "The nature of the firm." *Economica* 4: 386–405.

Cohen, R. B. (1981). "The new international division of labor, multinational corporations and urban hierarchy," pp. 287–315 in M. Dear and A. J. Scott, eds. *Urbanization and Urban Planning in Capitalist Society*. London: Methuen.

Darwent, D. F. (1969). "Growth poles and growth centers in regional planning: a review." *Environment and Planning* 1: 5–11.

Davis, H. S., G. W. Taylor, C. C. Balderston, and A. Bezanson (1938). *Vertical Integration in the Textile Industries*. Philadelphia: Industrial Research Department, Wharton School of Finance and Commerce, University of Pennsylvania.

Dawley, A. (1976). *Class and Community*. Cambridge Mass.: Harvard University Press.

Dicken, P., and P. E. Lloyd (1981). *Modern Western Society: A Geographical Perspective on Work, Home and Well-Being*. New York: Harper and Row.

Duncan, O. D., and B. Duncan (1955). "Residential distribution and occupational stratification." *American Journal of Sociology* 60: 493–503.

Dunning, J. H. (1981). *International Production and the Multinational Enterprise.* London: Allen and Unwin.

Evans, A. W. (1973). *The Economics of Residential Location.* London: Macmillan.

Fales, R. L., and L. N. Moses (1972). "Land use theory and the spatial structure of the nineteenth century city." *Papers of the Regional Science Association* 28: 49–80.

Feldstein, M. (1975). "The importance of temporary layoffs: an empirical analysis." *Brookings Papers on Economic Activity* 3: 725–744.

Florence, P. S. (1948). *Investment, Location and Size of Plant.* Cambridge: Cambridge Univrsity Press.

Fothergill, S., and G. Gudgin (1979). "Regional employment change: a subregional explanation." *Progress in Planning* 12: 155–219.

Foucault, M. (1980). *Power/Knowledge: Selected Interviews and Other Writings 1972–1977.* Edited by C. Gordon. New York: Pantheon/Random House.

Frank, A. G. (1979). *Dependent Accumulation and Underdevelopment.* New York: Monthly Review Press.

Friedman, A. L. (1977). *Industry and Labour.* London: Macmillan.

Friedman, J., and G. Wolff (1982). "World city formation." *International Journal of Urban and Regional Research* 6: 309–344.

Fröbel, F., J. Heinrichs, and O. Kreye (1980). *The New International Division of Labour.* Cambridge: Cambridge University Press.

Gad, G. H. K. (1979). "Face-to-face linkages and office decentralization potentials: a study of Toronto," pp. 277–323 in P. W. Daniels, ed. *Spatial Patterns of Office Growth and Location.* New York: John Wiley.

Gera, S., and P. Kuhn (1978). *Occupation, Locational Patterns and the Journey-to-Work.* Ottawa: Economic Council of Canada, Discussion Paper 121.

Giddens, A. (1984). *The Constitution of Society: Outline of the Theory of Structuration.* Berkeley, Los Angeles, London: University of California Press.

Goddard, J. B. (1973). "Office linkages and location." *Progress in Planning* 1: 109–232.

Goffman, E. (1959). *The Presentation of Self in Everyday Life.* Garden City, N.Y.: Doubleday.

Habermas, J. (1971). *Knowledge and Human Interests.* Boston: Beacon Press.

Haig, R. M. (1927). *Major Economic Factors in Metropolitan Growth and Arrangement.* New York: Regional Plan of New York and its Environs.

Hall, P. G. (1962a). *The Industries of London since 1861.* London: Hutchinson.

———. (1962b). "The East London footwear industry: an industrial quarter in decline." *East London Papers* 5: 3–21.

———, and D. Hay (1980). *Growth Centres in the European Urban System.* Berkeley, Los Angeles, London: University of California Press.

Harvey, D. (1973). *Social Justice and the City.* London: Edward Arnold.

———. (1985a). *The Urbanization of Capital.* Baltimore: Johns Hopkins University Press.

———. (1985b). *Consciousness and the Urban Experience.* Baltimore: Johns Hopkins University Press.

Helfgott, R. B. (1959). "Women's and children's apparel," pp. 19–134 in M. Hall, ed. *Made in New York.* Cambridge, Mass.: Harvard University Press.

Henderson, J., and A. J. Scott (1987). "The growth and internationalisation of the American semiconductor industry: labour processes and the changing spatial organisation of production," in M. Breheny and R. McQuaid, eds. *The Development of High Technology Industries: An International Survey.* London: Croom Helm.

Hershberg, T., ed. (1981). *Philadelphia: Workplace, Family, and the Group Experience in the 19th Century.* New York: Oxford University Press.

Hill, R. C. (1984). "Economic crisis and political response in the Motor City," pp. 313–338 in L. Sawers and W. K. Tabb, eds. *Sunbelt/Snowbelt: Urban Development and Regional Restructuring.* New York: Oxford University Press.

Hirschman, A. O. (1958). *The Strategy of Economic Development.* New Haven: Yale University Press.

Hodge, G., and C. C. Wong (1972). "Adapting industrial complex analysis to the realities of regional data." *Papers of the Regional Science Association* 28: 145–166.

Holmes, J. (1986). "The organization and locational structure of production subcontracting," pp. 80–106 in A. J. Scott and M. Storper, eds. *Production, Work, Territory: The Geographical Anatomy of Industrial Capitalism.* Boston: Allen and Unwin.

Hoover, E. M. (1937). *Location Theory and the Shoe and Leather Industries.* Cambridge, Mass.: Harvard University Press.

———, and R. Vernon (1959). *Anatomy of a Metropolis.* Cambridge, Mass.: Harvard University Press.

Huriot, J. M. (1981). "Rente foncière et modèle de production." *Environment and Planning A* 13: 1125–1149.

Hymer, S. (1972). "The multinational corporation and the law of uneven development," pp. 113–140 in J. N. Bhagwati, ed. *Economics of World Order from the 1970s to the 1990s.* New York: Collier Macmillan.

Isard, W. (1956). *Location and Space-Economy.* Cambridge, Mass.: MIT Press.

Jayet, H. (1983). "Chômer plus souvent en région urbaine, plus longtemps en région rurale." *Economie et Statistique* 153: 47–57.

Kaldor, N. (1970). "The case for regional policies." *Scottish Journal of Political Economy* 17: 337–348.

Karaska, G. J. (1967). "The spatial impacts of defense-space procurement: an analysis of subcontracting patterns in the United States." *Papers of the Peace Research Society (International)* 8: 109–122.

Kaserman, D. L. (1978). "Theories of vertical disintegration: implications for antitrust policy." *Antitrust Bulletin* 23: 483–510.

Katznelson, I. (1981). *City Trenches: Urban Politics and the Patterning of Class in the United States.* New York: Pantheon.

Kenyon, J. B. (1964). "The industrial structure of the New York garment center," pp. 159–166 in R. S. Thoman and D. J. Patton, eds. *Focus on Geographic Activity.* New York: McGraw-Hill.

Kohn, M. (1969). *Class and Conformity.* Chicago: University of Chicago Press.

Kornblum, W. (1974). *Blue Collar Community.* Chicago: Chicago University Press.

Lampard, E. E. (1955). "The history of cities in economically advanced areas." *Economic Development and Cultural Change* 3: 81–136.

Leijonhufvud, A. (1984). *Capitalism and the Factory System.* Institute of Industrial Relations, University of California, Los Angeles, Working Paper 79.

Levy, D. T. (1984). "Testing Stigler's interpretation of 'the division of labor is limited by the extent of the market.'" *Journal of Industrial Economics* 32: 377–389.

———. (1985). "The transaction cost approach to vertical integration: an empirical examination." *Review of Economics and Statistics* 68: 538–445.

Ley, D. (1983). *A Social Geography of the City*. New York: Harper and Row.

Lichtenburg, R. M. (1960). *One-tenth of a Nation*. Cambridge, Mass.: Harvard University Press.

Lipietz, A. (1986). "New tendencies in the international division of labor: regimes of accumulation and modes of regulation," pp. 16–40 in A. J. Scott and M. Storper, eds. *Production, Work, Territory: The Geographical Anatomy of Industrial Capitalism*. Boston: Allen and Unwin.

Lowry, I. (1964). *A Model of Metropolis*. Santa Monica: Rand Corporation, Memorandum RM-4035-RC.

Mackay, D. I., D. Boddy, J. Brack. J. A. Diack, and N. Jones (1971). *Labour Markets under Different Employment Conditions*. London: Allen and Unwin.

Malecki, E. J. (1986). "Technological imperatives and modern corporate strategy," pp. 67–79 in A. J. Scott and M. Storper, eds. *Production, Work, Territory: The Geographical Anatomy of Industrial Capitalism*. Boston: Allen and Unwin.

Marchand, B. (1986). *The Emergence of Los Angeles: Population and Housing in the City of Dreams, 1940–1970*. London: Pion.

Marglin, S. A. (1974). "What do bosses do? The origins and functions of hierarchy in capitalist production." *Review of Radical Political Economics* 6: 60–112.

Markusen, A. (1985). *Profit Cycles, Oligopoly and Regional Development*. Cambridge, Mass.: MIT Press.

Martin, J. E. (1969). "Size of plant and location of industry in Greater London." *Tijdschrift voor Economische en Sociale Geografie* 60: 369–374.

Massey, D. (1984). *Spatial Divisions of Labour*. London: Methuen.

———, and R. A. Meegan (1979). "The geography of industrial reorganisation: the spatial effects of the restructuring of the electrical engineering sector under the Industrial Reorganisation Corporation." *Progress in Planning* 10: 155–237.

Masten, S. E. (1984). "The organization of production: evidence from the aerospace industry." *Journal of Law and Economics* 27: 403–417.

Monteverde, K., and D. J. Teece (1982). "Supplier switching costs and vertical integration in the automobile industry." *Bell Journal of Economics* 13: 206–213.

Morgan, K., and A. Sayer (1985). "A modern industry in a mature region: the remaking of management-labour relations." *International Journal of Urban and Regional Research* 9: 383–403.

Morgan, W. T. W. (1961). "A functional approach to the study of office distributions: internal structures in London's central business district." *Tijdschrift voor Economische en Sociale Geografie* 52: 207–210.

Morrison, P. A. (1975). *The Current Demographic Context of National Growth and Development*. Santa Monica: Rand Corporation Publication P-5514.

Moses, L. N. (1958). "Location and the theory of production." *Quarterly Journal of Economics* 73: 259–272.

———. (1962). "Towards a theory of intra-urban wage differentials and their influence on travel patterns." *Papers of the Regional Science Association* 9: 53–53.

Munby, D. L. (1951). *Industry and Planning in Stepney.* London: Oxford University Press.

Myrdal, G. (1957). *Economic Theory and Underdeveloped Regions.* New York: Harper and Row.

Nelson, K. (1986). "Labor demand, labor supply and the suburbanization of low-wage office work," pp. 149–171 in A. J. Scott and M. Storper, eds. *Production, Work, Territory: The Geographical Anatomy of Industrial Capitalism.* Boston: Allen and Unwin.

Norton, R. D., and J. Rees (1979). "The product cycle and the spatial decentralization of American manufacturing." *Regional Studies* 13: 141–151.

Noyelle, T. J., and T. M. Stanback (1984). *The Economic Transformation of American Cities.* Totowa, N.J.: Rowman and Allanheld.

Oakey, R. (1981). *High Technology Industry and Industrial Location.* Hampshire: Gower House.

———. (1984). *High Technology Small Firms: Regional Development in Britain and the United States.* New York: St. Martin's Press.

Oi, W. Y. (1962). "Labor as a quasi-fixed factor." *Journal of Political Economy* 73: 538–555.

Panzar, J. C., and R. D. Willig (1981). "Economies of scope." *American Economic Review (Papers and Proceedings)* 71: 46–58.

Park, R. E., E. W. Burgess, and R. D. McKenzie (1925). *The City.* Chicago: Chicago University Press.

Peach, C., ed. (1975). *Urban Social Segregation.* London: Longman.

Pencavel, J. H. (1970). *An Analysis of the Quit Rate in American Manufacturing Industry.* Industrial Relations Section, Department of Economics, Princeton Universtity. Princeton: Princeton University Press.

Penrose, E. T. (1959). *The Theory of the Growth of the Firm.* Oxford: Basil Blackwell.

Perrin, M. (1937). *Saint-Etienne et Sa Région Economique.* Tours: Arrault et Compagnie.

Perroux, F. (1961). *L'Economie du XXe Siècle.* Paris: Presses Universitaires de France.

Pettman, B. O. (1975). "External and personal determinants of labour turnover," pp. 31–50 in B. O. Pettman, ed. *Labor Turnover and Retention.* New York: Wiley.

Piore, M. J., and C. F. Sabel (1984). *The Second Industrial Divide.* New York: Basic Books.

Pollard, S. (1959). *A History of Labour in Sheffield.* Liverpool: Liverpool University Press.

Pred, A. (1965). "The concentration of high value-added manufacturing." *Economic Geography* 41: 108–132.

———. (1974). *Major Job-Providing Organizations and Systems of Cities.* Commission on College Geography, Research Paper 27. Washington, D.C.: Association of American Geographers.

———. (1977). *City-Systems in Advanced Economies.* New York: Halsted Press.

Premus, R. (1982). *Location of High Technology Firms and Regional Economic Development.* A staff study prepared for the use of the Subcommittee on Monetary and Fiscal Policy of the Joint Economic Committee, Congress of the United States. Washington, D.C.: U.S. Government Printing Office.

Putman, S. H. (1983). *Integrated Urban Models*. London: Pion.

Pye, R. (1979). "Office location: the role of communications and technology," pp. 239–275 in P. W. Daniels, ed. *Spatial Patterns of Office Growth and Location*. New York: Wiley.

Rees, A., and G. P. Shultz (1970). *Workers and Wages in an Urban Labor Market*. Chicago: University of Chicago Press.

Rees, J. (1978). "Manufacturing change, internal control and government spending in a growth region of the USA," pp. 155–174 in F. E. I. Hamilton, ed. *Industrial Change*. London: Longman.

Richardson, H. (1977). *The New Urban Economics: And Alternatives*. London: Pion.

Robinson, E. A. G. (1931). *The Structure of Competitive Industry*. Cambridge: Cambridge University Press.

Rodgers, D. T. (1981). "Tradition, modernity, and the American industrial worker," pp. 217–243 in T. K. Rabb and R. I. Rotberg, eds. *Industrialization and Urbanization: Studies in Interdisciplinary History*. Princeton, N.J.: Princeton University Press.

Rugman, A. M. (1982). "Internalization and non-equity forms of international involvement," pp. 9–23 in A. M. Rugman, ed. *New Theories of the Multinational Enterprise*. New York: St. Martin's Press.

Sallez, A. (1972). *Polarisation et Sous-Traitance*. Paris: Editions Eyrolles.

———, and J. Schlegel (1963). *La Sous-Traitance dans l'Industrie*. Paris: Dunod.

Saxenian, A. (1983). "The urban contradictions of Silicon Valley: regional growth and the restructuring of the semiconductor industry." *International Journal of Urban and Regional Research* 7: 237–262.

Sayer, A. (1986). "Industrial location on a world scale: the case of the semi-conductor industry," pp. 107–123 in A. J. Scott and M. Storper, eds. *Production, Work, Territory: The Geographical Anatomy of Industrial Capitalism*. London: Allen and Unwin.

Schmenner, R. W. (1982). *Making Business Location Decisions*. Englewood Cliffs, N.J.: Prentice-Hall.

Schumpeter, J. A. (1950). *Capitalism, Socialism and Democracy*. New York: Harper and Row.

Schwartz, G. C. (1979). "The office pattern in New York City, 1960–75," pp. 215–237 in P. D. Daniels, ed. *Spatial Patterns of Office Growth and Location*. New York: Wiley.

Schwirian, K., ed. (1974). *Comparative Urban Structure*. Lexington Mass.: D.C. Heath.

Scott, A. J. (1980). *The Urban Land Nexus and the State*. London: Pion.

———. (1981). "The spatial structure of metropolitan labor markets and the theory of intra-urban plant location." *Urban Geography* 2: 1–30.

———. (1982). "Locational patterns and dynamics of industrial activity in the modern metropolis: a review essay." *Urban Studies* 19: 111–142.

———. (1983a). "Industrial organization and the logic of intra-metropolitan location I: theoretical considerations." *Economic Geography* 59: 233–250.

––––––. (1983b). "Industrial organization and the logic of intra-metropolitan location II: a case study of the printed circuits industry in the Greater Los Angeles Region." *Economic Geography* 59: 343–367.

––––––. (1984a). "Industrial organization and the logic of intra-metropolitan location III: a case study of the women's dress industry in the Greater Los Angeles Region." *Economic Geography* 60: 3–27.

––––––. (1984b). "Territorial reproduction and transformation in a local labor market: the animated film workers of Los Angeles." *Environment and Planning D: Society and Space* 2: 277–307.

––––––. (1984c). "Solidarity forever? The pursuit of bread in the age of runaway production." *Graffiti* 5 (October): 8–11.

––––––. (1986). "High technology industry and territorial development: The rise of the Orange County complex: 1955–1984." *Urban Geography* 7: 3–45.

––––––. (1987). "The semiconductor industry in South-East Asia: organization, location and the international division of labor." *Regional Studies* 21: 143–160.

––––––, and D. Angel (1987). "The U.S. semiconductor industry: a locational analysis." *Environment and Planning A* 19: 875–912.

Sennett, R. (1974). *The Fall of Public Man: On the Social Psychology of Capitalism.* New York: Random House.

Sheard, P. (1983a). "Auto-production systems in Japan: organizational and locational features." *Australian Geographical Studies* 21: 49–68.

––––––. (1983b). *Auto Production Systems in Japan.* Melbourne: Monash University, Monash Publications in Geography 30.

Silver, M. (1984). *Enterprise and the Scope of the Firm.* Aldershot, Hants.: Martin Robertson.

Sirmans, C. F. (1977). "City size and unemployment: some new estimates." *Urban Studies* 14: 91–101.

Sjoberg, G. (1965). "Cities in developing and industrial societies: a cross-cultural analysis," pp. 213–263 in P. M. Hauser and L. F. Schnore, eds. *The Study of Urbanization.* New York: Wiley.

Smith, A. (1776, 1970 ed.). *The Wealth of Nations.* Harmondsworth, Middlesex: Penguin Books.

Soja, E. W., R. Morales, and G. Wolff (1983). "Urban restructuring: an analysis of social and spatial change in Los Angeles." *Economic Geography* 59: 195–230.

––––––, and A. J. Scott (1986). "Los Angeles: capital of the late twentieth century." *Environment and Planning D: Society and Space* 4: 249–254.

Sraffa, P. (1960). *Production of Commodities by means of Commodities.* Cambridge: Cambridge University Press.

Steed, G. P. F. (1971). "Internal organization, firm integration, and locational change: the Northern Ireland linen complex 1954–1964." *Economic Geography* 47: 371–383.

Steindl, J. (1965). *Random Processes and the Growth of Firms.* London: Charles Griffin.

Sternlieb, G., and J. W. Hughes, eds. (1975). *Post-Industrial America: Metropol-*

itan Decline and Inter-Regional Jobs Shifts. New Brunswick, N.J.: Center for Urban Policy Research.

Stigler, G. J. (1951). "The division of labor is limited by the extent of the market." *Journal of Political Economy* 69: 213–225.

———. (1961). "The economics of information." *Journal of Political Economy* 69: 213–225.

Storper, M. (1985). "Oligopoly and the product cycle: essentialism in economic geography." *Economic Geography* 61: 260–282.

Storper, M., and S. Christopherson (1985). *The Changing Organization and Location of the Motion Picture Industry: Interregional Shifts in the United States.* Graduate School of Architecture and Urban Planning, University of California, Los Angeles, Research Report.

———. (1986). *Flexible Specialization and New Forms of Labor Market Segmentation: The United States Motion Picture Industry.* Working Paper Series 105, Institute of Industrial Relations, University of California, Los Angeles.

Storper, M., and R. Walker (1984). "The spatial division of labor: labor and the location of industries," pp. 19–47 in L. Sawers and W. K. Tabb, eds. *Sunbelt/ Snowbelt: Urban Development and Regional Restructuring.* New York: Oxford University Press.

Struyk, R. J., and F. J. James (1975). *Intra-Metropolitan Industrial Location.* Lexington, Mass.: D.C. Heath.

Stuckey, J. A. (1983). *Vertical Integration and Joint Ventures in the Aluminum Industry.* Cambridge, Mass.: Harvard University Press.

Takeuchi, A. (1980a). "Motor vehicles," pp. 152–162 in K. Murata and I. Ota, eds. *An Industrial Geography of Japan.* New York: St. Martin's Press.

———. (1980b). "The industrial system of the Tokyo metropolitan area." *Report of Researches, Nippon Institute of Technology* 11: 1–40.

Taylor, M. J., and N. J. Thrift (1982a). "Industrial linkage and the segmented economy: 1. Some theoretical proposals." *Environment and Planning A* 14: 1601–1613.

———. (1982b). "Industrial linkage and the segmented economy: 2. An empirical reinterpretation." *Environment and Planning A* 14: 1615–1632.

Teece, D. J. (1980) "Economies of scope and the scope of the enterprise," *Journal of Economic Behavior and Organization,* 1: 223–247.

———. (1985). "Multinational enterprise, internal governance, and industrial organization." *American Economic Review* 75: 233–238.

———. (1986). "Economies of scope and the scope of the enterprise." *Journal of Economic Behavior and Organization* 1: 223–247.

Thiry, J. P. (1973). *Théories sur le Phénomène Urbain.* Louvain: Publications de la Faculté des Sciences Economiques, Sociales et Politiques de l'Université Catholique de Louvain, Nouvelle Série 109.

Thompson, W. R. (1969). "The economic base of urban problems," pp. 1–47 in N. W. Chamberlain, ed. *Contemporary Economic Issues.* Homewood, Illinois: Richard D. Irwin.

Thorngren, B. (1970). "How do contact systems affect regional development?" *Environment and Planning* 2: 409–427.

Tilly, C. (1961). "Occupational rank and grade of residence in a metropolis." *American Journal of Sociology* 67: 323–330.

Timms, D. (1971). *The Urban Mosaic*. Cambridge: Cambridge University Press.

Tsuru, S. (1963). "The economic significance of cities," pp. 44–55 in O. Handlin and J. Burchard, eds. *The Historian and the City*. Cambridge, Mass.: MIT Press.

Uyeki, E. S. (1984). "Residential distribution and stratification." *American Journal of Sociology* 69: 491–498.

Vernon, R. (1960). *Metropolis 1985*. Cambridge, Mass.: Harvard University Press.

———. (1966). "International investment and international trade in the product cycle." *Quarterly Journal of Economics* 80: 190–207.

Vining, D. R., and A. Strauss (1977). "A demonstration that the current deconcentration of population in the United States is a clean break with the past." *Environment and Planning A* 9: 751–758.

Vipond, J. (1974). "City size and unemployment." *Urban Studies* 11: 39–46.

Ward, D. (1971). *Cities and Immigrants*. New York: Oxford University Press.

Warren-Boulton, F. R. (1978). *Vertical Control of Markets: Business and Labor Practices*. Cambridge, Mass.: Ballinger.

Webber, M. J. (1984). *Explanation, Prediction and Planning: The Lowry Model*. London: Pion.

Weber, A. F. (1899, 1963 ed.). *The Growth of Cities in the Nineteenth Century*. Ithaca, N.Y.: Cornell University Press.

Weber, A. (1929). *Theory of the Location of Industry*. Chicago: University of Chicago Press.

Westaway, E. J. (1974). "Contact potentials and the occupational structure of the British urban system." *Regional Studies* 8: 57–73.

Wheeler, J. O. (1968). "Residential location by occupational status." *Urban Studies* 5: 24–32.

Williamson, O. E. (1975). *Markets and Hierarchies: Analysis and Antitrust Implications*. New York: The Free Press.

———. (1979). "Transaction-cost economics: the governance of contractual relations." *Journal of Law and Economics* 22: 233–261.

———. (1981). "The modern corporation: origins, evolution, attributes." *Journal of Economic Literature* 19: 1537–1568.

———. (1985). *The Economic Institutions of Capitalism*. New York: The Free Press.

Wise, M. J. (1949). "On the evolution of the jewellery and gun quarters in Birmingham." *Transactions of the Institute of British Geographers* 15: 57–72.

Young, A. (1928). "Increasing returns and economic progress." *Economic Journal* 38: 527–542.

Zunz, O. (1981). *The Changing Face of Inequality: Urbanization, Industrial Development and Immigrants in Detroit, 1880–1920*. Chicago: Chicago University Press.

Index

Designer:	U.C. Press Staff
Compositor:	Auto-Graphics
Text:	10 / 13 Galliard
Display:	Galliard
Printer:	Princeton University Press—Printing Division
Binder:	Princeton University Press—Printing Division